LIVERPOOL
FOOTBALL TEAM 1986

LIVERPOOL F.C. /
Crown paints

No. 5 JULY

...AND HELLO

rting On Top Of The World

LIVERPOOL F.C.
OFFICIAL
DIARY
1986/7

LIVERPOOL F.C. / crown paints
Fan Club Member

NAME Carsten Nipper
NO.   P319

No.
Beatles
Perry and the pacemakers   06

Date _____   N.R.: _____
Source _____   Mono ☐ Stereo ☐

he loves you   You'll never walk
lease please me   ferry cross the Me
enny Lane   Don't let the sun catch
ello goodbye   Where have you been all
ol on the hill   I like it
little help from my friend   Walk hand in han
                                    I'll be there
                                    You're the reason
                                    I'm the one
                                    It's gonna be alri
                                    Away from you
                                    w do you do i
                                    about love

LFC Y 1 A

ANFIELD
RAP

Also available at all good book stores

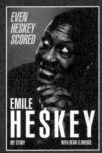

9781785315008

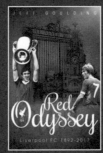

9781785313875

9781785314407

9781785315992

9781785313967

9781909626584

9781785313066

9781785311932

9781785314490

NOT GERMAN,
I'M SCOUSE

NOT GERMAN, I'M SCOUSE

A LIFELONG RED'S JOURNEY ABROAD

CARSTEN NIPPERT

First published by Pitch Publishing, 2022

Pitch Publishing
A2 Yeoman Gate
Yeoman Way
Worthing
Sussex
BN13 3QZ
www.pitchpublishing.co.uk
info@pitchpublishing.co.uk

A CIP catalogue record is available for this book
from the British Library.

ISBN 978 1 801500 555

Typesetting and origination by Pitch Publishing
Printed and bound in Great Britain by TJ Books, Padstow

Contents

To my mum

Who has always supported me unconditionally,
whatever I've done, wherever I've gone

To achieve the greatest possible self-fulfilment

That humanity can yearn for,
and to experience the ultimate feeling

Being a Red!

Acknowledgements

THE GODFATHERS of Reds autobiographies, Alan Edge's *Faith of Our Fathers* and Brian Reade's *43 Years with the Same Bird*, inspired me far more than the stranger whom I obtrusively pestered and bored with my endless Liverpool stories in the pub one night. He refrained from telling me to shut up but, just to bring my monologue somehow to an end, he advised me: 'You should write a book about this.'

Out of many Reds tales I've read, the adventures in Eddie Cotton's *The Voice of Anfield* and the stories of travelling Kopites Dave Kirby, Nicky Allt, Peter Hooton, Jegsy Dodd, Kevin Sampson, John Maguire and Tony Barrett in *Here We Go Gathering Cups in May* were certainly encouraging to eventually narrate my own experiences of a lifelong Red from abroad.

I also owe gratitude to the people who educated me and shaped my approach to a Red's life by their writing. The fanzines, Steve Kelly's *Through the Wind and Rain*, John Pearman's *Red All Over the Land*, Dave Usher's *The Liverpool Way*, Chris McLoughlin's *The Kop Magazine* and Gareth Roberts's *Well Red* were sent to Germany on a regular basis from their early beginnings. Their guiding Scouse spirit has accompanied me from an early age.

Thank you to all Scousers and all other Reds I've ever met anywhere in the world and with whom I enjoyed the banners, banter and singing, from Taksim Square to Salvador Dali Square. Everyone has a unique story to tell and could write his or her own book. Without you my story would never have been written. Even more important than the written words, however, are the memories we share in mind!

A very special thank you
to lifelong Kopites:

John Lyness
Brian Lyness
John Prior

Let Me Tell You a Story
of a Poor Boy

Who Was Born Far Away
from His Home

CHAPTER ONE

Searching for Heroes

PINK FLOYD are not the kind of band you listen to as an eight-year-old. They were the favourite band of my cousin Hans-Jürgen, who is five years my senior. I was naturally also into music – British music, of course. In the mid-1970s, pop groups from the UK ruled the world. They certainly ruled TV viewing habits in our living room on a regular basis. One Saturday each month, the German TV show *Disco* presented all the latest highlights from the rock and pop charts. It was an age when the technical term 'video' hadn't come into existence. There was nothing like flamboyant 'video clips' with visual effects enhancing the programme, but bands actually had to turn up personally to perform in the studio in front of an audience.

The application of the phrase 'perform' in this context might be a little exaggeration as bands very much relied on playback. But you never really bothered about that in those 3 minutes and 30 seconds when you were just glued to the TV screen. All you cared about was listening to those men in tight trousers and with long hair. No, actually, it wasn't to just listen, but rather to see or, to describe it even more appropriately, to absorb all those stars from the UK during those few precious moments. You never even perceived, let alone concerned yourself that their lip-syncing didn't even correspond with the lyrics you were listening to. You never scrutinised the vocal phenomenon of how a chorus could still sound as crystal clear and distinctive, even though the microphone was being swung in the air and was nowhere near the front man's vocal cords. Your complete attention focused solely on the sheer coolness of the guys' countenance, gestures and movements. They certainly left no doubt that they couldn't care less what the entire universe thought of them.

Those moments were the most precious highlights for a whole month and I never missed them. I mean, I did never ever miss them. Frequently I did succumb to a slight sense of envy towards the inhabitants of the UK, who, not knowingly and by birth right, were in an advantageous position to enjoy those highlights on their national TV, certainly on a regular basis. I realised that whingeing wouldn't get me anywhere and I had to come to terms with and get on with my underprivileged, handicapped, deprived, meaningless life.

One of the most important and time-consuming occupations at the time was the preparation for my cassette player's audio recording of new songs from the TV show. There were hits you only wanted to listen to a couple of times, some only once. After a while, you just wanted to get rid of them. Some you just wanted to keep for good. Those were the ones you let be part of your very personal 'best of' tape. It became a nuisance not to be able to listen to your favourite songs in one flow. You were compelled to wind forward to skip the ones that you couldn't remember why you had recorded in the first place.

Modern 24/7 technology of unlimited online or mobile download availability was still light years away. The luxury of obtaining the full song in high quality, whenever you felt like it, was completely unknown. If I wanted my 'best of' cassette to be of some sort of quality, I had to take care of that myself. It turned out to be a challenge, which was sometimes influenced by obstacles that weren't to be underestimated. The task I set myself was to develop an expertise to stop the recording of a song at the exact point to cut off the first note of the following song, which was designated to be deleted. Only then was the cassette properly prepared for the recording of a new 'best of' song. While stopping the tape too early may have wasted precious seconds, a split second too late would ruin the perfect transition. I was regularly caught between the devil and the deep blue sea.

Another factor responsible for a successful recording was a kind of profound psychological knowledge and personal estimation of the TV presenter's conduct. It required an enormous amount of instinctive feeling to be able to anticipate the exact timing of the presenter quitting his waffle. This was of fundamental importance for pressing the record button at the right moment in order not to miss the first syllable of the song's lyrics.

The most challenging task, though, was less of a technical one than of human nature. In fact, major obstacles were often detected within my very personal surroundings, such as family members as close as the first degree. Having overcome all sorts of preparatory problems, my own relatives were the most influential make-or-break factors. Every single person

NOT GERMAN, I'M SCOUSE

that was going to be in the living room watching the show had to be brainwashed to refrain from even whispering. A lot of charming, persuasive efforts on my part were needed to guarantee sufficient comprehension on the part of the others. Most often I addressed my loved ones with my begging plea 'to keep quiet' sensitively. In one extreme circumstance of inexplicably ignorant disobedience, I might have forgotten my good breeding and exclaimed full-throatedly, 'Oh, please shut up!' In the middle of a song, my mother forgot my beseeching and asked whether I had any intention of finishing my dinner, and thereby ruined my recording. Of course, this led to early bedtime. For me that was, not my mum, as she was, due to her hierarchical status, in a far superior position.

Our big family house organigram consisted of three generations. My grandparents came from Leinefelde and Thorn, both West Prussian towns that are now part of Poland. They were born before and during the First World War. Their childhood and teenage days were characterised by hardship and they had to help out in the fields at an early age. The aftermath of the war and its economic consequences in the 1920s was followed by a currency reform that made their small amount of savings worthless. It was a difficult time, not just for their families, but for the whole country.

People were fed up feeling suppressed and were searching desperately for a hero to take them out of their misery. A less able school drop-out, who had always found it difficult to come to terms with work on a regular basis and who claimed to be a professional artist, even though denied the final admission exam to art college, somehow managed to fascinate the masses of the German population in such an unquestioning way that they followed him blindly. When he marched towards Moscow, or to put it more precisely, let the masses march to Moscow, he enjoyed a kind of love and esteem he had previously lacked in life. When German soldiers were at some point bottled up by the Russian army at Stalingrad, the tide turned and the Russians marched towards Berlin. The German population more or less knew about the atrocities used against the Russian civil population. Fear rapidly spread about what the Russian army might get up to with German civilians in retribution once they reached German soil. My grandparents decided to leave their farm in West Prussia and flee westwards.

After the war, they bought a three-storey house to which they and two of their three daughters with their families moved, occupying a floor each. The biological begetter, who shared responsibility for my existence, diminished his personal appearance after a few years. However, financially, he proved to be exceedingly reliable for decades. Considering his economic support, my underdeveloped emotional and personal bond with him may seem, admittedly, extremely ungrateful on my part. I certainly would have given him a chance to impress me and become my hero, but I had to look elsewhere. What I couldn't seek elsewhere was my ancient middle name that I inherited from him and that I'm stuck with for the rest of my life. It's way too embarrassing to mention, but to deprive speculation its breeding ground, no, it's not Adolf!

The youngest generation in the house consisted of four cousins – two boys and two girls – and me. It was never boring as live entertainment was guaranteed in an environment full of youngsters.

'I Only Wanna Be with You' by the Bay City Rollers was the very first single my mother bought me. I kept playing it non-stop. As I considered myself at least as cool as the band members, I couldn't help playing it at full volume to let the entire house know. My grandparents, who had their living room right under my bedroom, constantly knocked with a broom on their ceiling. In my perception, and to my delight, the rhythmic knocking only enhanced the drum and bass sound of the song. A few moments later, a ringing sound that was in no uncertain manner out of harmony with the melody infiltrated my musical enjoyment. But even that stood no chance of gaining my attention. When the song slowly faded, I heard another knocking. This time, a real hard and loud knocking sound on our door startled me. I opened the door and saw my angry-looking granny in front of me.

'Why are you knocking so loud? You nearly gave me a heart attack! Can't you tap on the door normally?' I asked, perplexed.

After a moment of speechlessness, she only yelled at me, 'Keep this noise down!'

'Sorry grandma!' I respectfully obeyed, until next time.

I became my grandmother's personal trainer as she had to walk upstairs on a regular basis. After a few of those incidents, my grandmother instituted proceedings against me. When my mother came home one day, she took me downstairs and pointed towards the ceiling. The pushing of the broom had left some visible marks.

'Carsten, look at that. You can't do this!' my mother told me.

'It wasn't me, Mummy. It was Granny with the broom!' I declared with the most innocent facial expression. My mother, who always took time to explain to me explicitly and patiently the difference between right and wrong, failed to keep a serious look on her face. Speechlessness followed.

Bay City Rollers' Scotsmen, Les, Woody, Eric, Derek and Alan, became my first heroes. My personal 'Rollermania' went as far as to beg my mother to adjust my outfit to their main visual characteristics. My ankle-length jeans with a tartan pattern round the hems were my greatest pride. I didn't do anything or go anywhere without them. School, playing field, living room never witnessed me dressed in any other piece of clothing. We became inseparable to the point that I was forced to let them be washed as stains and fragrance left no other option. That fashionable, cool gear turned me into an absolute trendsetter at school. I was hot, I thought. This must be the perfect age to be at. I was good at primary school, could play footie as much as I wanted and was part of a world of my heroes. I led a carefree, wonderful life. Nothing could harm me.

My superior status experienced a gradual phase of decline, or rather an abrupt point of demolition, when Hans-Jürgen called me upstairs. He didn't really break the news in a sensitive way, but rather set up a presentation in the most sensationalist manner. He wouldn't let me know by just telling me. Of course not! No, he wanted to let me hear it, or even better, feel it. Before I could realise what was happening, I heard the first guitar tunes of a song. I felt benumbed!

'It's that other Bay City Rollers song I told you about. It's "Money Honey", a much more rock-like tune than before,' Hans-Jürgen told me.

For any philologist, it was the perfect setting for the invention of a new word. Combining 'flabbergasted', 'speechless' and a facial expression displaying my darkest desires to torture a person would have given birth to the latest contribution to the *DUDEN*, the German equivalent of the *Oxford Dictionary of the English Language*. Innocent childhood days were over. I had to deal with the fact that he had more pocket money than me. This disadvantage on the monetary front was no cause for concern in itself. The consequences it generated, though, were too much to bear. He made me lag behind in my own heroes' world. It was my band, they were my heroes. It just couldn't be that he possessed more records than me, thereby being closer to my heroes than me!

I pulled myself together as much as a manly eight-year-old could. All energy had to be concentrated in one big effort to refrain from bursting into tears. 'Oh, great, you got the new single then?' I asked in my typical cool manner. Lying on the sofa, he appeared as if he had already listened to it a million times and boredom had already crept in when he replied almost indifferently, 'Yeah, but there are other songs that are quite good as well.'

The combination of the words 'other' and 'songs' indicated that the pain-inflicting scenario hadn't reached its peak yet. I still couldn't grasp the magnitude of the drama and looked at him, confused.

'I got the whole new album,' he said. To describe my state after hearing the letters A ... L ... B ... U ... M would have taken an entire conference of psychologists to get a new definition into that bloody dictionary! This album highlighted the band's heyday with 'Money Honey', 'Rock and Roll Love Letter' and 'Yesterday's Hero'. But unfairness in life is never to last for long and I persuaded, no I actually convinced my mother to get me the album *Dedication* too.

'Mum, you do like them as well, don't you?!'

The following year, 1977, I was still very much into the Bay City Rollers. At the same time, other cool bands were emerging, which attracted my fascination. It hurt to realise, but Bay City Rollers' music became a bit girlish, too smooth and not really manly. What might have been the case is that their music had actually always been extremely girlish, but only then I personally realised that fact. I found myself in a situation where I had to part with my first heroes.

Fashion and music styles developing in the UK never passed by without leaving a significant mark on my psyche. The 1970s must have been a nightmare for parents and teachers, who were in charge of bringing up and educating kids. The *Rocky Horror Picture Show* made cross-dressing kind of socially acceptable. The Glam Rock era of David Bowie, Queen, T-Rex and Kiss was the perfect platform for revolutionary teenagers. In retrospect, the long-haired Beatles appeared comparatively model pupils. I never wore the outrageous clothes, make-up, let alone platform shoes, but I took to the long hairstyle and definitely the music.

The Sweet enjoyed their greatest success in Germany, where they were top of the charts eight times! They had six consecutive No. 1 hits in the short space of 1972 to 1974, starting with 'Little Willy' to 'Wig Wam Bam', 'Block Buster', 'Hell Raiser', 'Ballroom Blitz' and 'Teenage Rampage', the song I identified most with. I didn't understand a single word, of course. The screaming of the singer and the hard rhythm of the sound sufficed to define my new set of heroes in The Sweet. Although they had already passed their prime and released their hits long before, it was the right time for me to let them enter my world. By their looks they were rebellious, by their music they were very rebellious and by their screaming, even if only lip-syncing, they were very, very rebellious. I became the spitting image of front man Brian Connolly, although only in terms of hair length. I had straight hair and let it grow underneath my ears, like Brian. With my baby-faced cheeks I never managed to look as hard as him, though. It was a physiognomic condition that wouldn't improve over the following decades either.

My mother developed a manner in which she scrutinised everything I started to worship. It wasn't her intention to dispute about issues, but rather to educate me to bring to mind the reasons for my adoration. She wanted me to become a critical thinker rather than somebody who just followed the crowd. She once asked me what it was that made me like The Sweet that much. I casually argued that they were real hard rockers. To me, the phrase combined a mixture of really cool rock 'n' rollers and bikers. To my mother, it solely referred to bikers, and 'bikers' back in the day generally solely referred to criminal biker gangs. She pointed out that they were people who may become a bit aggressive towards other people if they don't get what they want. In the most explicit way, a horror scenario was unfolded to my mind of how brutal these gangsters were to innocent people, even mothers and even little boys like me.

'I'm not saying that all bikers are like that,' my mother said. 'I'm not even suggesting that this band of yours has anything to do with that. But if you say you like them because they are hard rockers, you should be aware what you're talking about.'

I didn't feel well after that conversation. Actually, it was a monologue as I couldn't speak. I was intimidated by my stream of thought. From that moment, I still liked their music very much, but was also a bit scared of Brian Connolly, Andy Scott, Mick Tucker and Steve Priest. They were still my new heroes, though.

Through these 70s music bands I made my first acquaintance with English lyrics and songs. I was still at primary school and foreign language lessons were a year away. 'Joining in' with the lyrics was reduced to very unconvincing soundless lip movements with the occasional utterance of an enunciation during the chorus with phonetic correctness leaving a lot to be desired. Some of the bands vanished quicker than they had emerged. Many of them wouldn't leave an impact on my further development. A few of them accompanied my life for a considerable time. One of them was to leave a lasting impression on me.

Hans-Jürgen's favourite band at the time was Pink Floyd. Their kind of instrumental music was the complete opposite to the mainstream taste I followed. He kept raving about this band with their ground-breaking, innovative ideas. There was one album, *Meddle*, he kept playing over and over. To be absolutely accurate, it wasn't the whole album, but rather only one song in particular. We always had our favourite songs on long-playing records. Instead of letting the record play through from beginning to the end and then flip over to the other side, we kept lifting the needle back to the start of our favourite song. In the case of *Meddle*, it wasn't even a particular song, but only two parts within the song. A new quality of replay was born. Approximately a million times, we didn't replay the song from the start but only those two parts over and over again. It was a brief sequence in the middle and an extended one at the very end. The name of that song, 'Fearless', impressed me very much in itself.

'What great, intelligent musicians they are!' Hans-Jürgen enthused once more. 'Never ever has anyone integrated fans singing in their songs!' Actually, two of my former favourite bands had recorded their own fans chanting and let it become a part of their hits. The crowd screaming, 'We want Sweet! We want Sweet!' at the beginning of 'Teenage Rampage', and 'Bay City Rollers!' at the start of 'Yesterday's Heroes' always sent shivers down my spine. Pink Floyd also decided to include singing fans in one of their songs, but in their case they didn't make use of their own followers. They employed a choir that never assembled at a concert. Pink Floyd availed themselves of not just any ordinary chant, but the anthem of that congregation. In the middle of 'Fearless', the music softened a bit without fading entirely. The guitar tune made way for the choir to emerge gradually. From a far distance, you could vaguely hear for a few seconds what sounded like thousands of people singing in a harmonious, spiritual and musical unity with fearless pride, power and invincibility. After only five seconds, these voices faded again and the song resumed properly. When the melody faded out completely at the end, the choir took up again. This time, the voices became louder and louder until they erupted at full volume: 'Walk On, Walk On, with Hope in Your Heart and You'll Never Walk Alone, You'll Never Walk Alone. Walk On, Walk On, with Hope in Your Heart and You'll Never Walk Alone, You'll Never Walk Alone.'

'Oh my god, what a brilliant idea to integrate the best football fans in the world into your music.' Hans-Jürgen rhapsodised about the greatness of his favourite band and the greatness of these best fans in the entire world again, again and again. It was an audition I had never ever been confronted with in my life before. My musical world consisted of loud and hard beats, fast guitar tunes and colourful, flashy, screaming men. This was something completely different; this was something utterly new. The sound was calm, the singers were composed, and yet the combined outcome was the most boisterous tune I could ever imagine. The force and intensity that characterised the closeness and unity of the choir wouldn't fade without leaving a lasting impression.

Listening to 'You'll Never Walk Alone' generated a mysterious power in your mind that would grip you and never let you off again. Never ever again! This choir symbolised unconditional support, unity, loyalty, determination, passion, love, addiction. The creators of that fellowship found their heroes for life and would stick with them for good. The foundation of this unique bond was no temporary trend, no superficial fashion, but an innate transcendental spirit. I felt envy as I wanted to be part of that parish. An awestricken admiration for those people, their common spirit and everything that was connected to their collective mission was born. An innocent admiration became a drug. Only a short taste of a contagious teaser turned the willing victim into an addict.

I was looking forward to the beginning of term after the summer holidays. Second class in co-educational primary school awaited me and no longer would I occupy the ignominious status of a first-former. Life was easy and trouble-free. Well, sort of free, if it hadn't been for two new women who, unsolicited, simultaneously entered my life.

One of them was older than my granny, the other one a middle-aged beast. Both of them were occupied with my education and were officially commissioned by the state to do so as teachers in my school.

Our new class teacher, Mrs Zaruba, was a total law and order disciplinarian representing virtues that didn't necessarily suit my personal approach to life. Actually, she insisted on being called 'Miss' Zaruba as she was still an untouched Fräulein despite being well past her best-before date. She impersonated all good old German virtues she must have learned in the League of German Maidens, the female branch of the Nazi Party youth organisation. After my first year at school with a mother figure-like class teacher, Mrs Junge – obviously and most certainly no 'Miss' Junge anymore by her looks – who was caring, lovable, extremely young and even bloody good looking, the second year was hell. Mrs Junge had her ups and downs, too. Sometimes she was even quite a moody bitch if she wanted to be, but she never lacked understanding and humour. Sometimes she did lack a sufficient sense of humour when she threw a bunch of keys at me or incarcerated me in the wardrobe for nattering away endlessly. But all in all she never made me not like going to school.

Now Mrs Junge was no more. Miss Zaruba was in charge of all but two subjects – art classes and physical education. One of the first and most alienating facts of my new life was that I was addressed by my surname! Not that it was necessary to command more respect, but by this measure she made us feel her undisputed authority. I felt like an inmate who wouldn't want to mess with the warden. As a logical consequence, I imposed a decision on myself to keep a low profile and not to make a spectacle of myself.

My personal teenage rampage had to be temporarily suspended. I had to take it like a man. My inner life was characterised by frustration, fear and a feeling of sickness. I tried to suppress what I felt deep down until one evening my mother asked me what the matter was. I hadn't spoken much that evening and it was quite obvious that I was bottling something up. After my lids fluttered, my chin twitched and my whole body trembled for a while, I burst out in tears and screamed, 'I'm not gonna go back to school anymore, never ever again, neeeeeeveeeer eeeeeveeeeeer!' I was virtually on the verge of resigning from school entirely and giving notice to Miss Zaruba.

My mother was very understanding, but also discussed with me the further options if I were to go ahead with my plan. From a purely objective economical point of view, opportunities to earn my own living without a certain certificate proving my presence at some kind of educational institute on a regular basis would have been very much limited. To weigh the pros and cons thoroughly, without taking German legislation on compulsory school attendance into consideration at all, I utilised respite for the following negotiation process. I came to the conclusion that under these terms and conditions: firstly, I had to get on with it; and secondly, I had to get it over and done with in the best possible way. Returning to school next morning was my personal option at least, I convinced myself. I wasn't forced into it and thereby didn't lose face. It was my decision!

I worked out how to cope with Miss Zaruba, and after a while we even got on together. There were certain conditions, though, that I never came to terms with. I was used to singing just being a part of the music lesson and physical exercise of PE lessons. Not so for Miss Zaruba. Whenever she caught sight of a free slot we had to sing endlessly. Good old traditional German children's songs. In a class of some 32 pupils she couldn't figure out who sang wrongly. This was our chance to get our own back on her. And I in particular got my own back on her big time.

She once complained that we didn't open our mouths as much as those choirboys on TV. 'The more you spread your lips the more distinctly and clearly you sing.' We willingly met her demand by tearing our gobs apart. The funny part was that we only made lip movements and didn't utter a single note. That referred to the ones she was looking at. The others tried to squeak as much as possible and thereby ruin the quality altogether. When she looked puzzled, I looked puzzled in the most unsympathetic way. How on earth can this choir be so bad?

We were tough boys, so we believed, and played footie in any weather condition any time. We usually even enjoyed playing outside in the school yard during our big break when it rained. Fresh air and a little run around were precious to us. Miss Zaruba had other ideas. As soon as a single raindrop was spotted, we had to stay inside. Of course, she wouldn't leave us alone but made us subject to her physical exercises as this would freshen up our minds and give us enough energy for the lessons to follow.

One of the few escapes was art lessons, in which drawing, painting and crafting was going to get the best out of my creativity, or so I thought. Mrs Kastner had other ideas. Actually she should have insisted on being called 'Miss', too, as no normal bloke with eyes in the right places ever went near her, let alone robbed her of her Fräulein status. When I reported to my mother what learning material lay ahead of us the following term, even she was a bit dumbfounded. We were going to learn knitting and crocheting for the entire school year.

One of the League of German Maidens' aims was to educate girls within the beliefs of the National Socialist system and to train them for their roles in German society: wife, mother and homemaker. Well, neither was I living in bloody Nazi Germany but in the rebellious 70s, nor was I becoming a wife, mother or homemaker. School was supposed to enable me to make a living economically, not make me stay at home. The content of education was to make me a respected member of society and, from a personal point of view, financially independent so that I could do whatever I wanted when I was a grown-up. After all, this was the bloody reason I voluntarily opted for going back to bloody school in the first bloody place! If that wasn't bad enough, Mrs Kastner had the unfavourable habit of yelling at you at every single opportunity. For a positive, healthy upbringing of a self-confident man it was a kind of unreal reality. One minute you looked up to your rebellious heroes singing about your teenage rampage and the next you were confronted with a middle-aged art teacher living out her personal rampage on you whenever you dropped a stitch! My dislike for her making me do these girly things turned into pure personal hatred.

Having encountered solely amiable members of the opposite gender until then, I had an absolutely healthy relationship with that species. My kindergarten teacher for a start had been kind, understanding and always gave me a smile. My hairdresser took my view on women to a higher level. I always went to this young, tall lady with short blond hair. She wore a black blouse and her bodily constitution on the upper tier was quite voluptuous. My mum always paid for the haircut, but her service, in my personal perception, went quite beyond that. Washing my hair was exceeded by massaging my head very intensively in a sensual way never experienced in this act of lavation before. While exercising her profession, she pulled my head slowly back until it casually touched her breasts. At the same time she ran her fingers casually above my ears. I couldn't figure out what she was doing, but I liked it. It didn't take me long to come to the conclusion that I liked women and what they can do. They were beautiful and gave you nice feelings. 'Mum, next time can I have my hair cut by her again?'

These rose-coloured glasses were taken off immediately the following morning by Mrs Kastner, who could deter any heterosexual young man from any kind of erotic purposes. For at least twice a week, in between yelling at me from behind, it was knit one, purl one, knit one, purl one, knit one, purl one, knit one, purl one, knit one, purl one.

I never took a particular liking to Smokie or Rod Stewart, but some of their songs even topped the charts, too. 'Lay Back in the Arms of Someone' was at number one in the German charts and 'I Don't Want to Talk About It' in the UK singles charts on 25 May 1977. We were going to watch newly crowned German champions Borussia Mönchengladbach in the European Cup Final on TV that night. They were a strong force in the German Bundesliga as they had been dominating the domestic league for some years, having won the championship in 1970, 1971, 1975 and 1976 previously, and the German Cup in 1973. They enjoyed their only

European success in the UEFA Cup in 1975. Three years earlier in the same competition, they had forced their way comfortably through to the final after overcoming in the most superior way Aberdeen 9-5, Hvidovre IF 6-1, local rivals Cologne 5-0, Kaiserslautern 9-2 and FC Twente Enschede 5-1 on aggregate. In the final though, they couldn't beat a certain team from England. A 2-0 win in the second leg in Germany wasn't enough after having been beaten 3-0 at Anfield in the first leg. This time, in 1977, the greats of Vogts, Bonhof, Stielike, Simonsen and Heynckes were going to play that English team again. That night, I was going to hear that choir from *Meddle* for real. That night, I was going to see Liverpool Football Club for the first time live on TV!

Most family members gathered around the TV before kick-off in an overcrowded living room. All of them supported Mönchengladbach, simply because it was a German team. My allegiance was very clear in advance, of course. In the Olympic Stadium in Rome, it was obvious that the travelling Liverpudlians were in the majority. Some 27,000 supporters from Liverpool made up around half of the overall attendance that night. The Germans had already succumbed to Liverpool in terms of numbers and atmosphere by their fans. It didn't take long for me to get my first physical, and in particular psychological, goose pimples.

When the players entered the arena and prepared themselves for kick-off, a visual impression immediately made me watch in awe. Borussia played in an all-white kit. The contrast couldn't have been more immense between the Germans' white and the Redmen's colour. Until 1964, the Reds were playing in red jerseys, white shorts and white socks with a red trim. Bill Shankly decided before a European

Cup home tie against Anderlecht to send his team out in all red. Shanks was convinced that the colour scheme would carry psychological impact, red for danger and red for power. Liverpool would be more intimidating. He came into the dressing room and threw a pair of red shorts to his captain Ronnie Yeats. 'Get into those shorts and let's see how you look,' he said. 'Christ, Ronnie, you look awesome, terrifying. You look 7ft tall.' To the press Shanks later confessed, 'He frightens me and he's in my bloody team!'

Shanks wouldn't have anticipated that this would carry some psychological impact on a little boy in a far off foreign land more than a decade later. Not only that the players wore an all-red outfit, but the red seemed to be redder than any other red I had seen before in my life. It was such a pure and glowing red that couldn't be matched by any other colour. It even appeared to be classed above any kind of colour scale. And yet the contrasting white trims and in particular the white numbers on the back didn't disrupt the beauty of the red but only intensified its impact. And if that wasn't enough, right out of the red depth there appeared a beautiful, slim yellow Liver Bird upon the chest. But it wasn't only Shanks who acted unaware of future consequences. Seeds of my life's predestination were sown on a global scale.

Hungarian dramatist and novelist Ferenc Molnár wrote *Liliom* in 1909. Liliom is a carousel barker who falls in love with a young woman. They both lose their jobs, and when the young woman becomes pregnant, Liliom is tempted to carry out a robbery, in which he dies. After some time in purgatory, he's sent back to Earth for one day to try to make amends. If he fails, he'll be eternally damned. On Broadway, the play was first staged in 1921. Orson Welles directed the radio adaptation for his programme in 1939.

The American songwriting duo of Richard Rodgers and Oscar Hammerstein created a string of popular Broadway musicals in the 1940s and 1950s. They created the innovative development of the musical play where songs and dances are integrated into a story. Drama and emotions became an important part of the new type of musical. Both initiated what's considered the golden age of musical theatre. They composed and wrote successful shows such as *Oklahoma!*, *South Pacific*, *The King and I* and *The Sound of Music*. They were awarded 35 Tony Awards, 15 Academy Awards, two Pulitzer Prizes, two Grammy Awards and two Emmy Awards. Their second musical *Carousel* was adapted from *Liliom*, the original setting of Budapest transplanted to the north-east of the USA. The show opened at Broadway's Majestic Theatre on 19 April 1945. In one of the songs, the cousin of the female protagonist Julie sings to comfort and encourage her when her husband Billy is killed during a failed robbery. The song is reprised in the final scene at Billy and Julie's daughter Louise's graduation. Billy watches this ceremony during his return to Earth. The song is called 'You'll Never Walk Alone'. The musical ran for 890 performances on Broadway before it premiered in London's West End at the Theatre Royal on 7 June 1950, where it ran for 566 performances.

A decade later, a Scouse band called The Mars Bars had to change their name after the Mars Candy Company refused their approval. The band, which then became known as Gerry and the Pacemakers, was managed by a man who was running a family business in Walton Road called North End Music Stores. Mr Brian Samuel Epstein also managed a certain group called The Beatles. The bands were part of the Merseybeat, the new pop and rock music genre that developed in Liverpool in the early 1960s.

The Beatles' first single release, 'My Bonnie', with Tony Sheridan, couldn't climb higher than No. 48 in the UK chart in 1961. 'Love Me Do' reached No. 17 the following year, followed by 'Please Please Me', which narrowly missed out on top spot in 1963. They were offered a song called 'How Do You Do It' by producer George Martin, but they declined to release it. One reason behind it was that John Lennon allegedly considered it 'rubbish'. Brian Epstein offered it to Gerry Marsden, who most willingly accepted it and Gerry and the Pacemakers had their first single release. In April 1963, it went to number one and a new star band was born. This was the moment when Gerry Marsden realised that being a musician was his business. Three weeks later it was replaced at the top by 'From Me to You', the Beatles' third single and first number one hit.

Gerry and the Pacemakers' next single, 'I Like It', also reached number one in the UK singles chart, but Gerry Marsden was also keen on ballads. However, he trusted Brian, and if he thought it was right to do rock songs he would do them. As long as this got them into the charts, Gerry didn't mind how they got there. These first two songs were similar beat songs. Now he wanted to do a ballad. Watching the musical *Carousel* in his youth, 'You'll Never Walk Alone' had been one of Gerry's favourite songs. He had a serious intention to make it his third single release. Brian Epstein and George Martin's response was that it was too slow. He would be wasting the one-off opportunity to make his first three singles number one songs as never had anyone done that before.

Gerry wasn't so much focused on getting another number one hit, but wanted to get a ballad into the charts. If he could succeed, he would be able to go on singing more ballads on records. He won the dispute and in November 1963 achieved a record that wasn't matched for over 20 years. 'You'll Never Walk Alone' hit number one and Gerry and the Pacemakers became the first act to top the charts with their first three consecutive single releases. They nearly achieved an even greater feat, but their fourth single release, 'I'm the One', was kept off the top by another Liverpool band, The Searchers.

The events in Liverpool in 1963 in music and football occurred at exactly the same time. The emergence of Merseybeat and The Beatles' supremacy coincided with Liverpool Football Club's own resurgence. After the dark ages of the 1950s, when the club even had to endure a spell in the Second Division, Bill Shankly hadn't only brought Liverpool back into the top flight, but made them the champions of England in 1963/64! Meanwhile, from April 1963 to May 1964, Liverpool artistes occupied the top of the charts for 51 weeks – 14 number one songs came from Liverpool: 'How Do You Do It', 'I Like It', 'You'll Never Walk Alone'; The Beatles' 'From Me to You', 'She Loves You', 'I Want to Hold Your Hand', 'Can't Buy Me Love'; The Searchers' 'Sweets for My Sweet', 'Needles and Pins', 'Don't Throw Your Love Away'; Billy J. Kramer & The Dakotas' 'Bad to Me', 'Little Children'; and Cilla Black's 'Anyone Who Had a Heart' and 'You're My World' all hit the top.

Football matches at Anfield were attended by capacity crowds. Fans on the Kop had to get in early to guarantee admission and therefore the terrace was packed some time before kick-off on a regular basis. The ground's DJ played top-ten hits to pass the time and Kopites joined in with the tunes. One Saturday in November 1963, the Kop joined in with Gerry Marsden's third number one hit and created a very unique bond with this song. After it dropped out of the charts and wasn't played any more, the Kop still kept singing it in the matches later on. As this didn't go unnoticed by the DJ, 'You'll Never Walk Alone' was played again and again until the tune, the lyrics and the chant became the hymn of Liverpool Football Club.

Now, over 23 years later, on a night in May in front of a TV screen somewhere in Germany, a unique bond was formed between that all-red kit, that very special hymn, that travelling Kop and me! Quite a few culprits participated in a series of events to exert influence on my personal development over the coming decades. My destiny was sealed long before the goals by Terry McDermott, Tommy Smith and Phil Neal were scored to secure a 3-1 victory against Borussia Mönchengladbach and the club's first-ever European Cup. That night in Rome, Liverpool took hold of me and haven't let go since.

CHAPTER TWO

First Time

SUBBUTEO TABLE football was my main occupation after daylight had vanished completely. Before dusk, my only thought after duly finishing my homework, or sometimes not so duly, was playing proper football. There was no higher force such as heat, cold, rain or snow that could interrupt or postpone, let alone cancel our footie.

The venue was, in the majority of cases, located in the park across the road. This setting of drama sometimes witnessed me obtruding myself upon the older boys to allow me to get into one of their teams. Sometimes, well rather quite a considerable number of times, I was painfully ignored and thereby left emotionally devastated. Occasionally, they had a soft heart and let me join, even if only to make up the numbers. Some of them had a builder's physique despite still sitting behind a primary school desk every morning. Due to their physical superiority, as well as my technical inferiority, I didn't really play a major role in my team's success. My shortcomings were compensated by my big mouth, though.

Big mouths don't really serve you well if you're younger, smaller, and physically as well as technically weaker. Big mouths serve you even less well when you're responsible for conceding the decisive goal for the opposition. A slap to my face was sometimes one of the consequences.

It was a rough area. Not only for cheeky little boys like me, but in general. Luzenberg, as a part of the industrial district of Waldhof, hosted some of the biggest employers in my home town, Mannheim. Our area was embedded right between French Saint Gobain's mirror glass factory and Daimler-Benz. Back in 1886, Carl Benz produced a three-wheeled vehicle powered by petrol and an engine, which was later regarded as the first automobile. In the 19th and at the beginning of the 20th century, the city played a generally important role in many technical innovations. Before the time of the motor, Karl Drais built the first two-wheeled running machine, the 'Draisine' in Mannheim in 1817. The Lanz Bulldog, a popular tractor, was first manufactured in 1921, and Julius Hatry built the world's first purpose-built rocket plane in 1929.

Luzenberg and Waldhof were traditionally pure working-class areas. Council housing in Germany was first established here. In both vicinities in the 19th century, the companies provided houses for their workers and their families. In Luzenberg, one block of these old barracks remained. It was only a five-minute walk across the park away from my home. It has become a listed building as one of the city's most famous sons lived there in his youth. Sepp Herberger was a local football player for SV Waldhof, who later, as manager of the German national team, rose to ultimate stardom. He led his team to the final of the 1954 World Cup and, against all odds, beat the favourites Hungary to win the Jules Rimet Trophy in 'The Miracle of Bern'.

The local football club SV Waldhof Mannheim 07 was the team everyone followed. Even though not everyone bothered to turn up for the match, they supported them in a sense that you just supported your local team. Strangely, I never developed any kind of bond with the club, whose ground was less than two miles away. The club even gained promotion to the first Bundesliga between 1983 and 1990 and once only narrowly missed out on qualifying for the UEFA Cup. They also produced some home-grown talents, some of whom developed at other clubs into national players, such as Bernd Förster, Karlheinz Förster, Uwe Rahn, Paul Steiner, Fritz Walter, Christian Wörns and Maurizio Gaudino, who had a brief loan spell at Manchester City in the 1990s. Jürgen Kohler even won the World Cup for Germany in Italy in 1990.

Another local lad who put Waldhof on the map was Charles 'Charly' Graf. He was born and bred in the 'Benz Barracks', temporary buildings that were constructed by the council for people who couldn't even afford the rent for council flats. In this particular area, poverty and all kinds of attached problems prevailed. As the kid of a mother from Mannheim and a black American soldier who shortly after his son's birth was called back to the States, Charly was treated as an outsider and discriminated against during his childhood. The only recognition he experienced was in sports. In his teenage years, he took up boxing and in reference to Muhammad Ali was soon called 'Ali from Waldhof" by the media. He then started to mingle with people from the underworld and became a criminal. Various offences, such as gambling, pimping and assault, led to him spending some ten years in prison.

While there, he took up training again and was even allowed to fight in boxing matches. In 1985, three years before being released from prison, he won the German heavyweight championship.

This rough working-class world we lived in was light years away from the posh areas where kids played strange sports such as golf or tennis. Just by mentioning that you were engaging in such an activity would have caused you severe facial damage in my world – big time. Later in school life I encountered such a breed in a culture shock period when I was enrolled at grammar school in the city centre. Eleven-year-old classmates who spoke about spending all Sunday on golf courses improving their 'handicap' made me seriously wonder why they boasted proudly about their disabilities. Others bragged about training at the same tennis club as Boris Becker or Steffi Graf, who were both born and raised in the greater Mannheim area. Those kids never experienced the hardship of being bullied or slapped by the big boys on a muddy playing field.

When there were no football matches on in the park, I chose the alternative of playing in our own stoned backyard. As I opted for this home venue on a regular basis, especially during summer breaks, my kneecaps were encrusted with blood from the beginning of June to the end of August. I had no action film heroes at the time, but these painful scars were as good as the bloodstained heroics of Bruce Willis a decade later. In my retrospective perception, my bodily wounds actually looked a lot harder than those the action film protagonist had to suffer.

There were major advantages to playing in our own backyard. You had two goals of just about the same size and height. One was the cellar wall and at the opposite end was our wooden garden shed. The sidelines consisted of another wall on one side and a high fence on the other. Both sides served as skilful one-two passing partners. The short distance between the goals of no more than 15 yards, and the walls and fences not being higher than 7 feet, didn't influence our style of play at all. We still played as if we were on a full-sized pitch. As a consequence, in some matches we spent more time climbing over walls and fences retrieving the ball than actually playing. If the ball was shot over the bar of the 'shed goal', it landed in the garden where our granny grew tulips, roses and other colourful plants, which were of no precious value to boys of my age.

As the wicket gate was locked, I had to climb over to get into the garden and again to get back. I was just able to clutch the top of the frame with both hands and press my left foot against the lattice fence to be able to set my right foot on the door handle. I would pull myself up and swing my left leg over the door until I sat on it. Another swing with my right leg and I was in the garden. Due to the circumstance that my feet pushed against the fence regularly, my left foot on the way in, my right foot on the way out, an obvious bulge in the fence could be noticed after a while. Praying that the ball hadn't destroyed any flowers, I would tiptoe in the direction I assumed the ball had landed. Despite the fact that tiptoeing in my granny's garden had become a regular exercise, I certainly hadn't attained perfection. My gran sowed the seeds or planted the flowers so closely together that it was a challenge not to leave any footprints, which would cause a clearly traceable path from the gate to the flower bed.

Compared to the noise created by screaming, shouting, hitting and bouncing when the ball was in play, the minutes during which we retrieved the ball were characterised by sudden silence. Our gran occasionally looked out of the kitchen window to observe the goings-on. Every so often the noise got out of control and occasionally an argument on the pitch led to tears. From time to time a tackle caused injuries. Now and then, gran took over the function of the referee, unauthorised by the players of course, and abandoned the match. She also figured out that an abrupt end to the noise wasn't necessarily an indication that we were taking a break or the match was over. The noticeable peace and quiet aroused a kind of suspicion that an unexpected incident might have led to an unwanted interruption of our play.

As Granny could smartly work out when the ball must have been gone missing somewhere outside the official playing field yet again, countermeasures had to be hatched. Whenever the ball disappeared out of reach and I had to get up on the fence once more, we slyly kept shouting and continued imaginary conversations as if we were in the middle of the game. The cunning plan worked most of the time and we played until our exhaustion reached the limit.

Later, when upstairs in the kitchen, I could hear my grandmother moaning from the garden: 'Carsten … oh my god!' I never knew when and how often she inspected the garden, but I assumed that she deliberately executed routine checks whenever I had been playing in the yard. As I was hiding, I never knew whether my grandfather inspected the state of the fence himself or whether Granny checked that as well. Anyway, the bulge had become even bigger and the most expensive and most beautiful flowers, which had only been planted two days before with the most loving care, had been destroyed.

When I appeared at the inquisition led by my mother, grandmother and grandfather, the hearing didn't really follow common procedure of examining evidence and charges. There were five of us kids, but it never appeared to be a question of who the main culprit was. Thus, I was the only one who was subpoenaed. The list of suspects was always narrowed down very quickly. Hans-Jürgen, of course, would avoid blame by claiming that a teenager his age wouldn't do this. The girls, Ingrid and Birgit ... well, they were girls. I had seen some Hollywood noir courtroom drama on TV and had acquired the necessary expertise to deal with the situation, but even in my self-defence I couldn't argue that the two girls could be involved in an action like that. And my little cousin Manfred was too small.

I referred to the heavy rain and storm a couple of nights before that must have been involved in the destruction. The traces, which the soles of my shoes left beside the dead plants, would contradict my feeble argument straight away, though. The matching of fingerprints hadn't been established in our house and a lie detector couldn't have been handled professionally by any member of the ruling hierarchy, but even if I had appealed to be allowed to undergo such measures voluntarily, the jury's verdict was out before I could start my closing argument.

'What have you got to say to that, hmm?' my mum asked.

'Well ... well, if Granny had left a bit more open space in between the planted flowers, I could walk easily through the flower bed without causing any damage. And because Grandad refuses to hand me a spare set of keys, and hereby I would like to point out that I've repeatedly asked him to do so, I have to climb over the fence.'

The jury looked at me. Speechlessness followed. As a consequence, all matches at the home ground were suspended for a few weeks. Most often it turned out to be only a couple of days before they were resumed.

A different kind of challenge was to not mishit the ball and let it cross the 'sideline', over the fence on to the street that bordered on a filling station. Cars, motorbikes and lorries entered and left the road all day long. It did occasionally happen that the ball was hoofed high up in the air, landed and bounced off a car's windscreen. Strangely enough, apart from the state of shock of the driver, no severe damage was ever caused.

One afternoon, the ball crossed the fence once again and rolled down the road underneath a neighbour's car. He had a big German shepherd watchdog, a pet I had respect for. A few men stood around the car chatting – the neighbour, the owner of the filling station, my granddad and some others. Confidently, I approached the car and crawled underneath it to retrieve my precious belonging – then I heard the dog bark. I was startled and got up quickly. Before I heard the men shout 'don't run!', I was on my way as quickly as I could. Within a few seconds I felt the dog's teeth in my back, while falling to the floor. A quite unmanly behaviour followed. I cried my lungs out and my granddad carried me home, where I recovered on the sofa.

I soon found myself surrounded by men in the living room. The dog didn't join them, though. 'Nah, he doesn't need a doctor!' my neighbour explained, before adding, 'Just ease the pain and clean the wound with strong schnapps.' These men had fought in the war. They must know. For some reason I fancied a rather profound professional medical examination, though. When my mother arrived home soon afterwards, she immediately took me to see a doctor.

The physical scars healed sooner than the psychological ones. Ever since, dogs have scared the shit out of me! It wasn't just the German shepherd I tried to avoid but anything hairy on four legs. This led to some very embarrassing situations when walking around with my mates. One day, five of us rang the bell to ask a friend out. I was on my bike, cycling in little circles, when his mother answered the door. Her tiny white poodle stepped outside. All it took was this little pooper to bark towards me and off I went. Forgotten was the lesson not to run or cycle away from dogs. I had a total blackout, not seeing or hearing anything around me. With all my efforts I pedalled away from this monster. As the beast wouldn't let me go and accompanied me down the road, I was speeding away on my bike for some 50 yards. In the background I could hear my mates taunting me with laughter. Verbal humiliation followed ever after!

The year of 1978 saw a kind of conversion. From my personal perspective, I turned into a bit of a soft kind of a man. The love story of John Travolta and Olivia Newton-John in the movie *Grease* certainly impressed me. I fancied innocent Sandy considerably more at the beginning of the film before she turned into a vamp in 'You're the One that I Want' at the end. So I started my emotional career off as a cuddling, smooching, canoodling sort of a guy. Cuddling, smooching, canoodling, though, was still light years away.

A new favourite band at the time entered my life that made me use make-up for the first time. Not on a regular basis and not when I went to school, though. I didn't use the colour to accentuate certain facial parts, but to cover my entire face with. The music that ruled my room and caused many more broom marks on my grandparents' ceiling, was Kiss. The two live double albums *Alive!* and *Alive II* even led me to 'play' their concerts. In my imaginary Kiss band I represented the lead singer Paul Stanley. I also liked Gene Simmons 'The Demon', Ace Frehley 'The Spaceman' and Peter Criss 'The Catman', but it would have been boring to do a whole concert being reduced to playing only an instrument. As Stanley's persona was 'The Starchild' I put a black star over my right eye. An ice hockey stick served as my guitar and I rocked the room for some two hours. In their concerts, Kiss used fireworks on stage, therefore a genuine Kiss concert just wouldn't be the same without them.

'Mum, pleeeeeaaase, if I promise to be really careful with the sparklers and cover the carpet so that it wouldn't be ruined!'

'Carsten! No!!!'

It was also the year of the World Cup in Argentina and I couldn't figure out why the greatest players on Earth who had just retained the European Cup in a 1-0 victory over Bruges at Wembley could do it for Liverpool but not for England. The Three Lions didn't take part in the tournament or in the one four years earlier in Germany in 1974. Reading the World Cup statistics in a history book, I firmly believed that England's lack of success must have been down to the players focusing more on their clubs rather than the national team. Well, that wasn't the worst of excuses anyway.

But to be perfectly honest, I was more interested in my personal Panini sticker album statistic anyway. It was my first-ever sticker album and, as with many firsts, it was very precious to me. This first time turned eventually into a nightmare, though. Apart from the fact that the whole project would have absorbed many years' pocket money if it hadn't been kindly subsidised by senior members of the working society, it stretched my nerves until the tournament itself was almost over. The World Cup produced stars like Argentina's Mario Kempes, whose name would never be forgotten on a global scale. But it was a rather unknown name that caused a very personal major concern that kept me occupied during the competition. The name that haunted me for a long time was a player called Cristóbal Ortega!

Having filled the entire sticker album, one bare space on the Mexican team's page caused me sleepless nights. Conspiracy theories erupted that his picture never went into print in the first place. While others boasted a full album, thereby invalidating my paranoia, I was embarrassed to admit that I still hadn't completed mine. If that wasn't bad enough, he was a kind of fringe squad player that no one had ever heard about as his only appearance came in Mexico's final and meaningless group fixture, which they lost 3-1 to Poland! Salt was rubbed into my open wound when classmates mentioned incidentally that they had already passed on the coveted sticker to friends in need as they had a spare one of him. 'A spare one!!!'

As the tournament approached the final, my torture continued as I was being left with a nearly completed album.

I tried to distract myself by playing the forthcoming match between Argentina and the Netherlands with a softball in my room. I was supported by some 75,000 wild Argentines by imitating their huge roars.

Argentina seemed to be invincible in front of their hysterical crowd, although they struggled when they had to face a proper opponent, losing 1-0 to Italy and drawing 0-0 with Brazil. One of the most impressive memories, besides the chant of 'Ar-gen-tina, Ar-gen-tina, Ar-gen-tina', was the confetti the size of A4 and copious use of toilet rolls. I seriously wondered how they provided themselves with sufficient supply before the matches, asking their mothers to buy more bog paper as they were 'going to see a football match', or if they just looted the sanitary rooms inside the grounds before each match. The latter, rather ignorant, option must have caused some irritating nuisance among other football fans who spontaneously felt no necessity any more of relieving themselves before kick-off when entering the lavatory. My supply was surplus. I kept throwing the bog paper, exceptionally clean and unused, up in the air and on to my carpet pitch, on which I was scoring Kempes's winning goals over and over again. Sliding the ball over the goal line on the slippery paper confetti made the look of the action even more authentic.

Finally, a few days before the final, I won my personal World Cup against Mexico. 'Oh, you still haven't got him? I've got him a few times.' I can't remember how many Rummenigges or whoever I exchanged in return, but I could finish my first-ever Panini sticker album. The Mexican squad became my most precious team and I never looked at any other pages more often than the one depicting 'Ortega'.

Having replayed the World Cup countless times in the park, in the backyard, in my room, I kept repeating the success on my Subbuteo pitch. To revive the proper atmosphere of the River Plate stadium I needed the appropriate utensils. I asked my mum to empty her hole puncher from the office, and those of her colleagues as well, to provide me with a sufficient supply of confetti. Standing in front of me she looked at me thinking there was something seriously wrong with her offspring. Speechlessness followed. I couldn't distinguish whether it was motherly love or a feeling of pity for the obviously deranged beloved only son that made her obey without reply, providing me with the contents of her puncher.

'That's all?!' I fumed when she produced a small handful of the coveted cut paper the next evening.

'I haven't got more, and you can't be seriously asking me to punch more office paper just to meet your demands!' she sternly replied.

Feeling ignored and neglected, I made her aware of the options that I had already explicitly explained to her the day before. 'Well, what about your colleagues? They must have more in their punchers!' When she realised that I actually did mean what I said, she challenged me with the personal embarrassment that she would be confronted with and therefore the lack of feasibility of the project.

'Do you seriously think I'm asking my colleagues to hand me over their punchers' rubbish?' Downhearted, rejected and depressed, I went to bed.

'I hope that's enough!' was all I heard when a big transparent bag of confetti greeted me the following evening. I was over the moon as I was now able to have a proper replay of the World Cup Final! I never enquired whether she punched fresh paper, asked colleagues kindly to hand it over voluntarily or whether she stayed longer to sneak from desk to desk to empty the punchers herself, trying not to be caught by anyone. It wasn't so much a matter of sheer ignorance, but rather a case of not bringing up the subject ever again! Never did I ask for the office's bog rolls though!

The World Cup and its confetti was only temporary fun, though. Soon I would move the venue from South America to Anfield. A Subbuteo match was never just a game, but a ritual, in which a genuine Anfield night came alive. In the evenings, lights were switched off and the angle-poise lamp from my desk provided the floodlights. Pink Floyd's 'Fearless' from the *Meddle* album provided the atmosphere. For night matches, I still needed a proper opponent for this staging. I begged my mum to make up the numbers, reminding her that I'm her only son and that it's in the nature of things to prove her undying love for me.

There was never a toss of a coin. Of course not! I was always red and, of course, I was always attacking the Kop End in the second half. The Kop End was always where the noise from the loudspeakers came from. These were positioned right behind the goal so that at high volume the Kop roar would be breathing the ball in. A minor problem remained. The singing of 'You'll Never Walk Alone' and chanting of 'Liverpool' only lasted about 75 seconds. As a consequence, I had to interrupt the match on a regular basis to get the needle back to the start again. These interruptions were artificially but necessarily prolonged as I didn't always find the exact groove on the record.

The opponent was not only disadvantaged by the noise but also by the constant interceptions in their attacking build-up play. My mother complained, 'I can't concentrate, Carsten, with all this noise behind me!'

I replied seriously and rather reproachfully, 'Do you seriously think that at Anfield the opposition goalie has a choice and complains to the ref that the Kop is too loud?!' No reply was received.

For me, it was a great night when I was winning, and it was still a great night when I was losing. For my mother it was bad when I was winning, and it was bad when I was losing. I can't recall any defeats though. It was the same unbeaten streak the Reds enjoyed at Anfield at the time. I just never lost when Pink Floyd was on. Detailed memories fail me, but deep down I remember some home victories being achieved late in added time. Sometimes the time added was long and the match terminated abruptly when I, the Reds, had just scored the winner.

The real Anfield experience was still reduced to the odd five minutes of highlights on late Sunday afternoons. The German TV sports programme *Sportschau* showed highlights from the English First Division on an irregular basis. They mainly picked Sunday's live broadcast from BBC or ITV. The chances that they would show a big Liverpool match were quite good, though. This was the case as long as it fitted in with their 30-minute time schedule. I was especially looking forward to the German Bundesliga winter break. They couldn't fill their time with post-match analysis, interviews and transfer rumours of the domestic league, so they looked abroad for quality sports to fill their programme.

Right from the very first match highlights I had the pleasure to enjoy, English football differed enormously from what I observed while watching the Bundesliga. English footballers seemed to be considerably stronger, faster and, what struck me most, much more emotionally committed to the game and the jersey they were wearing. Every single second of the match seemed to be the decisive battle for winning a cup final. The will to win was an integral part of every single movement. As a consequence, the game was much more physical. Players using rough tackles more often got away with them than in similar incidents on the Continent. Therefore, the fluency of play wasn't interrupted as often in England as in Germany. In the English philosophy, under no circumstance was any tackle ever considered as lost. You may even no longer have the ball under control, but it was only a question of seconds before you would recapture it.

Along with this attitude came the unconditional will to keep the ball in play rather than allowing it to go out. It seemed that the ball had to be kept on the pitch by all means, even if it would only be going off the pitch somewhere near the halfway line. Players didn't want to regain possession by a throw-in or a corner, but to win it back by themselves straight away by fighting for it on the pitch. No effort was spared in running after a ball that was rolling off the pitch in 'nowhere' areas. Unlike players' on the Continent, who considered the worthiness of a run after the ball before starting to move, English players only stopped fighting when it had actually crossed the line and the match was officially interrupted. No run was too long, no yard deserved to be given up too early. Every single effort might turn out to be the key to success, or might culminate in a decisive pass to create the winning goal.

This impressive never-give-up attitude on the pitch was perfectly demonstrated some years later in one of my all-time favourite Liverpool goals scored by my personal favourite Liverpool player at the time. In our 1987/88 title-winning season, Liverpool played Arsenal at Anfield. Just before the half-time interval in a scoreless first half there was a battle for the ball in Arsenal's half. John Barnes attacked on the left wing into the six-yard-box. Ray Houghton couldn't convert his pass and Steve McMahon's shot was blocked. Tony Adams cleared the ball that was then rolling off the pitch towards the main stand. Everyone expected a throw-in for Liverpool. Under any normal circumstances it would have been acceptable to let it go out of play and reposition yourself for the subsequent throw-in to start the next attack. Steve McMahon thought differently. He wouldn't let go and sprinted after the ball as if he wanted to prevent it from crossing his own goal line. He just about caught up with it and managed to keep it in play by putting his foot on it on the sideline before stumbling against the advertising board. Within a split second, McMahon turned his body around, rushed back and took possession of the static ball. He beat Adams, then another Arsenal player, before he passed it between two more defenders to Peter Beardsley, who stormed into the box. He passed it square to the far post where John Aldridge slid it over the goal line into the net. This goal may have increased Aldo's scoring account but it was definitely Macca's goal.

Apart from the speed and fighting spirit in matches, the entire atmosphere inside an English ground electrified me. Whereas in almost all German stadia a running track separated the pitch from the terraces, English grounds were purpose-built for football only. Terraces and stands were so close that from nearly all camera angles the movement of the crowd was an integral part of the coverage. Spectators weren't only audibly but also visibly a part of the spectacle. The close proximity of fans to players could look intimidating, especially during throw-ins and corners. The grounds always seemed to be packed to capacity. Pitches were encircled by four human walls, beyond which players couldn't escape. Teams became converted into gladiators, who were extradited into an arena where they were left stranded at the mercy of the fans until the final whistle.

At Anfield, the crowd seemed to have no spectators, no neutral observers who just attended a match. The masses came across as one unit. On the Kop, a cohesive wall often moved in waves. What made these impressions even more extreme was the fact that coverage only lasted some five minutes, in which all highlights were compressed. Nearly every single scene showed attacking play, shots on or off target and goals. You were led to believe that week after week for 90 minutes, Liverpool fans were spoiled with such an orgasmic ecstasy. I yearned for this ecstatic sensory overload that infected me.

What made matters worse and didn't stand me in good stead was the technical underdevelopment in my world. There was no such friend as a video recorder, who would let me rejoice at watching highlights again. My addiction was thereby reduced to those few minutes. My addiction was also subject to the mercy of German TV editors. In some winters, Germany did particularly well in some kind of sporting activity, such as ski jumping, biathlon, curling and the like. Pondering about how one can bring oneself to be interested in such happenings in the first place, I wondered how much one can report and enthuse about it. This extended coverage of German winter sports on *Sportschau* culminated sometimes in the *lèse majesté* to not show Liverpool at all, although it was announced at the beginning of the programme. 'Due to the extended highlights of this historic day in German snow sports we have run out of time to show you the highlights from the English First Division. We apologise, but we're sure you do understand!' I went berserk. When I realised I couldn't change the situation I just burst into tears. I felt marooned, held incommunicado, cut off from the outside world.

My German standard of living was good. I was part of the industrialised Western civilisation. We did have TV sets in Germany. We did have professional football clubs in Germany that were followed by masses of German fans throughout the country and their matches were shown on German TV. However, I wasn't interested. Due to lack of access to what was of a real major concern to me I felt as if I led an underdeveloped life. I felt as if I had been kidnapped in my postnatal period to be brought up in an environment my most inner instincts told me weren't mine. Once you've become addicted to a drug, you can't let go. The higher the quality and the lesser the availability of that drug, the more desperate you become. As emigration at my age was no option I had to put up with this no-win situation. My short-term, random and brief access to heaven was dependent on caprice by some German TV decision-makers. But when those five minutes of sheer heaven were granted, I was abducted into a different world of my own.

'They are playing Bayern Munich!' I screamed when I found out about the draw for the semi-final of the European Cup in the 1980/81 season. From those Subbuteo encounters, my mother knew exactly without asking what was going on in my head. I had already made my mind up – I'm going to Munich! Without taking into consideration my age, the minor obstacle of overcoming the distance of 220 miles to Munich and how I would transport myself to the destination, I knew I would be there.

What didn't cross my mind for a single second was the potential challenge of obtaining a ticket. The Olympic Stadium held over 70,000 people, the biggest capacity in Germany. Little did I worry about spare tickets. We would ring the ticket office and order the desired number. My mother was told a couple of times that tickets weren't on sale yet and we would have to wait. 'Sold out,' was the reply on the other end when she tried again a couple of days later. Selling arrangements had started before schedule and demand for tickets was high, of course. I had felt so close to seeing my beloved Reds for the first time and yet was so far away only because some **** from the ticket office, who was tired of answering early callers, led us into a false assurance. The fact that she messed ignorantly with my feelings filled me so much with scorn and anger that I cried for hours that afternoon. Homework had to be postponed that day.

My mother didn't give up and rang again after a few days to receive a stunning reply. They had 'opened a new allocation', whatever that meant, and 'tickets might be available again'. My mother asked to be put on the waiting list, no matter in which section of the ground. 'Oh, you would want to also get tickets for the North Curve?' This particular end, which had the same size as the home end in the South Curve, was the away section.

'Yes, of course,' replied my mother.

'Oh, no problem, we have got loads of those left.' Silence followed. Being absolutely puzzled by 'sold out', followed by 'a new allocation being available' and 'having loads of tickets in the away end available anyway', my mother didn't want to take any chances and made sure we would somehow get two tickets, no matter where in the stadium. She decided to place two orders.

'Please send me two tickets for the North Curve and also two anywhere in the stadium of the new allocation you might make available.'

A few days later, we received an envelope with two tickets. Yeeeeeeeeeeeessssssss!!! I had just received my adoption application papers! I was going to watch my Reds for the very first time. And it wasn't just any kind of match, but the return leg of the semi-final of the European Cup! And, as it happens, a couple of days later another envelope with another two tickets arrived!

My Red birthday was approaching and Bayern Munich captain Paul Breitner's comments after the goalless draw in the first leg at Anfield made the encounter all the more special. The Bayern skipper criticised the Reds for playing unintelligent football and promised the German media they would walk all over Liverpool easily in the return leg.

It was a beautiful, sunny spring Wednesday morning during the Easter break when we set off in my mother's red Fiat. I would like to point out that she had owned this car for a few years already and wasn't harassed by me to have it lacquered in the appropriate colour just for the big occasion. On the motorway drive down to Munich we passed by an untold number of coaches from Liverpool with red-and-white banners, flags and scarves decorating the interior around the windows. Seeing Kopites for the first time in the flesh made the build-up to the match and the journey on my back seat itself indescribably exciting.

Overtaking the coaches one after another over a very long period of time, I started to count them, multiplying times 50 fans on each of them approximately. After a dozen coaches my thoughts were trying to figure out how many more were still behind us that wouldn't pass us, how many more were still ahead that we may never catch up and how many had already reached the Olympic Stadium. In my imaginary geographical map of Germany I was seeing hundreds of red coaches making their way from the Dutch, Belgian or French borders to Munich, turning the motorway into one red stream throughout the country. The Red Army was marching, well, being driven, towards Munich, and I was part of it.

After arriving in Munich we went straight to the Olympic Park. Already from afar I could detect the unique construction of the stadium. A large sweeping and transparent canopy imitating the Alps was the venue of my first Liverpool match! My heart beat faster, my skin was covered with goosepimples, and shivers went down my spine. Yes, all at the same time! Around the stadium there was a festive atmosphere turning the area into a massive pub garden, which Liverpudlians had already seized in their masses. I spotted the same kind of Liverpool scarf over and over again and wondered whether there was a source nearby selling Liverpool merchandise.

Nervously, I approached a Scouser with my broken English pointing at his scarf. I had never ever spoken to a native speaker in English before. 'Where you've this?' was the best I could come up with spontaneously.

He smiled and replied in German, 'U Bahn'. He was proud to be able to answer in a foreign language himself. Right, there must be someone selling these by the underground station,

I thought. I walked further until I spotted a bulk of people surrounding a street seller. Fighting my way through men who were all at least three heads taller than me, I spotted my item of desire, a beautiful white scarf with thin yellow and red stripes above and below and capital letters L I V E R P O O L with red Liver birds on each end. I grabbed one and handed over 12 Deutsche Mark. Within a split second, the division between me and all other Kopites had vanished.

Filled with pride of being able to display my new uniform with the appropriate colours, I walked back to catch up with my mother. We were strolling around the park when we spotted a group of Liverpudlians and Germans gesticulating. They were obviously discussing something over a ticket. The Liverpudlian appeared to be lost in translation. My mother, being the kindest person on Earth and trying to help out whenever possible, approached them straight away. While walking over she remarked that the Germans might want to rip the Liverpool fan off. It was her time to interfere and fend off harm from the young Reds. One of the Liverpudlians held a ticket in his hand, but looked absolutely sad. 'They sold a child's ticket to this Liverpooler,' a German man informed us.

We learned that this Scouser had travelled the whole way from Liverpool down to Munich on a coach without a match ticket, hoping for the chance he might be lucky on the black market. Some German tout had offered him a ticket and enquired about the amount of cash he had with him. When he showed him the 30 Deutsche Mark he had, the equivalent of about £6.50, the deal was done. The ticket he showed us read 'Kinder 3DM'. He had been sold a child's ticket that cost officially 3 Deutsche Mark, some 65p, for ten times the original value. We just couldn't fathom how someone could bring himself to undertake a journey of almost 1,000 miles one way with virtually no money, hoping to get a ticket for a match that was officially sold out! The fact that he was now in possession of a valid ticket but still wouldn't make it through the gates as he was not four feet tall anymore was heartbreaking. He looked exhausted. Every minute of his 20-hour trip seemed to have left a mark on his face. He had a shy appearance and was absolutely shattered. My mother and I, just as the rest of the people around that poor fellow, felt for him but couldn't change his fate, could we? When we reaffirmed to him that he wouldn't get inside, he walked on.

We still had to find people looking for tickets to whom we could sell our spares. For face value of course! The poor guy wouldn't leave our thoughts, then I remarked, 'Would it hurt us if we gave him one ticket for nothing?'

'I don't think so,' my mother replied instantly and handed me over a ticket. I chased back through the hordes of people, and when I finally spotted him with his mate, I tapped him on his shoulder from behind. He ignored me at first, so I grabbed his arm and made him turn around. He gave me an irritated look, wondering about my intentions. I showed him the ticket and passed it to him. He wouldn't touch it and uttered, 'I've got no money.' I replied in my broken English, 'It's a present, no money.'

He reluctantly took the ticket and read the words on it thoroughly as if he didn't trust his luck. He was in a kind of state of shock and didn't say anything at all. With a very low and tired voice he then muttered, 'Thanks!' His mate went 'Yeeeeeesssssssssssss!' and tapped him on his shoulder. Clutching his ticket firmly with both hands, he walked away smiling. I made a brother happy. I felt like I had been admitted to my new family circle!

My mother and I both felt happy, too. Having sorted out the ticketless Scouser, it was time to get into the action and absorb the party atmosphere. Kick-off was still a few hours away, but the park outside the stadium was already packed with both sets of supporters. A group of Liverpool fans gathered on a small hill outside one of the gates, displaying their colours and enjoying their chants. It was a great view and exciting to witness the Kopites in action so closely. Some representatives of the rural Bavarian branch approached the group as if to mark their territory, on which foreign singing was obviously prohibited. One of the Liverpool fans walked up to him with a smile, reached out his hand and made a handshaking gesture. The German prat wouldn't respond. The Red didn't make too much of a fuss and left again.

Within seconds the Germans started a small fight. The Liverpudlians wouldn't back off and stood their ground. Just when it started to escalate I shouted to my mother, who stood behind me, 'Let's get out of here.' I moved away quickly through the crowd. All of a sudden I heard a glass bottle smash on the ground. My only thought was *Oh no, now it's getting nasty*! I looked back, trying to spot my mother, but she was not behind me. Walking back into the crowd I saw her holding both of her hands over her head. She was surrounded by other people trying to help her. Broken glass covered the floor around her. As a reaction to the Bayern fans' not-so-hospitable behaviour, some Red had thrown a bottle towards them from the hill. The intended flight course took a little detour via my mother's head before hitting the floor. Fortunately, there was no open wound and she soon recovered. After a few moments she smiled again.

We thought it would probably be better to get inside the stadium early before the crowds turned up at the gates. Bayern's club officials must have thought it would probably be better to inform their supporters how to get to the final early, even before the second leg had been even played. They were distributing leaflets everywhere advertising trips to Paris.

It didn't take long before the first rendition of 'You'll Never Walk Alone' could be heard, the very first I witnessed so closely. Shivers, spine-tingling and goosepimples jointly worked on me again. When the teams were announced, the scoreboard read Ray Clemence, Phil Neal, Richard Money, Colin Irwin, Ray Kennedy, Alan Hansen, Kenny Dalglish, Sammy Lee, David Johnson, Terry McDermott, Graeme Souness. I was about to see my heroes for the very first time! The match itself couldn't have started worse. Kenny Dalglish limped off after only a few minutes and was replaced by someone I had never heard of before, Howard Gayle. However, this injury-hit Liverpool team still managed to keep Munich at bay in the first half.

Bayern failed to put real pressure on the Reds, or rather Black-and-Whites on the night. The match itself was a tight, tense affair and characterised by a lot of rough tackling. Deep into the second half, nerves became increasingly frayed. In the 83rd minute, David Johnson beat a Bayern defender just outside the box on the right side. He played the ball to Ray Kennedy in the middle, whose 20-yard low drive with his right foot gave Liverpool the lead, and my first-ever Liverpool goal! Now Bayern had to score twice in the remaining minutes. Rummenigge equalised four minutes later, but the drama ended shortly afterwards when the final whistle was blown.

On our way out, we had to walk over thousands of soiled, crumpled or ripped leaflets littering the terraces. Liverpool were on their way to the European Cup Final!

CHAPTER THREE

Got My Education
from the Kop

MY PASSION for Liverpool generated a significant interest in the English language. One day I would stand on the Kop and be linguistically prepared to communicate properly with my brothers and sisters. At school I was able to learn the language of my heroes and at home I started to follow general news about cultural, social and, as long as I could make any sense of it, political issues from the UK on TV. The more I watched, the more I learned about the country's tradition and history. A fascination for everything British grew inside me.

The music and fashion movements of the 70s had gone and Glam Rock was taken over by the New Romantics and New Wave. OMD, ABC, Yazoo, Soft Cell, Spandau Ballet, Kajagoogoo, Tears for Fears, Howard Jones, The Human League, Dead or Alive, A Flock of Seagulls, Culture Club, Depeche Mode and in particular Duran Duran were the new paragons. Their influence on me went to the extent that they were responsible for my first-ever use of a hairdryer, which was necessary to obtain the desired perfect side-parting hairstyle.

During English lessons, my teacher perceived an increased interest and a more active participation in the subject. Initial joy on his part soon faded, though. I would get the appropriate application of correct grammar right on a regular basis, but to listen to the repetitive content of my illustrative sentences became rather arduous, if not tiring, when it was my turn to read out my homework.

Simple present: 'I watch every single Liverpool match on TV every weekend.' Apparently, English lessons became a setting to subconsciously vent my innermost wishful fantasy. They provided a psychological insight into the state of my soul that was characterised by escapism.

Present progressive: 'Liverpool are playing Tottenham on Saturday.' Nothing to worry about in that sentence as no psychological deviations from reality could be detected there.

Simple past: 'Liverpool beat Arsenal 5-0 at Highbury yesterday.' Creative writing can have such a liberating, relieving and satisfying psychological impact on one's positive mood.

Past progressive: 'While I was watching the Liverpool highlights on TV, the telephone rang, my mother called me for dinner and there was an electricity cut.' Obviously, English lessons also became a substitute support group to subconsciously vent my worst innermost fears.

Present perfect: 'I've supported Liverpool since I was a little kid.' I actually wanted to write 'since I grew inside my mum's womb', but then my environment would have thought that there was something seriously wrong with me.

Present perfect progressive: 'I've been replaying Liverpool's 10-0 away win over Everton on my Subbuteo pitch for hours.' No psychological salience could be identified in that sentence and the grammar was perfectly implemented anyway.

Past perfect: 'Liverpool had won more league chamionships than Manchester United before the start of the season.' Sometimes, even for me the reading out of example sentences was rather arduous, if not tiring, when the content was a boring fact.

Going to – future: 'I'm going to watch Liverpool in the European Cup Final.' Sure!

Will – future: 'Liverpool will win the league championship this year again!' That one went without saying.

I kept volunteering for reading out my essays in class until I was ignored. No one was interested in me taking a ferry across the Mersey in 'My best vacation trip'. I did perceive a kind of lack of comprehension for Rushie scoring four goals at Everton in 'My greatest role model'. 'My favourite TV show' produced, according to my taste, the most cringy outcomes from all the others, but no one was interested in my *Match of the Day* experience, a show I had never seen but only read about, either.

The development of my pure theoretic knowledge about the UK as well as the mere abstract use of the English language reached a stage when I felt it was time to obtain first-hand practical experience. My mother found a trip to England a sensible decision to invest in my education. In August 1983, I set foot on holy ground for the first time. An organised trip with a language school took me to Southend-on-Sea, where I spent three weeks with a host family. Paul Young's 'Wherever I Lay My Hat' topped the charts during those weeks. I intended not only to improve my English but to absorb and internalise as many ingredients of British culture as possible.

My host family were eagerly determined to do a good job in teaching me their way of life, after I had made my intentions clear to become a true Brit at heart. The first opportunity wasn't long in coming. Having arrived at my temporary new home in early afternoon, I unpacked my bag and spent the time until dinner in front of the TV. Cricket was on. How exciting! I had heard of that sport before and was fired up for getting the gist of what was one of the most typical of British sports. People in love tend to see and evaluate things through rose-coloured or sometimes, as in my case, just blurred glasses. I tried to convince myself that cricket was a sport I was going to like. I was committed to understanding the rules by watching it all afternoon. It would certainly only take me a tiny, little while to comprehend for sure.

Soon I figured out that maybe it would take me a tiny, little bit more than a while as there wasn't so much action going on. Men in all-white outfits were standing around. Occasionally a ball was thrown, occasionally a ball was batted, but most often men in all-white outfits were standing around. It appeared to me that the protagonists were of a different class. Nor did they look tense, nor would they shout, let alone sweat while exercising their sport. Their supporters seemed to be of a different class too, as they made no efforts to cheer their team on. To their defence, occasional clapping could be heard, though. It was a rather tedious first encounter with UK culture. Cultural differences culminated in confusion after a few hours when the match ended without a final whistle or at least some team celebrating. To my irritation, there wasn't even a winner or loser. They were going to take up the following day where they just left off. 'What?' There must be more to typical British life than that! More enjoyable opportunities were certainly to come.

'Oh, what's this?' I asked enthusiastically the following morning at the breakfast table.

'Oh, you'll love it, it's so typically English!' was the even more enthusiastic answer. Of course, I had the option of butter or jam on my hot, crusty toast. I even had the choice of butter *and* jam on my hot, crusty toast. But I opted for this new stuff. Well, I had to. I was promised to be entertained by something traditionally British. I was passed a glass with a liquid, dark content. As soon as I removed the lid, a rather interesting odour reached my olfactory system. Within a split second, an old familiar question emerged inside the parts of my brain that were still functioning. It was a question that had been asked a million times before in my life, but never answered properly. It was a question I confronted myself with: 'Carsten, why?' Why couldn't I have just come down, sat at the table, enjoyed my normal breakfast, kept a low profile and not get myself in any kind of situation that I had no clue whatsoever how to get out of?

I was surrounded by mama, papa, the little daughter and little son, all with a smiling, expectant look on their faces. It was our very first breakfast on the very first morning and this moment was to be a defining one for the following three weeks. You could sense the pride in their eyes that they were duly accomplishing the first culture lesson that I had begged them for. Chickening out of it wouldn't only have disappointed them but also questioned my serious intention to become acquainted with the British way of life.

'It tastes great and is healthy!' the little bugger added. On the outside I tried to maintain my countenance and smiled. On the inside I was focused on persuading myself to develop a positive perception from some angle. The indefinable and unprecedented scent tried to persuade me that, at least, it didn't look too challenging. The indefinable and unprecedented sight tried to convince me that, at least, it might not taste too challenging after all. I was caught in a trap. In the seconds to come, all highlights of my rock bottom culinary life unveiled like a horror movie in front of my eyes. The first time my mother asked me to eat a whole raw tomato. The first time she made me drink a full glass of carrot juice. The first time my grandmother ran after me to get me back to the table in order to eat an overfilled dish of spinach.

When I became conscious again, I spotted the little boy greasing his entire toast with the black paste and biting into it with the widest possible width of his mouth with relish. He munched happily as the stuff drooled out of both corners of his mouth and down his cheeks. I dipped my cutlery cautiously into the pot until only the smallest possible part of the knife point was covered. I avoided any kind of shovelling movements so as not to accumulate an additional amount on the knife's surface. Carefully I withdrew the knife from the goo, hoping that slow motion would lead to a few more drops dripping off. I applied the remains from the knife to one corner of my toast and ushered it into my mouth. The flavour explosion that followed made me fearful of what culinary excursions were to follow over the coming weeks. I managed to keep a straight face, affirmed my appreciation for the experience and explained in a credible argumentation that German people would rather eat spicy food at a later time of the day. For breakfast I would stick to jam and butter on toast. I would ignore that glass for the remainder of my stay. My eyes would only catch a final glimpse of the label to make sure I would never forget the name. It read 'Marmite' and I haven't forgotten it to this day. Love it or hate it? Well!

However, there was one tradition that perfectly typifies Britishness that I did fall in love with at the breakfast table. I had always hated tea. Herbal tea was the only kind with which I was acquainted. Peppermint, rosehip and chamomile tea were the sort of drinks I only ever endured when I had to stay in bed with flu. Black tea was no different at first sight. But I did become addicted to PG Tips when my host mother served me one with milk! And she served me one not only for breakfast, but now and then during the course of the day.

Tea seemed to be an integral part of British life. Tea was drunk all day long. As soon as two people started to chat, tea was always the additional companion. My foreign observation of this cultural importance was substantiated while watching British programmes on TV. I never got the gist of what the poor creatures living in *Coronation Street* mumbled, but they obviously liked their tea. On another trip to England a couple of years later, I watched a few episodes of *EastEnders*. What these Cockneys with their even more unbearable accent had in common with their Mancunian counterparts was, apart from spending half their days in a pub, their preference for hot drinks. Their consumption figures reached epic scales though. I seriously wondered whether that London soap, produced and screened by the commercial-free BBC, was actually an infomercial by the tea industry. Tea was used in excessive overdose as a problem solution-finder. You either saw someone standing with a cup in his or her hand, someone coming into the room holding a mug, or the kettle just being filled with water or just being switched on. In case of a crisis, someone would no doubt suggest, 'I'll make a cup of tea,' 'Fancy a cuppa?' or 'I'll just put the kettle on.'

When I returned home, my mother was rather surprised at the amount of tea I consumed all of a sudden on a regular basis. She was even more flabbergasted when I asked her not to forget milk when doing the shopping. I had always detested milk but my trip to England somehow seemed to have worked wonders on my nutritional education. She was very happy, but still wouldn't stop asking me for a long time whether I was really sure about putting milk into my black tea, a tradition Germans hadn't been acquainted with. Healthy drinking was sorted! What did worry her a bit were my new eating habits. A constant lack of variation between my favourite breakfast and dinner meals caused a kind of concern. To me, sausage, beans, eggs on toast and ham in the morning, and sausage, beans, eggs on toast and chips in the evening was varied food of a creative cuisine at its best!

The next logical step was to keep working on the lingo. I decided to buy a British newspaper regularly. Of course, it had to be the famous *Times* to start with. Flicking through the pages, I very soon came to realise that my vocabulary wasn't sufficient to grasp any kind of content in any of the articles, not even in the sports section. I didn't want to give up, though, and decided to start at a lower level. Tabloids had much bigger letters, much shorter sentences and more pictures. I soon found out that the language wasn't always in line with the grammar that was taught at school. Puns as a linguistic tool seemed to be used in headlines in particular. This didn't make it any easier for me to comprehend the meaning of any Liverpool articles. But after a while I started to get the gist, and the more I read the more I developed a sense for the language. Some football technical terms I only understood by reading them over a long period of time in various contexts over and over again.

My brain's intellectual thirst for information and language skills was complemented by a desire driven by a deeper force. Considering the fact that I was only 14 years of age, a nice side-effect in buying British Fleet Street papers was the legitimate access to pictures of attractive young women with very little clothing covering their upper bodily parts on page three. Samantha Fox was a very likeable companion, but Linda Lusardi developed into my favourite friend in the long run. Not many people usually keep a daily paper longer than the day itself, but there were editions I kept forever; 'forever' in the sense of a considerably long time, not that I'm still in possession of them now.

The only place where British newspapers could be bought in Mannheim was the newsagency at our central station. On Sundays, I took the tram to the station before breakfast. I was always looking forward to the ritual and treat of reading the paper all morning while sipping my milk in my black tea. I always checked the back pages first, and whenever I spotted a Liverpool article I chose the paper. In the case of Liverpool being on all back pages, I made my decision on the length of the respective articles before I picked one to buy. Often I couldn't make up my mind and bought the whole lot.

After a while, mere post-match analysis didn't suffice any longer. It was time to be part of the pre-match warm-up too. It became a common procedure after school on Saturdays to take the trip to the station and then back home to enjoy my precious and coveted source of information. Pre-match concentration could be seriously disturbed, if not ruined, when I entered the newsagent and found out that the last copy had just been sold. Out of this concern, I rushed out of the classroom after the final lesson to guarantee a happy weekend.

Classmates who wanted to stay for a chat after school were left confused when I ran off just shouting back, 'Sorry, have to go, I need to get my English newspaper, see you Monday!' They looked on in disbelief as they couldn't figure out why I was doing this, but soon accepted my behaviour. After all, I was a likeable person despite my obvious psychological salience.

Having learned the Liverpool newspaper articles by heart, I also turned to the other sections in the paper and thereby picked up phrases you wouldn't learn in school. Of course, I used the newly acquired words, technical terms and phrases in English lessons whenever an opportunity arose. This not only improved my marks but also elevated me in the pecking order from my teacher's view. Other teachers from chemistry or maths approached me, asking why I couldn't be bothered to develop a similar interest in their subjects. The arithmetic in updating the league table on a regular basis just wouldn't really make me a better maths student, though. Despite the fact that I spent hours on running through the season's remaining fixtures and prognosticating three points for a win and one point for a draw for the Reds and their closest rivals for the league title, it just wouldn't improve my abilities for probability calculation.

Living in my Red world, my mental state cast a spell on my entire environment. It virtually took over home. My mother decided to go for a weekend trip to London in the following summer. She had watched the European Cup Final in May on TV with me when the Reds beat AS Roma in their home stadium. Before the match I pleaded with her not to distract me while watching the match again as she had three years before when Liverpool were playing Real Madrid in the European Cup Final in Paris in 1981. On that occasion, just as the ball went out of play and Ray Kennedy prepared for the throw-in, she engaged me in yet another conversation while she was ironing. I missed Alan Kennedy's run into the box to score the winning goal. When my eyes moved back to the screen he was already running behind the goal to celebrate in front of the travelling Reds. That night in Rome, she would question the fairness of a final to be staged in one of the finalists' home stadiums. When our goalie Bruce Grobbelaar did his wobbly legs during the penalty shoot-out, she brought up the subject of fairness again but the question quickly made way for the query: 'Is this allowed?' Before she further engaged in discussing the laws of football, she burst out laughing and enjoyed the Italians missing their penalties by Brucie's antics alone.

That year marked the 20th anniversary of Liverpool's total autocracy. Just as the Reds and Merseybeat dominated the world back in Shanks's first championship season, Liverpool again ruled the roost on the footie as well as on the musical front. Joe Fagan's Reds triumphed in an unprecedented way, winning the treble for the first time ever. Having won the

League Cup Final, they retained the league title and then marched on to win the European Cup.

Apart from Frankie Goes to Hollywood conquering the world, Scouse artistes dominated the charts at the start of that year: Frankie's 'Relax', Paul McCartney's 'Pipes of Peace', Joe Fagin's 'That's Livin' Alright', John Lennon's 'Nobody Told Me', China Crisis's 'Wishful Thinking', Echo & The Bunnymen's 'The Killing Moon' and Icicle Works's 'Love Is a Wonderful Colour'. There were even more Scouse acts in the Top 20 than in 1964. Frankie Goes to Hollywood then went on to reach number one in the UK singles chart with 'Two Tribes' and 'The Power of Love', becoming the second Scouse band, and only second band of all time, to achieve this feat with their first three single releases after Gerry and the Pacemakers did so two decades before.

One early Saturday morning in mid-August, we took off with British Airways from Frankfurt to London Heathrow. A pity that the football season wasn't already underway, I thought. It wasn't easy to gain access to the fixture list of the upcoming season anyway. They were certainly released some day during the summer, but it would have been tough to guess which of the close season's 100 days was the one worth making the trip to the station's newsagent for. What a dream would have come true if Liverpool just happened to be playing away at a London team like Tottenham, Arsenal, West Ham or Chelsea. But even if there had been a match on, there's no way I could have hassled my mum on our holiday sightseeing weekend to make the trip to north, east or west London to spend the precious short time in England watching a football match. Still, I was looking forward to guiding my mother through London and showing her all the sights I had been to before.

We stayed in a hotel in Earl's Court. It was a lovely sunny day and we didn't waste too much time unpacking our bags and went straight back to the street to get to the nearest underground station. We had a tight time schedule as I had planned the whole day, actually the whole weekend, thoroughly. Big Ben was the first stop, obviously. We took the tube to Westminster and were looking forward to a great, joyful day in England's capital. After Big Ben I was going to turn right into Parliament Street, to take her to Whitehall, passing Downing Street, and then off to Nelson's Column on Trafalgar Square, before turning into The Mall to walk up to Buckingham Palace. Nothing would interfere with my professionally organised high-quality plan.

Just as we turned away from Big Ben, we passed by a souvenir shop and dropped in just to have a look. In between umbrellas, cups and pencils displaying Union Jacks or Her Majesty's head, I spotted something rather familiar, a Liverpool hat. The positioning of this wasn't on a shelf for sale, but on a man's head. *Wow, a Liverpool fan showing his colours while doing his sightseeing tour in London*, I thought. On holidays in Spain I had often seen British people wearing jerseys of their football teams. On the beach, holidaymakers from all countries wore nothing but a suntan and swimming trunks. British people, most often with a kind of pink skin caused by a sudden and careless exposure of a very white body to the sun while not applying the sun-cream competently, tended to show off their kits all day long. Even in restaurants for breakfast, lunch or dinner, where everyone else was wearing smart clothing, the British marked their territories with their football outfits.

I walked on, when suddenly I bumped into a girl wearing a Liverpool scarf. *Hang on*, I thought, *this is the most touristic area in London and there are so many Liverpool fans around wearing LFC clothing? Can't be!* When I turned around I spotted even more people wearing something red and white with 'LIVERPOOL FC' all over it. I got heavily suspicious. I said to my mother, 'Look at them, Liverpool fans in London.'

'Ask them what they're doing here. Maybe Liverpool play here,' she replied.

'Noooo, the season hasn't started yet.'

'Just ask them!' she insisted.

I approached the man and started to speak in my still broken English. 'Excuse me,' pointing at their Liverpool outfits, 'what are you doing here?'

'We're going to the match!' was the answer. A silent pause on my behalf interrupted the conversation.

I stuttered, 'Liverpool is playing?'

'Yeah!' 'Where? In London?'

'Yeah, at Wembley.'

'At Wembley?' Now I was confused. Wembley was for internationals and cup finals.

'Who are they playing?'

'Everton.'

'Everton?'

Now I was totally lost. Two teams from Liverpool playing in the middle of the summer in London and of all places at Wembley? My unbelieving and confused face must have aroused compassion from the man, who was surrounded by more and more people in Liverpool outfits. It was his family apparently. He started to explain to me why Liverpool were playing that day and that they had come to watch them. I could hear his voice but was unable to listen. My mind wandered off, drifted light years away to a world of thoughts on its own. All I could grasp was the explanation that the champions play the cup winners in the season's opener at Wembley.

When my brain arrived back in the presence of the souvenir shop, my eyes stared at him, realising that LIVERPOOL were in town! 'Are there tickets?' I asked.

He smiled and said, 'Oh no, it's been sold out for six weeks. No chance!' Paralysis of my soul took over my entire body. I intended to force a smile upon my face but only managed a slight twitch of my labial angle. The entire world's injustice burdened on my shoulders! Coming so close and yet being so far away would bother me for the remainder of our weekend. The whole London trip was ruined for me after we had only started our tour five minutes before. I was shattered, gutted and on the verge of wallowing in self-pity.

'Let's go and try to get a ticket,' my mother suggested. Despite acknowledging her kind support, I declined. Wembley was miles away and I wanted to avoid increasing the pain by wandering aimlessly around the holy ground asking cheerful ticket holders for spares in vain. My mother sometimes has this 'let's just do it' attitude, which convinces you of just doing it before you can give it a second thought.

She insisted, 'Come on, Carsten! If we don't get tickets you can still at least have a look around the famous Wembley Stadium from outside. That's worth it too, isn't it?' That convinced me. Thus, we followed the Red family to the station. On the train, Reds and Blues mixed in a great atmosphere. I was on the march with the Red Army to Wembley. The journey felt like hours, although we were only heading to a suburb on the outskirts of the same city. With every minute passing by, excitement was infiltrated by a strong feeling of sadness. I would be part of the party only as far as the turnstiles. The all-too-familiar feeling of envy crept inside me. This sense of self-pity soon made way for a guilty conscience towards my mother. She had sacrificed her first day in London for sitting on a musty seat on a train leading us far away from Buckingham Palace or the Tower of London.

After leaving the train, we followed the masses. Soon, we realised it wasn't going to be much of a stroll around Wembley, but rather a strictly organised march with policemen on horses directing the way. Walking along the road there were loads of people shouting or holding up pieces of paper asking for tickets. My initial belief of having no chance of obtaining tickets was confirmed. The slightest hope of getting lucky by chance was dashed dramatically by being surrounded by so many competitors longing for the highly coveted spares. All these people must have already made a big effort to get tickets for weeks. They had probably spent all day in London and at Wembley, approaching anyone wearing red or blue colours, only to be turned away.

It felt somehow a naive decision to have come here in the first place. We walked on with no hopes in our hearts. Police horses pushed us up the road, the riders shouting at people who tried to pause on the side of the road. It was a weird feeling of having paid a lot of money for an unforgettable sightseeing weekend in London and now finding ourselves in some of the capital's suburbs being shouted at by policemen, who looked at everyone in a very derogatory way and treated you as an inferior citizen just because you belonged to an anonymous crowd of football supporters.

Arriving outside the ground we could move freely again as the police decided not to escort us further through the turnstiles to the inside of the stadium. Typical, isn't it – they're never there when you actually need them! The hectic, busy atmosphere was comparable to an Arabian bazaar. It was about a quarter of an hour to kick-off and the masses moved towards the entrances. There were people shouting everywhere around us. The one and only word you kept hearing was 'tickets'. We approached one group of people who we thought might be discussing a ticket deal, only to be turned away. 'No, sorry, luv.' Some fans mistook us for potential sellers and came up towards us asking how much a ticket would be. We were confused, and explained that we were looking for spares ourselves.

Kick-off time approached and the area visibly emptied. Amongst hordes of grown-up men, a tourist mother and her tourist teenage son, who looked a bit lost, must have made a strange impression to some onlookers. But maybe it was this helplessness that drew the attention of a man who suddenly approached us. 'Ticket?' he said.

I replied, 'No, no, we have no ticket,' and was already about to turn away. He pointed a finger at me and repeated, 'Ticket? You want a ticket?'

Now I was pointing to myself, interpreting his words. 'Ticket for me?' He nodded.

Disbelieving, I turned to my mother and told her about his offer. In a very strict voice she exclaimed, 'Show me ticket!' He produced a piece of paper that looked very much genuine. In no time we were surrounded by loads of other people trying to interfere with our discussion, only to be turned away by this man. He meant to do business with us. Suspicion infiltrated our thoughts. There must be a snag. Either the ticket would be a fake or the guy just a tout. There must be something wrong.

'How much?' I asked. He showed me the ticket and pointed to the £4. 'Four pounds? How much is the ticket?'

'Four pounds,' he replied.

'But what's your price?' I remarked in a rather unfriendly way, as if to imply that he shouldn't take the piss out of me.

He smiled and nodded. 'It's four pounds.'

My mother and I looked at each other, both thinking why is he doing this?

'Why are you doing this?' I asked. He explained that he got the tickets a long time ago for his son and himself. His son had become ill and he didn't want to go on his own. He had already sold one ticket and now had a spare one left. Speechlessness followed on my behalf. Whereas I couldn't grasp what was happening, my mother forked out the money.

My 'thank you' in this moment to this stranger was the most grateful and sincere one I had ever uttered in my life. He smiled again and left. 'What about you?' I asked my mother.

With a smile, she said, 'Don't you worry about me. I go shopping around Wembley. Meet me at this very same spot after the match.'

There I was, standing outside Wembley Stadium with a valid ticket to watch Liverpool! I gripped it with both hands, pressing thumbs against my forefingers, while being careful not to inadvertently tear the holy paper apart. Making my way through the turnstile was the most unreal feeling. At about ten to three we would probably now have been walking to Piccadilly Circus if we had stuck to my schedule. Now I was just entering Wembley Stadium! Not only was I about to watch Liverpool Football Club live in England for the very first time, but also at Wembley of all places, and against Everton of all teams.

Walking up the steps to the lower tier I found out that my spec was right behind the goal. And what was even more important, it was in the Liverpool end. The upper tier soon started to get the songs going. A choral competition started with the Blues at the opposite end when I noticed that quite a few people around me joined in with the Evertonians. I was surprised to witness such a massive mixed zone with Blues here and Reds in the Blues' end. It felt a bit strange but I was looking forward to the mutual banter, most of which I wouldn't get the gist of anyway.

Bruce Grobbelaar received a special reception from the travelling Kop, although in the second half he became the tragic figure of the match by scoring one of the most bizarre goalkeeping own goals ever at the Everton end. I tried to follow the match itself, but I was more occupied with happenings off the field. I was completely taken aback by the whole atmosphere that 100,000 Liverpudlians created all around. It was electrifying being right in the middle of a red, white and yellow sea of scarves, flags and banners that I had only ever seen on TV before.

The moving masses kept shifting me around. Within a few seconds I found myself three steps down, then five straight back up again. A four-foot move to the left was followed by a six-foot move back to the right. In between the shoving and pushing I tried to reserve enough energy for the songs. I recognised most of the tunes but had no chance of comprehending the lyrics. But I joined in most vociferously when 'You'll Never Walk Alone' was intoned or 'Li-ver-pool, Li-ver-pool, Li-ver-pool'. Even the fact that my pubescent vocal change hadn't been successfully completed entirely didn't diminish my joy in joining in! Occasional sudden squeaks in my singing wouldn't be perceived amongst the screaming masses anyway. I hoped!

There was one chant that kept erupting with most intense passion during the whole match again and again. The fact that both sets of supporters sang it was astonishing. By the look of the faces and the singing with such gusto, I couldn't figure out at first whether it implied a very unfriendly message towards each other or rather comprised a kind of solidarity of Reds and Blues. As the whole stadium sang it synchronously, I figured it must be something unifying. It had the same familiar tune of 'Li-ver-pool, Li-ver-pool, Li-ver-pool'. I didn't care about the meaning and just tried to sing along with it.

Trying to lipread the Kopites around me was more important than the match itself, which we were losing anyway. As a teenager staring at strange, older men's lips for longer than just a moment caused irritated looks towards me. My autodidactic crash course in Scouse pushed me from auditory to articulatory phonetics, which culminated in me belting out 'Me-ssi-sseye, Me-ssi-sseye, Me-ssi-sseye'. Screaming out my new favourite chant, the passion in my voice and eyes didn't differ at all from the born and bred Scousers all around me. I didn't have a clue what I was screaming about, but I stood for 'Me-ssi-sseye' as for nothing else. When I got hold of the Sunday papers next day and read the back page headline 'Merseyside', I felt some pride that I wasn't too far off the original vocable, phonetically at least.

My mother and I managed to catch up with our sightseeing schedule on Sunday and concluded the most perfect trip to London.

Reminiscing about my Liverpool Football Club live match history and also the way I got hold of tickets, I came to one conclusion: I was very blessed. I had attended the semi-final of the European Cup away to German champions Bayern Munich and now the all-Merseyside derby in the Charity Shield encounter at Wembley. In future, I couldn't expect to push my luck anymore and for fate to come to my aid. It just wouldn't happen!

CHAPTER FOUR

Any Spares for a European Cup Final?

'I'M GOING to Brussels!' I remarked rather casually one Saturday afternoon. My mother looked puzzled, not really grasping what I was referring to. 'Liverpool will be playing in the European Cup Final in Brussels.' That was quite a confident remark as we were in early April and would actually still have to overcome our Greek opponents Panathinaikos in the semi-final first. Confidence also characterised my mindset on finding ways to obtain a ticket. After the experience at Wembley at the beginning of the season, everything seemed to be possible, especially if you plan it thoroughly beforehand. I firmly believed in the universal law of attraction.

By focusing on positive thoughts, one can bring positive experiences into one's life. In my personal interpretation it basically meant that the power of obtaining anything one desires, may it be health, wealth or happiness, lies in your own hands ... well, my personal health, wealth and happiness was grounded in the acquisition of a European Cup Final ticket.

Unlike to Munich in 1981 and Wembley in 1984, I would have to sort it out in advance and I would have to sort it out myself. There was no way my mother could find a way to aid me in this matter. As I couldn't figure out how to find any official access to tickets from a German source, there was no alternative appearing on the horizon but to contact Liverpool Football Club directly. I formulated the sentences I was going to speak on the phone a thousand times. I practised articulating these sentences out loud a million times.

'Hello … my name is Carsten. I would like to know when I can buy a ticket for the European Cup Final in Brussels.' The use of 'if' in a conditional clause instead of 'when' didn't even cross my mind.

Maybe it would arouse compassion if I emphasised my disadvantageous situation living abroad. 'Hello … this is Carsten from Germany and I would like to ask you how I can buy a ticket for the European Cup Final in Brussels.' This kind of straightforwardness, combined with my cleverness in settling the purchase before tickets officially went on sale would certainly sort me out with a ticket.

Thus, I rang the Liverpool ticket office enquiring about the general ticket sale the day before the return leg in Athens. Liverpool had won the first leg 4-0 at Anfield. I kept pressing the dialling code 0044 151 for ages but couldn't get through. Disappointment grew inside me as I suspected other canny fans had the same smart idea to enquire about selling arrangements before tickets actually went on sale. A free line signal made my heart beat faster. A female voice answered the phone. Before I could even finish my sentence 'Hello, this is Carsten from Germany and I would like …' I was cruelly reminded of my personal deficits in understanding the local language of my beloved football club … Scouse. In the souvenir shop outside Big Ben, I could at least make use of international sign language. On the terrace at Wembley, I could at least try hard to read people's lips to comprehend. But on the phone, I had been plunged in at the deep end! Within the scope of my comprehension, she informed me that Liverpool would have to play the second leg encounter the following day first. Good point! She pointed out that the ticket allocation might not be sufficient to cover the demand and that season ticket holders were served first. *Oh,* I thought, *they do have a ticketing qualifying scheme,* a fact that made sense but had never really crossed my mind. Still, this minor challenge couldn't interfere with my plan to go to Brussels.

It turned out to be a Liverpool v Juventus final, an encounter between record title winners of the English and Italian leagues respectively. Indeed, it turned out that demand for tickets exceeded the available allocation. I contacted the German Football Association and other institutions. Someone somewhere, somehow, must have some kind of complimentary tickets for honorary reasons or simply for raffles. Destiny, kismet, karma will be on my side, I was convinced, but time went by without showing any signs of a merciful fate.

I had to involve my mother. She was good at sorting out difficult tasks. Of course, she would be fundamentally against her 16-year-old son going on his own on a 270-mile train ride to Belgium. However, just like back in the old

Subbuteo days, I had a very strong influence on her psyche. 'You're my only mother, I can't turn to any other.'

One pro argument was that the final was being played during a week's school holiday, so I would be able to make the trip without interfering with my education programme. Although she totally opposed the whole idea, my mother had already started to look for some accommodation for me in the meantime. Being convinced that I would be going anyway, she wanted to make sure that I was having a safe stay over in Belgium at least. She rang a couple of hotels but was always turned away immediately. Brussels was fully booked. I made it quite clear that I would still be going, even without knowing where to stay. Brussels' nights at the end of May would be warm enough to sleep rough. Speechlessness accompanied by a look that indicated the serious question of whether she had brought up an insane teenager was followed by a straight return to the phone the next evening to dial a few more hotel numbers.

One night shift reservation manager wasn't able to offer any vacancies either, but he was different from all others answering her phone calls. He was rather friendly. He introduced himself and offered his support. Abdullah promised to stay in touch and, in case one room reservation was cancelled, he would help us out. Great stuff! At least I had reason to be optimistic on the accommodation front, but what about the ticket?

I started to become as desperate as you could get. There was no naive measure too embarrassing that I would refrain from daring to attempt. I even placed a classified ad in our local newspaper: 'Mannheimer Morgen: 1 Karte für Fußballspiel Liverpool/Turin in Brüssel 29.5.85 gesucht. Tel.

0621/...' A local paper in some town in Germany to get me a ticket for the biggest encounter in club football was my last chance. Subconsciously, I was hoping for a tout to get in touch with me. Response to the ad was a bit limited, or to put it more precisely, zero!

Thoughts of going anyway wouldn't leave me. The Liverpool guy in Munich back in 1981 did it and was lucky to get inside, just as I managed it at Wembley. My intention overstrained my family. 'Carsten, I as your mother won't allow you, my underage 16-year-old son, to travel alone to a foreign country without a match ticket and no room to stay for the night!' This was followed by an enumeration of laws by the German state concerning her duty as a parent to look after the well-being of her child. Additionally, she confronted me with judicial facts that, by my doing, she would personally get into conflict with the law if such and such paragraph was neglected. She never studied law, nor did I ever give her cause to occupy herself with legal advice, but in that situation it just came pouring out of her. I had to laugh. Not because I didn't take her seriously, but because I sensed that she was convinced I would become obsessed with my idea and actually go ahead and realise it. My mother considered me as a crazy and thereby a proper Liverpool supporter. I liked that! I calmed her down by reassuring her I wouldn't go.

Another call to Abdullah brought some kind of good news. As there was no sign of any room cancellations, he offered to let me sleep in a room in the cellar. 'It's nothing special. It has no window. It's just a room with a bed. It's for hotel employees who sometimes have to stay overnight,' he explained. Great! Accommodation problem solved, at least!

'Mr Abdullah, do you think there's a chance to get a ticket as well?' my mother politely asked.

'No chance,' he replied. 'The city is full of people looking for tickets. There are tickets available, but you wouldn't want to pay that money. The latest I heard was over one thousand Deutsche Mark.'

My mother gave the impression that she was contemplating this for a split second, but said, 'No, Carsten, I can't.'

'But I'll keep an eye on it for you,' Abdullah said, trying to end the conversation on a positive note.

By the time the week of the final arrived, there was no other topic at home but Brussels. I asked my mother on Monday night, 48 hours prior to kick-off, to call Abdullah one more time. Again, we sat down, she rang the Belgium code, then the one for Brussels and finally the hotel. Abdullah answered the phone. When he realised it was my mother he immediately exclaimed, 'Aaaah, where are you?' We looked at each other, not knowing how to interpret this question. 'Where's this son of yours? I'm waiting for him!'

My mother asked him what the story was and he replied what none of us could comprehend: 'I've got your ticket!' Silence at our end. Abdullah explained that some Italian was wandering around for days trying to sell his ticket on the black market. 'But the Liverpool fans wouldn't talk to him and his offers.' The price for the ticket was now down to 120 Deutsche Mark, some £30. I was in a trance. I couldn't grasp what I seemed to hear. Two nights before the European Cup Final, I had my ticket! 'But it's not in the Liverpool end, it's in the neutral section.'

I wasn't able to follow the rest of their conversation. From some million light years away I heard my mother confirm everything and settle the details about when I would arrive and that I was bringing him the money and so on. When she put down the phone, we looked at each other and the biggest 'Yeeeeessssssssssss' followed that I had ever screamed in my life! I was about to witness my first-ever Liverpool European Cup Final. What a great, unforgettable day it was going to be!

Leaving early Wednesday morning on 29 May 1985 from Mannheim main station was a very proud moment. I was wearing my yellow Liverpool away strip with thin red lines, and the scarf I had bought in Munich four years earlier. Amongst business people commuting to their jobs in Frankfurt, I stood out in my football gear. My mind envisioned the evening to come.

In Cologne I had to change trains to get to Belgium's capital. Walking by the compartments on the train looking for a free seat, I spotted two English guys who I sat next to. They were from Nottingham and served in the British Army in Germany. A bit later another young German in LFC colours joined us. He was born in Dresden in East Germany but now lived in Sweden. Neither of them had match tickets. The soldiers taught us a couple of Liverpool songs and this time it didn't take me long to comprehend the lyrics: 'We're on the march with Fagan's Army, We're all going to Brussels, And we'll really shake 'em up, When we win the European Cup, Cos Liverpool are the greatest football team.' I loved it! It was the first encounter with Liverpool fans who I could have a proper conversation with. In retrospect, by the fact that they originated from Nottingham in particular, I wonder whether they were real Liverpool supporters or just making the trip to watch another English team, which was nothing unusual back then. I told them about my ticket and the story of how I got hold of it.

After arriving in Brussels, they joined me in a taxi drive to my hotel. We hoped that my source might provide further availability. But, as expected, their hopes were dashed immediately. A colleague of Mr Abdullah, who himself would be on the late shift that night, handed me the precious envelope. Enquiring about more tickets, he warned us that there were a lot of fakes doing the rounds. We decided to split as the others wanted to try to find some spares on the city centre's main square. I dropped off my bag in my room and headed straight to the stadium, despite it being only early afternoon. When I received my ticket, I read 'Bloc Z' and the letters 'XY' next to it being painted over black. I couldn't wait to get to the Heysel as soon as possible to absorb every second of the final's atmosphere. On the metro, I was sitting with English and Italian families. They were all smiling and joking. Apart from facial expressions, communication was reduced to sign language. Holding up fingers in numbers on each hand indicated everyone's prediction for the outcome of the match.

Getting off the train, my excitement had already hit boiling point. Never ever had I been to a match on my own, let alone to one of this magnitude. To get to the stadium you had to cross a massive meadow. The whole area seemed to be taken up by supporters in black and white colours. There wasn't any red to be seen. The Liverpool fans on the train had disappeared in various directions. Within seconds I was on my own. I kept walking through masses of Italians and was soon the focus of their attention. Not understanding any word they were shouting at me, I was definitely a victim of their banter. I could easily sense that they were purely joking in a friendly way. Some of them approached me quite closely and tried to involve me in sign language communication. Family fathers and their kids, groups of men, and young guys were smiling at me, giving me finger salutes, indicating Juve were going to win 2-0. I replied, of course, the opposite. I was fully overwhelmed by this friendly party atmosphere full of laughter and jokes but always with respect.

All of a sudden, I was confronted by a bunch of Juve fans surrounding me. At first I was a bit irritated but then I began to understand their intention. One guy gesticulated that he wanted to buy my jersey off me. I tried to make him understand that I was from Germany and had no easy access to buy Liverpool kits myself. The fact that he spoke as much English as I was acquainted with Italian didn't help the situation. When he started to grab my shirt I panicked a bit as I was totally outnumbered. It would have been no big deal for them to strip my jersey off me. *Why did I have to take the route right through the Italian end on my own?* I thought.

But then I realised that his physical approach was in no way aggressive towards me, but happened out of sheer despair on his behalf. His facial expression and his voice made me understand that he was actually begging me to give him my jersey. One of his mates, who smiled all along and observed us both being lost in translation, tried to intervene by playing interpreter. He could speak a bit of English and he translated to me that his mate wanted to offer me his Juve jersey, Juve scarf and Juve flag in return for my jersey. He wanted to give me everything he had in exchange. I felt sorry for him, but it never crossed my mind seriously to wrap up that deal, though. Still, it mattered to me that he understood that my decline wasn't down to sheer ignorance, but my personal lack of availability in my country. I apologised politely for not accepting his generous offer. When I eventually got my message across to him, he was on the verge of crying! He accepted my decision and thanked me for the encounter. We both wished each other good luck for the match.

Feeling relieved to have escaped unscathed, I walked over to the red end of the ground. There were innumerable Liverpool fans with Juve scarves, hats and flags and Juve fans with LFC colours everywhere. Only then did I realise that it was obviously common practice to swap colours that day. No wonder he was surprised that I refused to participate in this sign of friendship!

It was a very hot day and I decided to get a few cokes, sandwiches and chocolate bars. Yes, at that age booze hadn't entered my life. To my amazement, walking around the stadium I couldn't find a single stall selling drinks or food until I eventually spotted a supermarket on the high street behind the main stand. Reds were swarming in and out as it seemed to be the only source of supply in the whole area. Inside the shop some Reds asked a question I interpreted as where they could find certain food. Again, I was confronted with a Scouse phonetic challenge. I had to apologise that I couldn't understand. Then I had to admit my foreign status and my German roots. Pure humiliation!

They seemed quite surprised to hear the name of my country and see the Liverpool gear on me. 'Germany, you're from Germany?!' You could tell their confusion about why a German would travel to Belgium to watch an English team play an Italian team. 'That's cool!' In that moment I somehow grasped that Liverpool Football Club was actually still a local concern. They were the record winners of the English league as well as holders of the European Cup and had a worldwide viewing audience on TV, but they were still only a 'local team'. Wherever they played, the following supporters would all be from Merseyside or at least had their roots in that area. By their smiles I could sense a kind of pride they felt that someone from a foreign land would support their team and dress and travel like they did themselves. This kind of acknowledgement from true Kopites caused me to burst with pride! One of them patted me on the back and wished me all the best. 'Enjoy it, mate!'

As there wasn't really anything to do in this area, I decided to go straight back to the gates of the blocks X, Y and Z. To the very right, a large group of people in black and white were already queuing outside the entrance for block Z. There were only Juve fans and I couldn't spot one single Liverpool supporter. I soon realised I didn't really fancy standing on my own in the middle of Italians. I wanted to enjoy being in the middle of the travelling Kop. I wanted to sing and celebrate with my fellow Reds. As the black-and-whites gathered in ever larger numbers, I decided to stay with the Liverpool lot outside blocks X and Y.

The sight of an ever-increasing Italian crowd over at the other end made it quite clear that this wasn't a neutral section at all. It was apparent that the allocation going on general sale to the Belgian public had been snapped up by Italian locals who provided themselves and family members at home with tickets. Although it had been an entirely friendly atmosphere until then, I didn't really fancy the idea of being the only one wearing yellow amongst an all-zebra-stripe dress code and be the subject of the contest to 'spot the Liverpool fan in the

Juventus crowd'. My plan was to get inside the ground and get a position as close to the Liverpool section as possible. Maybe I could climb over a fence if I wasn't observed. Maybe some steward would even let me get to the other side when he realised that I was in the wrong section. In my mind, I occupied myself for a long time about how to overcome the official organisation of the authorities, who would have been given orders to strictly implement segregation. They would have prepared stewards and policemen inside the ground to control the blocks professionally to the highest security standards for this event. In the end, I scrapped all ideas and decided to just stick with the Liverpool supporters. I would try to get in the middle of a crowded queue and put my thumb on the letter 'Z' when showing my ticket. I hoped that they would be too busy to check each ticket thoroughly.

At around 4pm, some Reds decided it was time to get in. The outer fence was joggled a bit but there were no stewards or policemen anywhere near to prevent them from going further. After a few minutes, the fence bent to the point that it tore down altogether. We all walked over it and towards the entrance to wait there for the checkpoints to open. All of a sudden, Belgian policemen appeared from inside the ground, the first I had seen all day. Soon afterwards, police on horseback joined them. The uniforms were screaming at us in a way I had last witnessed in some old Nazi films. These guys were definitely not to be messed with.

The crowd grew bigger and after a while they decided to open the gates. Every little shove would be penalised with a hit of a stick. There were quite harmless people such as couples, families and myself amongst the crowd, but we were all treated like potential offenders. Some of the policemen seemed to be waiting for a reason to exert any kind of aggression. I tried to present a well-behaved impression and pressed my thumb firmly on the big Z on my ticket. They didn't even bother checking tickets at all, to my surprise. They were solely concerned about keeping the crowd in order. I kept on walking and felt great relief when I was inside. I had made it into the Liverpool section.

My pure happiness was soon infiltrated by a disappointment caused by the obvious state of the stadium, though. I had never envisioned it before too much, but I certainly never expected the view that unfolded before my eyes. Most steps on the terraces were broken. Rusty steel pieces hung out of the concrete. Weeds grew all over the place. Barriers were corroded. I had been to a few football stadia, even some old grounds, but never had I seen an arena so unfit for a match, let alone a European Cup Final. Heysel Stadium appeared to be an abandoned place where no football match had been staged for ages. This was the venue of the most important match of European club football?

I needed a pee and headed back upstairs to go to the toilets, but could only find an open wooden hut with a roof. Standing at the urinal trying to relieve myself, I spotted fans throwing their tickets over the eight-foot-high stone wall to their mates outside.

Even the wall was crumbling and had holes, through which tickets could be passed. One Liverpool fan came running into the hut being chased by a policeman, who hit him with his stick. As quickly as they both appeared, they vanished again at the other end. Other policemen were screaming at supporters who tried to make use of the holes in the wall. All while I was trying to have a slash.

The situation seemed to have got out of hand as the police obviously had a problem in getting the chaos under control. The severity with which they handled the entire circumstances seemed to be an attempt to make up for lost ground, as they weren't present outside when the fence had been crashed earlier on. Their aggressive and brutal behaviour might also have been grounded in their awareness of being outnumbered. It was still afternoon and only a few hundred fans had to be handled as most Reds were still on the main square in the city centre. In any kind of normal situation, it wouldn't have been all too challenging a task to deal with this amount of people, provided that a professional organisation of a sufficient amount of police and stewards had been promptly and strategically instructed.

I walked around the top of the terrace looking for a stall selling drinks. The heat had got worse and so had my thirst. But there were no drinks available, not even water. The only refreshment I could get hold of was ice cream. Not for a single moment did I contemplate leaving the stadium to get back to the supermarket for some cans. It was still more than three hours before kick-off, so overall it would be some six hours before I could get access to something drinkable in town again. The experience was just too unreal but at least I was in the Reds' end and could take my position directly behind the goal, where Brucie might be doing his antics tonight again.

Looking at the fence that separated the two sets of fans only a few yards away, I realised that I shouldn't have worried too much about finding my way into block X and Y. It didn't really provide an obstacle to overcome. It was a rusty, weak wire mesh fence, which could easily be climbed over. Furthermore, apart from one single policeman and his dog on the running track, there wasn't a single steward or policeman to be seen on the entire terrace. There were no officials installed to guard the segregation between blocks X, Y and Z. I had everything I desired so desperately, but my mood had somehow totally changed over the course of the previous quarter of an hour. I tried to get rid of all my negative impressions mentally and focus on looking forward to the big match. Everything will calm down. Everything will be fine. Everything will be great for us! The terraces became gradually more and more crowded and the singing got going.

Every single Liverpool supporter who attended the match that day will have his or her individual perception and own personal recollection of the events that followed.

Some ten yards away from me somebody threw what looked like a lighter over the fence into the Italian crowd. There was no response from the other side. After a while another piece was thrown from our end over to block Z. Again, no response followed. When yet another missile was tossed across the blocks, some object was returned. A mutual throwing of little items started. The frequency of throws increased and missiles got bigger. When a firework rocket was launched, it started to become really nasty. I quickly moved away from the middle of the terrace over to the safer corner flag area. I took it only as a temporary, precautionary measure and would return to my former spot later on. Surely there will be a sufficient police force to intervene soon and bring the trouble to an end before it has a chance to escalate. I was looking around to see whether any officials had turned up in adequate numbers to be effective but, from my view, there was still not a single policeman anywhere on either side of the fence to take responsibility and appropriate action to stop the aggression. They were probably still busy sorting out the problems outside the stadium.

After a while, the unprotected fence was torn down from our side and fighting broke out. Only at this stage did the police turn up, but they failed to get the situation under control. It was too late. They were right in the middle of it. The Juventus fans in block Z tried to escape and fled from the middle towards the outer parts of the terrace. You could clearly see masses of people crushing into the bottom corner. Then all hell broke loose all over the place. There was so much violence to be witnessed everywhere that you couldn't be sure where it might break out next. Suddenly, a massive scream of tens of thousands echoed around the stadium, coming from the opposite end. I couldn't figure out what it was. Just like most of the people around me I was looking towards the pitch. I asked a guy next to me what had happened and he just shrugged his shoulders. What I only learned afterwards but didn't know in that moment, as I never saw it, was the collapse of the wall in block Z due to the pressure of the fleeing Italian supporters.

From a distance I saw more and more Juventus fans at their end climbing over the fence and running over the running track towards our end. Some fans in my area started to make their way up the steps to get outside. 'Fucking stay where you are!' a man in his fifties screamed at them. 'Fucking stay!' That man's quick reaction was the most sensible there could have been in that situation. Not only did people keep calm but also signalled that we were to stand our ground. When the Italians arrived in front of our end there wasn't much they could do. I just kept wondering what would happen if they were able to run around the stadium to storm our block from behind. Would there be enough policemen to keep them out? They couldn't even manage to keep ticketless fans from bunking in. Helicopters were flying above us. Ambulances were driving around all over the place. After a while it quietened down a bit. Little brawls could be seen here and there but the war-like atmosphere had gone. Policemen formed a human chain and walked over the entire pitch to clear it and separate both sets of fans. Looking to my right, block Z was completely cleared of people too. It looked like an abandoned battlefield.

An English voice, which people around me soon identified as Liverpool's captain Phil Neal, spoke over the PA system to the crowd, but I couldn't understand a word. A bit later our manager Joe Fagan walked over to our curve and by his gestures tried to calm emotions down. A long time passed by and I was actually expecting and waiting for the announcement that the match was to be cancelled. At some point, both teams walked out of the tunnel, and at around a quarter to ten the match actually kicked off. It was the time when I had expected to await the final whistle to celebrate our fifth European Cup win. The match got underway, but I wasn't at all in the mood to be bothered. I was shattered, sad and ashamed.

After the match on the tram back to my hotel, I stood next to two Italian men. I couldn't understand a word of their conversation, but then overheard the word 'morte'. From my Latin class at school I comprehended the meaning of it. I dared to interrupt them and repeated 'morte?' They just nodded. That was the first time I learned that people had died. Back at the hotel, I had no chance to get through to the reception desk as everyone wanted to make phone calls to relatives back home. It was way past midnight. It was already some five hours after the wall had collapsed and news had broken to the watching TV audience at home that people had been killed. My mother at home still didn't know that I was alright. When I spotted Mr Abdullah's name badge I called his attention. He rang my mother, handed me over the phone and I could assure her of my well-being.

When I returned from Brussels the next evening, my mother picked me up from the station. I was wearing the only change of clothing I had with me, a shirt depicting 'LIVERPOOL – Pride of Anfield' in big letters. After the most relieved hug she could give me, she whispered something into my ear that I couldn't make any sense of. 'How on earth can you bring yourself to wear that Liverpool shirt?' I looked at her quizzically. 'The atmosphere here all day has been so hostile and full of hate for that club of yours. Everyone from the newsagent to the tram driver is talking about it. We'd better get out of here quickly!' My mother sometimes tends to exaggerate, but while walking to the car some people really did look askance at me. On the way home, she explained in detail that there had been no other topic of conversation everywhere all day.

In the evening, the scheduled TV programme was cancelled completely and there were only special broadcasts about Heysel, Liverpool Football Club and Liverpool as a city in general. Sitting exhausted and depressed on the sofa, I still couldn't come to terms with what had happened some 24 hours earlier. Even my mother found it hard to believe that I hadn't been aware of the fatalities while I was inside the ground. If she knew about the deaths in her living room hundreds of miles away, how could it be that I didn't know about it, being less than 100 yards away? There was a wider story to be told than that presented on TV. Events were reduced to the fact that Liverpool hooligans stormed the Juventus section, where a wall collapsed and 39 people died. End of story! The round-table discussion completely lacked any kind of deeper analysis of any organisational failures.

The main focus was on Liverpool fans and conversation led to discussing Liverpool people in general. Footage of the Liverpool 8 uprising and burning houses in Toxteth a few years earlier were shown, of course. Unemployment rates were mentioned and Margaret Thatcher got air time to contribute her personal views. She described Liverpool as 'a city possessed with a particularly violent nature'. The population of an entire city was quickly denounced over the behaviour of some individuals. Facts wouldn't fit into Mrs Thatcher's argument at all, least of all that these supporters had previously had a comparatively good record while travelling around Europe. And this in view of the fact that Liverpool FC had played more matches in European competitions in the 1970s and 80s than any other English club and had reached no fewer than six finals before 1985.

They also explained the roots of the tragedy and made viewers comprehend the complexity of Liverpudlians living in general decline. The editorial team even excavated some documentary out of the archive, which showed some footage about an 'average Scouse family'. An unemployed family father was portrayed. His daughters were also out of work and had a couple of children by different fathers. Alcohol, sex and crime were the sole contents of life in a typical Liverpool household. A simple, but perfect causal link between Liverpool's state and events in Brussels was presented. This undifferentiated view unfairly attacked all fellow Reds and their families. The media did its best to influence public opinion that cried for collective punishment.

I was shocked! I was angry! I was hurt! In the days that followed I stood no chance of arguing against the general stance. What relevance did it have that thousands of true Liverpool supporters were swapping their shirts with Italians before the match? I could have told long stories about the friendly party atmosphere. What significance had the fact that there were also people from out of Liverpool who weren't even following the Reds, but looking for trouble? I could have related brief encounters with German hooligans; for example, the two guys from Cologne standing next to me during the match, who told me they came only to seek trouble and intended 'to smash every Italian's face' they bumped into when they got back to the city centre after the match. What implications on the entire outcome it might have had if there had been proper policing in place. I could have counted the limited number of policemen I came across all day. People were listening to my stories but they were simply not interested in the details. I couldn't be bothered to argue against them, so I started to keep quiet on the whole matter and never talked about it.

The negative connotation of Heysel associated with Liverpool FC kept resurfacing for years. Whenever I proudly proclaimed which club was assured of my unconditional allegiance, people gave me a questioning look. Without asking me why, most of them assumed that it must be a kind of admiration for their 'hooligans'. What else?! There could be no other reason for a German who was born and bred in Germany and never lived outside of Germany to not support a team from Germany but from England. And Liverpool of all teams!

Sometimes I felt gutted, I felt sick. Out of a general condemnation of what I loved by the outside world, my emotional relationship with Liverpool grew even stronger. This bond not only referred to Liverpool Football Club but to the people of the city of Liverpool.

REST IN PEACE

Rocco Acerra
Bruno Balli
Alfons Bos
Giancarlo Bruschera
Andrea Casula
Giovanni Casula
Nino Cerullo
Willy Chielens
Giuseppina Conti
Dirk Daeninckx
Dionisio Fabbro
Jacques François
Eugenio Gagliano
Francesco Galli
Giancarlo Gonnelli
Alberto Guarini
Giovacchino Landini
Roberto Lorentini
Barbara Lusci
Franco Martelli

Loris Messore
Gianni Mastroiaco
Sergio Bastino Mazzino
Luciano Rocco Papaluca
Luigi Pidone
Benito Pistolato
Patrick Radcliffe
Domenico Ragazzi
Antonio Ragnanese
Claude Robert
Mario Ronchi
Domenico Russo
Tarcisio Salvi
Gianfranco Sarto
Amedeo Giuseppe Spolaore
Mario Spanu
Tarcisio Venturin
Jean Michel Walla
Claudio Zavaroni

CHAPTER FIVE

From Away Ends
to the Sacred Terrace

WHAT WAS supposed to be the start of my away travelling career in Europe turned out to be the very end, at least for the foreseeable future! First media reports claimed that a ban for Liverpool in any European competitions would last until the year 2000. I quickly calculated and realised that I would be in my early thirties. Furthermore, the already limited coverage of highlights on *Sportschau* on Sunday afternoons was scrapped indefinitely. I was about to be completely cut off from Liverpool.

During the World Cup in 1982, I spent the summer holidays in S'Illot on Mallorca. One afternoon, I spotted a little three-year-old boy with a Liverpool hat playing on the beach. Merchandise wasn't available in Germany in those days, so I hesitantly approached the father. After explaining where I came from, I asked him in my broken school English whether I could buy the hat from him. He consulted the proud possessor of the hat about my request, but his son demonstratively declined. We exchanged addresses and he promised to send me some Liverpool souvenirs. To my surprise, a few weeks later a parcel containing a hat and a few more items arrived at my home. No, I wasn't over the moon, I was bloody jumping from Mercury to Neptune. From that day I began to realise what kind of excitement our relatives in East Germany felt when they received another care package from granny. What Western coffee and chocolate meant to them, Carl's surprise package meant to me. We have stayed in touch ever since by exchanging letters from time to time.

At 17 I felt the time had come to visit Anfield. I was prepared to rob my piggy bank and make the trip to Liverpool. Of course, it wouldn't be just any fixture. Only a home match against Manchester United would be the adequate framework for my premiere. The minor issue of obtaining a ticket wouldn't cause me too many sleepless nights. My self-confidence knew no limits after my Munich, Wembley and Brussels experiences. I mentioned my plan in one of my letters to Carl. In his reply, he pointed out that it would be very difficult to get a ticket for this match. Being a Liverpool supporter, he had tried several times in vain. As a trip to Liverpool was now out of the question, he invited me to stay with his family to watch it live on TV. Therefore, my first trip 'up north' took me to a place called Ramsbottom near Bury.

After they had picked me up at Manchester airport on the Friday evening, over dinner we talked about the weekend that lay ahead. It was a warm-hearted welcome and they disclosed to me that they had decided to take me to Liverpool the next day. Even if I couldn't watch the match on Sunday at Anfield, they would take me there to have a look around outside the ground. I was thrilled and filled with excitement. Father and son were, besides following their local Bury FC, both Liverpool supporters. That evening meal was great, and when they asked me whether I had any favourite food for breakfast, I replied in a friendly way, 'Um, well, I eat anything. I mean, just Marmite is maybe something I don't necessarily eat every day.' Potential predicament preventively sorted!

Next morning was a cold but beautiful, sunny day. My gustatory nerves were treated with eggs on toast, beans and tea. My mind was thirsty for my first visit to Liverpool.

'On the way, we have a quick stop in Manchester to take a look at Old Trafford as well,' Carl informed me.

'Okay, yeah, why not? Good idea!' was my acknowledgement. A feeling of impatience grew inside me as I sensed an unnecessary, unworthy delay in reaching the most sacred place on Earth. I persuaded myself to consider the entire trip as a well-matched circular tour from hell to heaven. The transition would be a dramatic means to make the final destination and highlight even more beautiful and thus more enjoyable, having started off the journey in the depths of blatant ugliness. 'Thank you, Carl! It's a great idea!' I added.

Outside Old Trafford there wasn't a lot to be seen and I didn't bother to spend too much time on this dump anyway. Walking back to the car, we passed by some windows, which looked like the ticket office. On an A4 lateral format sheet of paper sellotaped to the window I read 'STILL TICKETS AVAILABLE'. My legs wouldn't take me any further as my eyes gazed at the letters. Most definitely this must refer to the upcoming next home league fixture or some cup tie, I thought.

The others stopped and tried to figure out what had hit me. I looked at Carl and pointed towards the paper as if I had just discovered the Holy Grail. He looked at me in disbelief and approached the ticket office. From some ten yards away I couldn't hear anything but observed a nodding person behind the counter. Carl returned towards me and, before he could say anything, I exclaimed 'Yeah, of course!'

Before he could finish telling me that I would have to be aware that this ticket was for the away end, his son intervened with a very resolute 'No! I can't be going with Carsten. All me mates from school are Man U fans and they will spot me and they know that I'm a Liverpool fan and ...'

'Okay,' Carl said, 'I'm going with Carsten then.'

We bought two tickets and I just stood there looking at this piece of paper I held in my hands. I couldn't believe what was happening. One moment ago I was going to listen to BBC's John Motson and now I was going to listen to the Kop sing 'You'll Never Walk Alone' inside Anfield. I would stand in the away section with the Mancs, but I couldn't care less!

In the car on the way to Liverpool, I didn't speak very much. In fact I didn't speak at all. I convinced myself to believe in karma. Giving that spare ticket to the Scouser in Munich must have stood me in good stead and the Scouse universe was reimbursing me now. At Anfield, we parked the car at Walton Breck Road and took a stroll around the ground. What attracted my attention straight away was that the stadium was embedded in a housing area. The courtyard outside the main stand and the backyards of the terraced houses were only separated by a wall with broken glass embedded on top of it. When I passed the big golden Liverpool Football Club crest on the black iron gate, a picture

I had looked at so often in one of my football books, I felt like I was finally at Anfield! I didn't realise it though; it just wouldn't sink in. It was a surreal experience, which was highlighted in reading 'YOU'LL NEVER WALK ALONE' on the Shankly Gates. My heart beat faster and, in those moments when I didn't forget to exert it at all, my breathing got heavier.

During the whole walkabout my speech was intermittent. When it resumed its functions we were at the Pier Head having sandwiches and coffee overlooking the Mersey and the beautiful Liver Building, Cunard Building and the Dock Office. The visit to Liverpool was supposed to be the highlight of the weekend, but now it was only the emotional preview to the following day.

Matchday's tension couldn't have been greater. There was certainly a noticeable strain at the breakfast table. The excitement in my stomach, heart, soul and every drop in my veins were equally matched by the anxiety running through every single nerve pathway of each member of my host family. My broad, never-ending grin induced my host family to remind me of the seriousness of the imminent venture. I received repetitive final instructions not to signal in any imaginable manner, not only verbally but also facial expression, that I'm a Liverpool supporter. I wasn't allowed to talk about Liverpool on the way to the ground. Neither should I comment, clap, or move conspicuously if something on the pitch happened in favour of the Reds. In more explicit detail, I was advised not to use that grin that had been covering the surface of my face all morning at all. Under no circumstances should I act in any way that might expose me. Under no circumstances should I act in any conceivable way that might expose me and the member of my host family who would be stuck with me in the away end.

Father and son still hadn't concluded their discussion about which of the two victims would have to join me. 'Carsten, it's important you understand. We do want you to enjoy your first trip to Anfield, but you have to obey our advice. There's nothing similar you would have experienced before! You've understood, right?' Carl pleaded.

'Yes, sure, I understand,' I reassured him before I added, 'Will there be a chance to buy a Liverpool scarf outside the ground?' Their bodies and facial expressions froze to the state where they looked like pale shop window dummies. 'I just wanna buy one and then hide it quickly underneath my jacket, okay?'

After a moment of respiratory arrest, they looked at each other and the fear in their eyes signalled unambiguously: 'We made a mistake!' After quoting to me again and again, sensitively, the Ten Commandments of the etiquette manual *How Not to Behave As a Single Liverpool Supporter in the Mancs' Away End*, I promised not to approach any souvenir seller on the way to the ground and on the way back to the car. Father and son had a brief family conference with the final outcome that it might be safer after all for the offspring to join me for the match.

Carl parked the car a mile away from the ground, so I had quite a distance to pull myself together. Soon we were walking in the middle of the street as the crowd expanded as more people joined from the side streets. To my amazement, none of them wore any club colours. In Germany, home and away supporters going to a match always wore kit, scarf or hat. It was always easy to recognise affiliation. Walking down Utting Avenue, then Arkles Lane, passing by Stanley Park, before turning into Anfield Road, I couldn't tell who was who.

'Are all these people from Manchester?' I whispered. A very quick nod, followed by a quiet 'Shush!' enlightened me. The latent aversion between the two clubs was more apparent over at the main stand before the match, where a tear gas attack greeted Ron Atkinson's men on their arrival when they left the team bus. When we arrived at the ground I totally forgot about the creatures around me. My inner excitement increased while clicking through the turnstile and walking up the steps until I finally caught sight of the Kop at the opposite end.

On Sunday, 9 February 1986, at around 2.45pm, I entered Anfield, holy ground of Liverpool Football Club for the very first time, to stand side by side with ... Mancs! Life's ultimate pleasure was accompanied by the oppression of not being allowed to live it out to ecstasy. It was as if I was just about to have sexual intercourse for the very first time with the woman of my dreams under the condition that I would have to let my fat, hairy, odoriferous, drooling, peeping Tom of a neighbour sit in the armchair in his stained underwear to watch us. As if those circumstances weren't bad enough, I had to watch the Mancs throw 50p coins at Reds in the Kemlyn Road end. Some of them seemed to be more occupied with hitting Scouse heads with their dough than the match itself.

As in field studies, I began to observe the breed and their actions around me. I couldn't really detect any species diversity. They all very much looked, behaved and mumbled the same. The anonymous antagonists in Danny Boyle's horror film *28 Days Later* would be my best spontaneous categorisation. Only that those around me didn't appear as scary as in the movie. Maybe those funny creatures in Edgar Wright's *Shaun of the Dead* were a much more appropriate comparison. Linguistic observation proved a rather limited Mancunian vocabulary, which was subject to a perpetual overuse. Liverpool supporters were continually addressed by a present participle verb that described love-making in a rather superficial manner, followed by a noun of a derogatory parlance that specified the most private parts of a member of the female gender. These impressions characterised my first encounter with the population of Manchester, a very unfriendly bunch of chaps to the neutral observer. Fucking ***** was my personal assessment of them.

My recollection of the match was, apart from reminding myself not to look open-mouthed at the Kop or Rushie attacking the Manc goal, that we should have easily won the three points. In the middle of the first half, Colin Gibson's shot was blocked by Grobbelaar. Our goalie fumbled it and Gibson scored from the rebound. A shove in my rib was the friendly reminder to clap hands whenever something positive happened for the Mancs. A few minutes before the interval, Jim Beglin passed the ball to Sammy Lee, whose shot hit the far left post. The ball bounced away and rolled close to the goal line towards the other post, where John Wark arrived in time to kick it into the back of the net. My first Anfield goal! It was scored only some 20 yards away from where I stood in the Annie Road end corner, and I couldn't even jump and scream. The match ended in a draw but the result was actually not all that important. I had experienced Anfield for the very first time and that was all that mattered.

The closer I got to my desire, the more emotionally attached I became. This love allowed no respite for an hour, a minute or even a second. Your heart shapes your soul and your soul develops your identification and grows into a ubiquitous sense that leaves no space for anything else.

My first trip to Anfield had brought me even more emotionally close to my spiritual home. It was the culmination of a gradual development that had started a long time before. This visit turned into a trigger that had a severe impact on my perception of life on a general scale. Not only did I love everything connected with Liverpool but also felt indifferent to whatever wasn't linked to it.

This applied, for instance, to the German national team, for which I couldn't care less anymore. Whereas in the World Cups and European Championships in 1976, 1978, 1980, 1982 and 1984 I followed my national team and wanted Germany to lift any cup available, I completely lost interest.

It was the summer of the World Cup in Mexico in 1986. We had just won the league and FA Cup double over our beloved neighbours Everton, leaving them behind in the title race and beating them at Wembley as well. The application of the personal pronoun 'we' in regard to Liverpool had been established naturally in my vocabulary without any further thoughts wasted on it. For international tournaments, national teams stand above all club allegiances. Rivalries were put aside temporarily to unite the various 'we' into one 'we' in support of your nation. In the weeks before the World Cup, I felt that this other, temporary meaning of 'we' couldn't pass my lips anymore. When classmates referred to 'us' winning the World Cup, I became conscious that I didn't feel a part of this natural unity anymore. I still viewed the tournament as an attractive, high-quality football competition and watched every single match, but felt emotionally detached. As a matter of fact, I slowly developed a liking for Liverpool's national team, England.

To carry matters to an extreme, an uncontrollable urge grew inside me to follow all nations who were represented by a Liverpool player. This new way of thinking led me to become *persona non grata* in my own household. As it happens, in the World Cup group stage Germany were drawn against Steve Nicol's Scotland and Jan Mølby's Denmark.

'Mum, you have to understand!' My very understanding mother's attitude towards my life was that as long as nothing interfered with my well-being, especially health and safety, everything was fine. There were typical motherly but totally unjustified fears that her son might one day take a liking to pleasures in life that would have a long-lasting negative effect. Therefore, from my early teenage years she talked insistently to me about the potential consequences. By discussing openly how I might fall prey to temptations she tried to have a positive influence before it could happen, thereby making sure it would never happen. On her personal 'Carsten's Don'ts List' none of the boxes for SMOKING, DRUGS, DRINKING (not yet) and such could be ticked. But she didn't have LIVERPOOL on her list and it was too late to intervene. It would neither endanger my health nor my safety, but she still didn't want her son to be like that!

'Carsten! You! Just! Can't! Be! Serious!' The accentuation indicated an exhaustion I hadn't experienced in our conversations before. She must have hoped for her son's most insane development to have already peaked, only to realise his mental trip was on a never-ending journey and the pinnacle nowhere near. Her indignant outcry was accompanied by a desperate look, fully aware that it was already out of her hands.

'You're saying we can't watch Germany together anymore as we used to because your Liverpool Nicky and Molly are playing for Scotland and Denmark? Have you totally lost your mind? Are you crazy?' I never asked her, but often wondered whether, given the chance, she would have traded me following Liverpool's various national teams for me taking drugs instead.

This development caused some general confusion in my personal surroundings. At the beginning, people found it entertaining. When they realised that there was a seriousness rooted in my views, they considered it weird. After a while they accepted it as a new part of my personality. It was difficult at times to distinguish my remarks from being a serious statement or an entertaining joke. I enjoyed being considered a genuine and serious Liverpool supporter by my friends and family. From time to time, this enjoyment was augmented by new notions I announced for my personal amusement.

My grandfather had kept asking me for ages whether I would join the army. We were still in the middle of the Cold War and Gorbachev's implementation of *Perestroika* and *Glasnost* had only been in the fledgling stage. Germany had national service for all men reaching the age of 18. Alternatively, you would have to do community service in a hospital or similar institution. As I emphasised that I would rather take that option instead of undergoing military instructions, he continuously brought up the subject to persuade me to go the other way. One afternoon, the situation seemed right to seize the initiative to start the topic once more.

'Granddad, this decision about joining the army and all, you know …' He looked at me with great anticipation. 'You know, Liverpool is the most important part of my life.' He looked puzzled as he couldn't connect *Die Deutsche Bundeswehr* with football. 'If I seriously join the army and someday Germany would go to war with Britain, I might stand opposite to my Red brothers. There's no way I would ever shoot at someone from Liverpool.' In the geopolitical age of NATO against Warsaw Pact, there wasn't really even the slightest possibility of such an event but in that moment it didn't matter. The entire global conflict potential between world powers and their allies was redefined. My grandfather still looked at me but withheld any comment. This was the moment that could be a turning point for future discussions, so I continued and took my stance to the next level.

'In fact, I've decided to join the British Army. I wanna stand side by side with my Liverpool brothers.'

After what was only a few seconds he broke his silence. He leaned forward towards me and asked, 'Would you shoot against Germans?' I knew that this would be the perfect opportunity for a killing answer. 'Well, if I have to, sure!' There was no further reflection on how I, being a born German with a valid German birth certificate and passport, would manage to join a different country's army. I had mentioned countless times before that after I finished school I would emigrate, apply for British citizenship, move to Liverpool and become a Kop season ticket holder. Even if I had been confronted with plausible arguments about Her Majesty's probable decision to not let me join her forces,

I would have made up some independent British Foreign Legion I had read about. I couldn't assess my grandfather's silence of disbelief, but in the months that followed the subject never came up again.

Sometimes I would overdo playing mind games or discussing my latest ideas without noticing the consequences. Admittedly, my poor, innocent mother was the victim in most cases. At the time, I was very much into Scottish folk rock band Big Country. Their albums *The Crossing*, *Steeltown* and *The Seer* were running up and down all day long. I knew most lyrics by heart. One of my main occupations was to rewrite the lyrics of my favourite songs to adapt them somehow with a reference to Liverpool. One song on the album *Steeltown* was called 'Where the Rose is Sown'. It was about a soldier's thoughts on the battlefield and contained the words: 'If I die in a combat zone, Box me up and ship me home. If I die and still come home, Lay me where the rose is sown.' The last five words 'where the rose is sown' were substituted for 'near the trophy zone'. I had heard about Liverpudlians, whose last wish was to rest their ashes in peace at Anfield. This ultimate spiritual bonding for eternity fascinated me, a new injection to elevate me to an even higher level of irreversible unity with my Kopite family.

A few weeks before, I had received another care package from the UK, which contained a tape recording of the entire double-winning FA Cup Final in 1986, including extensive pre-match build-up and post-match interviews. One afternoon, I was watching the tape yet again. I plugged in the headphones and at times turned the sound up to listen at full volume to 'You'll Never Walk Alone' and 100,000 Scousers jointly singing 'Are you watching, are you watching, are you watching Manchester? Are you watching Manchester?' I kept rewinding back to the 84th minute of the match when John Motson commentated: 'This is Rush … Mølby again … oh I say, his vision there was lovely … Whelan … and Dalglish … and Rush is on the far side. Is this three? It is!!!' My visual ecstasy was followed by listening to my favourite songs of my favourite bands. This sensual composition heated me up to high-altitude euphoria. In that moment of frenzy I listened to that Big Country song. While Alan lifted the cup again and again in my mind, I kept belting out 'lay me near the trophy zone'.

In that state of legal insanity, for which I could comprehensibly not really be held accountable, I went to the kitchen to see my mother. 'Mum,' I started the presentation of my latest idea when I entered the kitchen where she was preparing dinner. 'I'm your only son and you love me, correct?!'

When I began my sentences like that, her facial expression was a combination of 'yes, you know that' and 'oh my god, what's coming now!' Both thoughts produced the answer, 'Carsten, what kind of question is that, hmm?'

My cautious strategy to feel my way resulted in the question, 'You'll do me any favour, right?'

'Carsten, I can't answer that. It depends on what you want.'

'Mum, are you indicating that your love is not unconditional but dependent on the content of my request?' Her countenance was irritated but curious. In my prelude, I summarised briefly the main points of the importance of Liverpool Football Club in the overall context of my life, yet again. For once, she refrained from rolling her eyes. Then I cited the adapted version of 'Where the Rose is Sown'. I translated the lines and explained the meaning of the 'trophy zone'. She could follow my description of Liverpool's trophy room at Anfield, but not my causal connection related to 'shipping the box home'.

'Son, I don't understand you.'

It was time to inform her about the project that lay ahead of her. 'Mum, this is serious. Just in case I die. I mean, I hope I don't. But if I do, can you please make sure, can you please swear to me right now that you'll honour my most important wish and last will to ship my body home to Liverpool and make sure my ashes are scattered on the Kop?'

I don't know what it was she had in her hand but it dropped into the kitchen sink as soon as I finished my plea. Tears were rolling down her twitching cheeks. Only then did I realise that I had breached the household's constitutional laws of 'you must not place yourself in danger whatever you do', followed by 'you must not even use any kind of language that might invoke dark forces to cause any bodily harm to you'.

When she calmed down and found her voice again I expected to get an earful. But she just sobbed, 'I'll never get this through the authorities.' Now I was the one who didn't get it and needed enlightenment. She explained, 'You're a German living in Germany with a German passport. How could I manage to convince the British authorities to let a dead German body be shipped to their country?' Whereas I was feeling a little guilty about imposing this macabre request on my mother, she had accepted my loss, was willing to fulfil my last wish and was now already being overwhelmed by the organisational challenges of my shipment. I reassured her sensitively that my project wouldn't be burdened on her shoulders and that I had no intention of leaving this world before her anyway.

It was a very quiet dinner that evening. I convinced myself that it might be in the general interest to never ever again bring up the subject. I mean 'never' as in 'never ever again'; 'ever' as in 'never ever again'; and 'again' as in 'never ever again'. Nonetheless, constitution was enhanced by a new law: 'You must not officially declare a last will that might cause an excessive coordinative international arrangement between Her Majesty's Immigration Authority, Her Majesty's Authority for Moving a Corpse, the German Foreign Secretary and my mother.'

During the summer holidays I always had various summer jobs but once I got a job at our local brewery, Eichbaum, I kept going back for several years. The work could be physically strenuous but the hourly wage was great and for a pupil there was no difference between gross salary and net pay. Therefore, after eight hours a day, five days a week and four weeks a month you could accumulate the wealth that was required to subsidise your holidays and Liverpool trips. As a temporary worker you also enjoyed the same perks as a permanent employee. Every person on the brewery's payroll received a very generous amount of free beverage coupons. My extended family was provided with water and soft drinks. Even if I had thrown a party twice a week, I wouldn't have been able to consume all the bevvies I was entitled to by my vouchers.

Different tasks were assigned to me. One of the more routine jobs was working in a group responsible for sorting crates of returned empties on the appropriate pallets. We were outside all day with the sun burning on our heads and the sweat running down our foreheads for hours. I was simply dying for a thirst-quencher all the time. Now and then the pallet drivers, who had direct access to fresh and cold drinks inside the brewery, would provide us with refreshments. Simple mineral water would have duly satisfied my modest expectations. Not even the diversity of carbonation degree was of any relevance to me and I didn't give a flying one about 'still', 'medium' or 'sparkling' as long as I could get some bloody water down my throat. All the pallet drivers most certainly meant well, but the only variety in their treat for us was an alternating delivery of pilsner, export and wheat beer.

I once dared to ask one of them to get us some water, for which in return I only got a questioning look and a derogatory grin. He made me feel like an unappreciative philistine who had just told the starred chef that he would actually prefer an ordinary burger with chips to his complimentary five-course menu. When the driver returned, he pointed to the fresh lager he had brought for us. I couldn't figure out whether he believed I had been ironic and used 'water' as a synonym for asking for more 'beer', or whether he deliberately refused to comply with my request to challenge me with the question, 'Are you a man or a mouse?'

Simply killing your thirst with booze turned into a daily ritual at around 2pm. We had one, two, then another one and ... Some afternoons, we got a move on to finish work early, a long time before we could clock our time cards. There was a little piece of meadow where we would lie or lean on the pallets in the shade and empty a full crate. Occasionally, one of us got up to pretend to be busy working by shifting something from here to there and back again. This was just a precaution as one of the managers from the office sometimes paid a surprise visit for an inspection. But most of the time it was paradise. We made lots of cash, were out in the sun all day, had a good laugh, got drunk on drinks that were already paid for and even got paid for the time drinking it! Life could be so beautiful!

Sad news reached me when I learned that I would be needed elsewhere over the following days. My new position turned out to be that of the delivery driver's assistant. The comfortable afternoons with the boys in the sun seemed to be gone. My shift would start at 6am. We met up, perused the order list of the day, arranged the pallets, loaded the lorry and trailer, and then went on our tour at around 8am to deliver our cargo to local pubs and supermarkets. My very first delivery route consisted of only one outlet. We loaded a full truck and drove an eternity to a destination in the middle of nowhere. Driving on a long road through a forest, we wouldn't see anybody at all.

When we reached the pub, a rural landlady in her late forties welcomed us. First, she flirted with my boss and then, while I was unloading the crates, gave me looks I wasn't used to from members of the opposite gender of an elderly generation. She kept making ambiguous remarks, which made me work faster … a lot faster. Even when I had a break I pretended to be busy. I had seen films in which innocent, helpless travellers were stranded in abandoned countryside. This village pub wouldn't too often see many new customers other than brother, uncle and priest. Whenever fresh meat would enter their premises she and her mates would definitely have a go, especially if brother, uncle and priest were the same person. On the way back, I was relieved to hear that we would only deliver to her once a month!

The following days were more entertaining in a rather different way. When we finished our first delivery at a pub, we sat inside and my boss would do the paperwork. The landlady joined us, poured a bottle of beer in a glass and put it on the table for my boss. 'You wanna drink something?' she asked me.

'A Coke, please.'

They looked at each other and my boss replied, 'He's just a kid.'

Next stop was another pub and the same procedure. I handed down 45 crates per pallet and the gaffer moved them inside. Another job done, more paperwork to be done. Another pint was served without asking, but this time for both of us.

'Fancy a shot?' the landlord offered my boss.

'Yeah, why not!' This was Monday morning at a time when most office sitters in these time zones between Hammerfest and Cape Town had just arrived at their desk contemplating getting a coffee from the kitchen. In Britain it would be tea, of course, and in all East London offices they were already asking each other whether they fancied a cuppa or were just about to put the kettle on. I was still half asleep and had to ponder whether not only to have my first beer of the day but also my first shot.

I quickly came to the conclusion that this round-table business meeting between our customer, my boss and me was official working time. By declining the offer I would breach business etiquette and there was no second chance for a first impression. To avoid an affront, I just had to bow to discipline. 'Yes, thank you, sir!'

Whereas having a pint, or three, surreptitiously in the afternoon with the boys was a personal option, getting ineffably pissed was now an official work instruction. This procedure continued all morning, all day. Every day! By noon hiccups and burps in the cab were familiar sounds. When our tour finished early we would stay in the last pub for several hours. We spent the time accomplishing personal quality control checks on the goods we had just delivered to our trade partner. As appropriate statistical quality control requires, more than one sample had to be randomly examined. To neutralise the taste on our gustatory buds, we were served schnapps between the pints here and there, too. By knocking-off time in the evenings, I felt replete and had no further need to redeem any of my personal vouchers.

I had some explaining to do one day for taking an afternoon off. Bayern Munich announced a testimonial in pre-season for their long-serving striker Dieter Hoeneß at the Olympic Stadium. The opponents they invited were Liverpool! The Reds had signed Peter Beardsley, John Barnes and John Aldridge for Ian Rush, who left for Juventus. It was Liverpool's first pre-season match and the very first match all three played together. The Germans scored three times before John Aldridge and John Barnes got two back. After the match, I headed straight back to catch the night train to Mannheim where I arrived at 3am. Instead of getting a few hours' sleep before my shift started at 6am, I watched the entire match again, as my mother had videotaped it on some regional TV channel for me. When I entered the factory premises I must have looked like the walking dead.

My boss asked me again, as if he hadn't believed me the first time, 'Did you really travel all the way to Munich to watch a Bayern friendly match for the Dieter Hoeneß testimonial?'

'No, I did travel all the way to Munich to watch a match with the greatest-ever Liverpool team the world will ever see.'

One year later, with enough cash from my summer job, Spain was the holiday destination again. One night, I bumped into a group of Scousers in a pub when I was wearing my Crown Paints home jersey. We chatted the whole night and met up nocturnally over numerous rounds of San Miguel. Like a sponge I soaked up every little story and detail they narrated about the club and the city of Liverpool. I was an eager disciple and hung on their every word. Whenever I could keep up with any kind of knowledge about a Liverpool FC topic, I was flowing like a waterfall. The conversation turned into an oral examination, only I didn't answer any questions, but presented answers about anything I knew about the history of the club anyway.

This kind of obtrusive boasting provoked them to take me on at a different level. They felt it was time to introduce me to their lingo. 'You may know everything about the club, but do you understand Liverpudlians as well?' Norman challenged me with a grin on his face. 'Do you speak any Scouse, Carsten?' My humble reply related to the fact that we had been talking for ages and that I understood everything they said. They smirked at each other. 'No, we mean proper Scouse.'

They started off with 'Unit 1: Scouse Words and Phrases'. 'You know the meaning of he's sound, that's boss, he's just a woolyback, go 'ed, I'm made up, that's nice clobber, it's chocka, me bird's doin' me 'ead in?' Reluctantly, I had to admit that I hadn't the faintest idea what they were on about. After they had disclosed the meanings of the phrases, they continued with 'Unit 2: Scouse Pronunciation'. I learned about the use of the rolling 'R', the 'K' that turns into 'kh' and the 'T' that's enriched by an 'S' to become a 'ts' wherever possible. 'I'm rreading a bookh about the historry of the Liverpool dockh.' 'Fancy some chickhen on yer butty for yer breakhfast?' 'Our Tsom was sittin' on a tsree in tsown.'

What made the amusement on their part greater and my personal predicament even worse was the fact that I was a keen student. I wanted to get it right so badly. But the harder I tried, the more ludicrous I sounded. Late at night, before the landlord called for last orders and closed the pub, we would leave the clubs in time to return to the pub and made sure we were provided with a few more rounds. We would sit outside long after all the others had gone and the daylight dawned on the horizon. When everyone was tired, every joke had been told and everyone hung bevvied up in his chair, the night would be concluded with 'Unit 3: Scouse piss-take out of a German wannabe Scouser'.

'Carsten, c'mon, one more try. The sentence is: They do that though, don't they though. It's easy, isn't it? In Scouse we say: Dey do dat dough don't dey dough.' I knew that they would be in stitches again with tears rolling down their cheeks in a few seconds, but I still made the best of efforts: 'Dee do da dou, dontee dou.'

The first one who could recuperate and breathe again encouraged me: 'Carsten, come on. One more ti …' but he couldn't finish his sentence as the sheer thought of me repeating it again made him burst into laughter anew. I had to come to terms with the reality check that you can't just choose to be a Scouser, but you had to work hard on becoming one.

As we walked back to our accommodation early in the morning, we passed by some hotels where the first Germans were already up and out to place their towels on the sunbeds by the pool. They would return upstairs to their beds and only come down to take up their reserved spot where they had marked their territory after they had eaten their breakfast some three hours later. Our plans were slightly different.

'Alright Carsten, don't forget, we meet up straight after brekkie at two o'clock at the beach bar for a few.' When we went our separate ways and were almost out of sight, I heard a shout. 'And don't forget your practice. Dey do dat dough …' More fading laughter was heard from afar.

After the holiday, we arranged to meet up in Liverpool a few weeks later. On the train up to Lime Street I travelled with the Tottenham fans, who were our opponents that afternoon. 'Oi fink we can ge' a resul' up there, know wha' oi mean, mai'?' I was glad that I wouldn't have to stand in the away end again with these Cockney geezers with their unaspiring, lowbrow, unchallenging language. On arrival, I had to get out of their mob to ensure I wasn't forced by the police to be escorted to Anfield.

The lads picked me up and we drove directly to Anfield. We were queuing along the wall outside the Kop on Walton Breck Road. It was an ecstatic wait for the turnstiles to open. I was trying to listen to all the Kopites around me, figuring out whether I would be as lost in translation as the lads had tried to suggest before. Surely they were only having me on again! I was an eager learner and had practised my understanding of Scouse from videos of some Liverpool TV series. I had memorised *Brookside* dialogues between Ricky Tomlinson and Sue Johnston and repeated them to perfection. The Boswell family in *Bread* were no phonetic challenge either, and Joey's 'Greetings' had become part of my personal repertoire of sayings. Holly Johnson was a Scouser and I understood every word he said while addressing the audience at a Frankie Goes to Hollywood concert a year before. If our Danish midfielder Jan Mølby had learned English with a Scouse accent, so could I, I was convinced. I was prepared, I was ready and I was raring to have my very first encounter with the Kopites. They would incorporate, adopt and identify me as one of their own as we all spoke the same language, our love for Liverpool FC.

From nowhere, my first proper encounter with the real-life Scouse street language would come thick and fast. Some 11-year-old approached me, looked up and told me something in a singing voice that I perceived as 'Eeeeh laaaah, gizza fockhin' ciggie matesssss.' I just turned to Norman with a look that cried for attention. He just laughed and told the kid to go away and that he shouldn't smoke at his age anyway, before enlightening me about the content of the boy's request.

On Frankie Goes to Hollywood's album *Welcome to the Pleasuredome*, the prelude to the song 'Born to Run' was a dialogue in Scouse. I hadn't listened to any song on that album more often than that part. The written language would have disclosed the following conversation: 'I'm sorry I left my card at home!' 'Well you're late as well; that's three times on the run. If you're late again the supervisor said we're gonna put you on daily sign-in.' The spoken language wouldn't let me practise a single sentence as I didn't understand a single syllable of it! On the Kop that day I realised that this wasn't creative hyperbole as part of the band's artistry, this was reality!

I was standing on the Kop and I was scared. I was standing on the most sacred terrace for the very first time in my life and, just as much as I prayed that the Mancs in the Annie Road end a few seasons before wouldn't speak to me, I wished all fellow Reds around me would just ignore me, pleeeeaaase!

My fear of the language barrier went when 26,999 Scousers, and me, jointly sang 'You'll Never Walk Alone' together for the first time. It was the perfect day! It would have been too perfect, or maybe too much to ask for, I suppose, if I was also to witness my first-ever victory, too. With a bit less than a quarter of an hour to go, Peter Beardsley scored. It looked like a happy ending, if only Terry Fenwick hadn't equalised shortly afterwards. It was another draw in my personal LFC match history yet again. It couldn't tarnish my mood at all, though, especially when I experienced my first-ever Liverpool nightlife later on. It wouldn't take long before they would start: 'Come on, Carsten. Let's see how you practised. Dey do dat, don't dey dough ...'

CHAPTER SIX

At Home in a
Far Foreign Land

FAMILY RELATIVES in East Germany once told me that they had access to 'Westfernsehen', West German TV. Behind the Iron Curtain, most East Germans used the Western TV as an alternative source of information as the news on their own communist TV station was considered to be less reliable. I had also learned that there were regions like the greater Dresden area where inhabitants weren't able to receive those TV stations and were therefore living in the so-called 'Valley of the Clueless'. I comprehended that feeling as I regarded myself a poor clueless inhabitant of such a faraway valley being cut off from BBC and ITV.

In one of Liverpool's match programmes I read about the club's official LIVERPOOL F.C./Crown Paints Fan Club. A few pounds fee brought me, if only mentally, closer to Liverpool. It also provided me with a pennant presenting my name and proving my official member status. One advantage of the membership was a news sheet being sent to your home on a monthly basis. Compared to my *Match* and *Shoot* subscriptions being sent over from the UK, which didn't really provide me with any inside information, the club's leaflet certainly did.

It also provided me with a shivering fit when they advertised the release of a video cassette called *The Official History of Liverpool FC*. The most excruciating anticipation ever followed the days and nights in between placing the order and receiving the parcel. By day I couldn't concentrate, at night I couldn't sleep. I began to sympathise with people who were diagnosed with attention-deficit hyperactivity disorder. The ailment ceased on the Saturday when the package waited for me after school. I opened my long-sought-after coveted 'bible' by carefully pressing play on the remote control and 'The Book of Genesis' unfolded before my eyes.

In the beginning there was chairman John Houlding. He had accommodated some football team and their directors in his Garden of Eden. A serpent more crafty than any of the wild directors led the board into temptation to provoke the chairman's goodwill. Houlding expelled the rental nomads from Anfield and cursed them above all that they will crawl on their belly and they will eat dust all the days of their life. These ungrateful dispossessed were stripped of their home, but still felt no shame. They went on to play across the park in their own new ground under the name 'Everton Football Club'. The creation of Liverpool's 'Team of the Macs', the christening of the Kop by *Liverpool Echo* sports editor Ernest Edwards, Liverpool's first legend Elisha Scott, the Kop getting a roof ... fundamental knowledge denied for such a long time finally reached me!

Emotions reached boiling point when old black-and-white footage started. The narrative introduction of Shankly: '… and when in December 1959 Liverpool's next manager was welcomed by chairman T.V. Williams, the whole outlook and destiny of the club was about to change', followed by some moving film clips accompanied by stirring music, gave me the shivers. A BBC *Panorama* clip highlighted the Reds' title-winning match against Arsenal in 1964. Before the match, a journalist standing next to the goal in front of the Kop enthused about the Liverpool supporters:

> The gladiators enter the arena, the field of praise. Saturday's weather perfect for a historic Scouse occasion. Liverpool in red shirts were playing before their own spectators for the last time this season. The desire to win was an agonised one. They would be the champions of England and they wanted their own people to see them become so. They care so much about football. This season over two million people on Merseyside have watched Liverpool or their neighbours Everton, last year's champions. But, they don't behave like any other football crowd, especially not at one end of Anfield, on the Kop. The music the crowd sings is the music that Liverpool has sent echoing around the world.
>
> It's to be thought that Welsh international rugby crowds are the most musical and passionate in the world. But, I've never seen anything like this Liverpool crowd. On the field here the gay and

inventive ferocity they show is quite stunning. The Duke of Wellington before the battle of Waterloo said of his own troops: 'I don't know what they do to the enemy, but by god they frighten me.' And I'm sure some of the players here for this match this afternoon must be feeling the same way.

An anthropologist studying this Kop crowd would be introduced into as rich and mystifying a popular culture as any South Sea island. Their rhythmic swaying is an elaborate and organised ritual. The 28,000 people on the Kop itself begin singing together. They seem to know intuitively when to begin. Throughout the match, they invent new words usually within the framework of old Liverpool songs to express adulatory, cruel or bawdy comments about the players or the police. But even then they begin singing these new words with one immediate huge voice. They seem, mysteriously, to be in touch with one another, with Wacker, the Spirit of Scouse. The spirit's good humoured and generous when they are winning, but not necessarily when they are losing. On Saturday they were certainly winning!

On Merseyside, football is the consuming passion. It's hard to persuade people to talk about anything else. Except perhaps the beat groups, which the Kop crowd do a lot to explain ...

Just when the video was about to end and I was looking forward to finally breathing in again, Gerry Marsden intoned 'When you walk ... ' As if emotional overload hadn't already become too great to bear, the video also provided the full version of our hymn 'You'll Never Walk Alone'. It was the first time ever I could listen to it in full length.

From Saturday midday to Sunday night, I kept rewinding the tape and watched the 1hr, 23min and 56sec over and over and over again. There was no time for even contemplating going out that Saturday night. In fact, I wouldn't even leave my room for lunch or dinner, but took my meals in front of the TV.

'May I bring you a chamber pot as well? You could place it right next to the armchair and wouldn't have to move at all? You know, just to make sure ...' my mother suggested.

After a split second of weighing up the pros and cons of her offer, I declined, to her surprise: 'Thanks Mum. I would actually indeed interrupt watching just to pay a visit to the bathroom in person.'

I had heard about sects who indoctrinated their disciples with their religious views to the extent of their unmitigated, submissive self-abandonment. Footage of lifting the FA Cup for the first time in 1965, Shankly on his lap of honour after winning the league at Anfield in 1973, the night of the first leg of Liverpool's UEFA Cup Final at home against Mönchengladbach in the same season, the European night at Anfield against Saint-Étienne in 1977, and Rush putting four past the Blues at their own ground in 1982 were the most extreme brainwashing liturgy a man could ingest. Ministering was now possible at any time of the day and night. It was the open gate to my Garden of Eden.

Regular access to live match coverage still remained a rather challenging task. Medium-wave frequency was a radio source I had never used due to its bad reception, let alone its sound quality. It had been invented before the mid-1980s but it was only then I discovered that the BBC World Service broadcast an entire second half live commentary of one English First Division match every Saturday afternoon. A new life began when I heard what appeared from afar as a live football commentary sound for the very first time. The voices of Alan Green, Bryon Butler and Mike Ingham transferred me live to Anfield Road, but also Carrow Road, Highfield Road, Loftus Road or Maine Road. My traditional ritual every Saturday followed a determined procedure that couldn't be interfered with by any exterior influencing factors.

Getting my paper from the station's newsagent, eating lunch, sitting in the armchair in my room reading the paper and sipping my black tea with milk, getting into the right mood by listening to my Beatles and Gerry and the Pacemakers 'best of' cassette an hour before kick-off before tuning in to the BBC World Service for the second half live commentary.

Just 'tuning in' would be the most simplified and exaggerated description of a fairy-tale happy ending. The actual perpetual fine-tuning of the adjuster kept me occupied for most of the 45 minutes most Saturdays. Sometimes my fingers were moving back and forth the entire match only to snatch a bit of reception. My ears were glued to the loudspeakers, anticipating when I would catch a sentence I could make any sense of. Some Saturdays I hoped to hear the Kop sing and celebrate as this would at least indicate a positive scoreline. I panicked and prayed that in connection with a scream none of the names Grobbelaar, Hansen, Lawrenson, Nicol or Gillespie was mentioned as this would indicate we must have conceded a goal or a penalty. I hoped to hear the names of Rush, Aldridge, Barnes, Beardsley, McMahon, Whelan, Mølby or Houghton, as this rather implied we had scored. When I picked up 'Rush', I wasn't sure whether this was meant to be Ian or if it meant 'they are in a rush'. In a rush for what? Were they in a rush to score the first goal or another goal or to equalise? And what team was in what kind of bloody rush anyway? I picked up a scream. Was it a goal? Maybe it was a missed sitter? Was it a goal disallowed? Was a penalty awarded? Even if I could figure out what it was, the question attached was always 'for whom???' You could get paranoid.

Some afternoons, you had a full-length reception of a very high quality. Most afternoons, listening to live commentary mainly consisted of a massive noise usually connected with a building site or dentist. Sometimes the noise faded completely and nothing could be heard at all. A new personal characteristic had to be learned and developed: patience. To the outside world, I gave the best impression of a train-spotting anorak, who just sits there waiting for something to happen. In my inside world, I was busy picking up a voice for a split second. My mother occasionally entered the room because the unbearable noise of what sounded like a percussion drill had lasted for 20 minutes. Sometimes she entered the room when nothing at all could be heard. In both cases, she saw me sitting there, leaning towards the loudspeaker with a concentrated facial expression. Enquiring about what I was doing, she would hear me respond, 'Psst, I'm listening to the Liverpool match.' Silence followed and she looked seriously worried about the mental state of her only son.

Some afternoons, a proper reception only improved after the final whistle. As the BBC World Service not only had the official assignment of providing me with my Liverpool result, but all people in the world who are interested in the outcomes of all professional football encounters in England and Scotland, longanimity would have to become my best companion. There were days when a quality reception didn't resume in time, or got lost again for a few seconds just before the Liverpool result was being read out. By the time West Ham or Wimbledon as the home teams were mentioned in the correct alphabetical order, I came to realise that I had missed my result and would have to wait even longer for a repeat later on. I knew what I had to endure, yet again! My eyes closed and my head dropped slowly until it was buried in my arms.

The English First Division consisted of 22 teams, which meant 11 results to be read out. However, it was also only one part of the Football League, which consisted of four divisions altogether. The English Second Division's 22 teams produced 11 further results, and the English Third and Fourth Divisions' 24 teams each generated another 24 scorelines in all. Oh aye, and if that wasn't enough, there was always the Scottish league after that, which consisted of another three divisions. The Scottish Premier Division's 12 teams produced six results. And as if the Scottish First Division's 12 clubs creating six more results wasn't enough, the Scottish Second Division had 14 teams creating another seven results on top of that. Oh, have I mentioned English non-league football yet?

What made matters even worse was that the reading out of the results wasn't really like a final countdown of the pop charts, as quick as possible before disclosing the latest number one in the BBC Top 40. It was rather a stage for a reading competition, in which participants made the greatest of efforts to speak as slow-ly ... clear-ly ... and ... dis-tinc-tive-ly ... in ... each ... of ... the ... hun ... dreds ... of ... syl-la-bles ... as ... they ... could. Miss Zaruba would have been choked up with emotion. As if listeners weren't competent enough to grasp that the result of a match is imparted after the number of goals of the second team of a pairing was announced, they would pause for seconds before the next pairing had their turn. 'Ply-mouth Ar-gyle ... Shrews-bu-ry Town ... *Pause* ... Ches-ter-field ... Ro-ther-ham U-ni-ted ... *Pause* ... Pe-ter-bo-rough U-ni-ted ... Har-tle-pool U-ni-ted ... *Pause* ... Heart of Mid-lo-thi-an ... Ha-mil-ton A-ca-de-mi-cal ... *Pause* ... Dun-ferm-line Ath-le-tic, Air-di-reo-ni-ans ... *Pause* ... Sten-house-muir ... Cow-den-beath ... *Pause* ... Frustration gradually turned into psychological torture, which slowly developed into mental hypnosis. My mind drifted away and only woke up way over 50 results later when I heard, 'And now, again, today's scores in the English First Division.'

Cable TV conquered Germany in the mid-1980s. This applied to some regions, at least. The particular area I lived in wasn't top of the priority list they would provide with the new technology. My suburb would have to wait a few years longer than the more plush quarters. It didn't really bother me. It did awaken my attention a few years later, though, when I was told about the new Super Channel. The English satellite TV station would broadcast programmes from the UK in Germany. Rumours spread quickly that they were going to show English football. As I was a susceptible believer and just everybody knew I would fall for news of that kind, I was an easy target to be made an April fool. This applied not only on 1 April, but on any day of the year. I couldn't be positive about whether people who claimed that they knew from a serious source that the TV channel would show highlights of the Reds would be trustworthy or were just trying to get back at me for being the victims of my jokes previously. Liverpool were never a joking matter, though, let alone TV highlights in Germany.

Nobody was joking! Super Channel did show highlights every Tuesday night – 'every' as in 'each and every one throughout the season without exception' – from all English First Division matches – 'all' as in 'I don't give a shit what other teams they are showing, but Liverpool will definitely be on' – every week. There are few certain moments in a man's life that he will just never forget. When this news broke, the emotional mixture of satisfaction and happiness I sensed was only comparable to the day, or rather night if I remember correctly, when I discovered for the very first time that the external male genitalia can fulfil additional pleasant functions other than releasing urine from the bladder through the urethra to the outside of the body.

A new social age broke. People were no longer divided into conventional categories of 'I like her', 'I fancy her', 'I like her but I don't fancy her', 'I don't like her but I fancy certain bodily advantages of her' or 'He's a good mate', 'He's a prat', 'I can't fucking stand the fucking idiot'. Borders were lifted and all categories were merged in the first step only to be divided into two plain groups: 'Has Super Channel' and 'Has not Super Channel', or to be more precise: 'Has Super Channel and video recorder' and 'Has not Super Channel'. As if matters weren't already complicated enough, another very important factor had to be considered. Although VHS had been generally accepted as the main video format by that time, there were still households with out-of-date formats such as Betamax, VCR or Video 2000. To categorise the two groups appropriately, I divided my environment into: 'Has Super Channel and VHS video recorder' and 'Has not Super Channel'.

Apart from redefining social aspects, verbal and non-verbal behaviour had to adjust as well. I depended on people who were lucky enough to receive the channel and had a state-of-the-art video recorder, but didn't necessarily comprehend the importance of English First Division football. Courtesy, compliments and charm had to be applied on a regular basis. I had never realised what a sycophant I could turn out to be! My entire universe pivoted on Wednesdays when I would receive my tape and watch it straight after lunch. The wait for that day could be agonising, especially after we had won a big match the weekend before. It goes without saying that I expected to be handed over the video cassette on the day after the broadcast without delay. My ignorant, reckless, outrageous environment, though, sometimes dared to leave the tape at home and an unthinkable torment had to be sustained. I would have to wait for Thursday. A reliable long-term solution had to be found.

A very well-performing go-between was my little cousin Manfred. He had a couple of mates living in the holy land of cable TV. One of the girls in his class fancied him and would do anything for him. 'Be nice to her,' I pleaded. She was willing to do the weekly job. I didn't know her, but I loved her. It went so well for some time and my problem seemed to be sorted for good. So I hoped.

One Wednesday, after one of those big matches, I got the tape, pressed the button, waited and waited. I wound forward and all I saw was a programme about locusts. I wound forward again and again until the locust baby had turned into an elderly locust. She had recorded the wrong channel! Love can vanish very quickly. I had to come to terms with the fact that these emotional setbacks are a part of life. It would make me stronger! It would be an important component in the process of growing up, becoming an adult, becoming a man! Would it fuck! Despondency and depression would be my companions whenever such a stroke of fate hit me time and again. Super Channel's coverage of English football eventually ceased a couple of years later. Therefore, the recording problem was solved as a consequence, too. And my garden gate to Eden was latched again.

* * *

On 15 April 1989 I couldn't wait for another FA Cup semi-final, against Nottingham Forest. It was a beautiful sunny spring day. We were on the march with Kenny's Army again and not only going to make up for last year's painful Wembley defeat against Wimbledon, but also to win our second league and cup double. Radio reception was acceptable but it was coming and going. I just picked up that something was going on and the match would have to be delayed. 'Fighting' was mentioned. 'People on the pitch' would make the delay even longer. 'Cancellation' of the match I couldn't make any sense of. 'Casualties' was a kind of information I couldn't grasp at all. Why? What happened? I didn't know what was going on at all.

The horror unfolded when news broke on German TV an hour later. The report showed pictures of Liverpool fans trying to escape over the fence on to the pitch. On the sports programme later that afternoon occurrences were explained in extended coverage. Peter Beardsley hit the crossbar at the Forest end after a few minutes. Showing highlights of the match that only lasted six minutes indicated that even German TV people didn't realise the magnitude of the tragedy they were reporting on. I saw fans walking into the penalty area at the Reds' end trying to gain the attention of Bruce Grobbelaar. An ambulance was driving on the pitch towards the Liverpool goal when there were already innumerable people trying to rescue the injured by using advertising boards.

One Liverpool fan spoke into the camera: 'Why didn't they give us the big end when they knew we had more supporters? Why?' TV programmes were full of it. Another football catastrophe involving Liverpool fans quickly assumed that it was yet another 'act of hooliganism'. Official statements by Prime Minister Thatcher and FIFA's General Secretary Blatter substantiated this perception. Just as quickly as both their predetermined stances were expressed, memories of Heysel and the rush to judgement came to my mind.

On the Monday, Norman rang to inform me that he was alright. They had been to the match with a couple of mates. One of them got lost and was still not in contact again days later. This was the last I heard from him as he moved out of town to seek a job elsewhere, and in the pre-mobile phone times, we lost touch.

When you think you've already hit the roughest rock bottom and you're convinced that nothing could cause the ground to open up for an even deeper fall …

I went to the station every single day to get any kind of inside information from just any newspaper. English sources were closer to details and facts, I was convinced. They might provide me with information the German media might filter and find not worth mentioning in its entirety a couple of days after the tragedy when attention would gradually fade here. On the Wednesday I picked up a certain piece, which read on its front cover: 'THE TRUTH'. I just flicked through the smaller headlines underneath, bought it and put it in my pocket. A sick feeling crept inside my stomach. I walked slowly to my favourite pub, got a pint, sat down in a quiet corner and read through it thoroughly. Under the headline 'THE TRUTH' and a picture of Liverpool fans crushed against the gate there were three subheadings and the following text:

Some fans picked pockets of victims
Some fans urinated on the brave cops
Some fans beat up PCs giving kiss of life

Drunken Liverpool fans viciously attacked rescue workers as they tried to revive victims of the Hillsborough soccer disaster, it was revealed last night. Police officers, firemen and ambulance crew were punched, kicked and urinated upon by a hooligan element in the crowd. Some thugs rifled the pockets of injured fans as they were stretched out unconscious on the pitch. Sheffield MP Irvine Patnick revealed that in one shameful episode a gang of Liverpool fans noticed that the blouse of a girl trampled to death had risen above her breast. As

a policeman struggled in vain to revive her, the mob jeered: 'Throw her up here and we will **** her.'...
One furious policeman who witnessed Saturday's carnage stormed: 'As we struggled in appalling conditions to save lives, fans standing further up the terrace were openly urinating on us and the bodies of the dead.'

A 'high-ranking' police officer was quoted as saying: 'The fans were just acting like animals. My men faced a double hell – the disaster and the fury of the fans who attacked us.'

I felt sick ...

I had to rely on 'news' like this because I had no access to alternative sources. I had to explain, defend and justify happenings, which I never believed in the first place. It was an emotional throwback to the days after Heysel. Over the following years, the media's coverage tied the city of Liverpool only to negative news. It appeared that writers had no intention to report on a certain topic specifically and thoroughly, but always relished going back to the same old preconceptions and on a general bashing of the people of Liverpool.

For many years, the same puzzle pieces were applied to present a certain picture of Liverpool again and again: unemployment, radical politics, strikes, decayed areas, Liverpool 8 uprising, Heysel, Hillsborough, James Bulger murder. All were mentioned in the same breath as coherent facts attached to Liverpool. As if this kind of coverage didn't suffice for the neutral observer to believe in Liverpool's continuous self-inflicted shame, readers would have to be convinced that Liverpudlians should be accused of wallowing in their victim status. One headline 'Self Pity City' summarised the mainstream's tenor in the years that followed. This article wouldn't leave my mind ever again. My view on media, especially London-based newspapers, became distanced. I still read papers but started to question articles more and more.

When people in power, be it media, police or politics abuse their strength and attack what you love with a vile, rotten agenda, you instinctively close ranks. You sense a rift that cracks further apart over the years. Your own mentality becomes 'us against them'!

REST IN PEACE

John Alfred Anderson (62)

Colin Mark Ashcroft (19)

James Gary Aspinall (18)

Kester Roger Marcus Ball (16)

Gerard Bernard Patrick Baron (67)

Simon Bell (17)

Barry Sidney Bennett (26)

David John Benson (22)

David William Birtle (22)

Tony Bland (22)

Paul David Brady (21)

Andrew Mark Brookes (26)

Carl Brown (18)

David Steven Brown (25)

Henry Thomas Burke (47)

Peter Andrew Burkett (24)

Paul William Carlile (19)

Raymond Thomas Chapman (50)

Gary Christopher Church (19)

Joseph Clark (29)

Paul Clark (18)

Gary Collins (22)

Stephen Paul Copoc (20)

Tracey Elizabeth Cox (23)

James Philip Delaney (19)

Andrew Devine (55)

Christopher Barry Devonside (18)

Christopher Edwards (29)

Vincent Michael Fitzsimmons (34)

Thomas Steven Fox (21)

Jon-Paul Gilhooley (10)

Barry Glover (27)

Ian Thomas Glover (20)

Derrick George Godwin (24)

Roy Harry Hamilton (34)

Philip Hammond (14)

Eric Hankin (33)

Gary Harrison (27)

Stephen Francis Harrison (31)

Peter Andrew Harrison (15)

David Hawley (39)

James Robert Hennessy (29)

Paul Anthony Hewitson (26)

Carl Darren Hewitt (17)

Nicholas Michael Hewitt (16)

Sarah Louise Hicks (19)

Victoria Jane Hicks (15)
Gordon Rodney Horn (20)
Arthur Horrocks (41)
Thomas Howard (39)
Thomas Anthony Howard (14)
Eric George Hughes (42)
Alan Johnston (29)
Christine Anne Jones (27)
Gary Philip Jones (18)
Richard Jones (25)
Nicholas Peter Joynes (27)
Anthony Peter Kelly (29)
Michael David Kelly (38)
Carl David Lewis (18)
David William Mather (19)
Brian Christopher Matthews (38)
Francis Joseph McAllister (27)
John McBrien (18)
Marian Hazel McCabe (21)
Joseph Daniel McCarthy (21)
Peter McDonnell (21)
Alan McGlone (28)
Keith McGrath (17)
Paul Brian Murray (14)
Lee Nicol (14)
Stephen Francis O'Neill (17)
Jonathon Owens (18)
William Roy Pemberton (23)
Carl William Rimmer (21)
David George Rimmer (38)
Graham John Roberts (24)

Steven Joseph Robinson (17)
Henry Charles Rogers (17)
Colin Andrew Hugh William Sefton (23)
Inger Shah (38)
Paula Ann Smith (26)
Adam Edward Spearritt (14)
Philip John Steele (15)
David Leonard Thomas (23)
Patrick John Thompson (35)
Peter Reuben Thompson (30)
Stuart Paul William Thompson (17)
Peter Francis Tootle (21)
Christopher James Traynor (26)
Martin Kevin Traynor (16)
Kevin Tyrrell (15)
Colin Wafer (19)
Ian David Whelan (19)
Martin Kenneth Wild (29)
Kevin Daniel Williams (15)
Graham John Wright (17)

YOU'VE NEVER WALKED ALONE
YOU'LL NEVER BE FORGOTTEN

CHAPTER SEVEN

A Golden Sky at the End of a Storm

AFTER MY A level oral examinations in early May 1989, for which I didn't really prepare well and basically couldn't care less due to the circumstances, I had lots of spare time. My social service in a home for mentally ill people, which I opted for instead of joining the German army, wouldn't start before December. I hadn't applied to join the armed forces of the Scouse Republic of Liverpool after all.

I took on lots of jobs to earn some money, which was useful when you have so much spare time at that age. I spent a couple of weeks in the summer at the brewery again, worked as a dishwasher in restaurants and as a poll worker at local elections.

I signed up with a temporary employment agency that immediately placed me in a bread factory. I earned less money than I used to but it was a regular job, five days a week, which would sort me out for six weeks. Compared to the requirements of the brewery, the work was at first impression less physical. Soon I would find out, though, that standing eight hours from 6am at an assembly line that set the pace and the breathers for you, was a strain of a different kind. After a couple of weeks I was put on the night shift, which began at 2am.

This was the time when my happy-go-lucky, I'm-only-here-to-earn-some-quick-bread attitude ended. I realised that a job would not only have your night rule over your day, but could dominate your life completely. Far from finding any sleeping rhythm, I didn't even know what rhythm would be suitable at all. I could never fall asleep straight after getting home by around 11am. Then I had a nap from around 1pm. I wouldn't sleep more than three hours maximum, which meant I was totally knackered by the time I turned up at work again. My whole body clock was screwed up. In my final week I decided to stay up all day as long as possible until I could no longer keep my eyes open, around 4pm, set the alarm for 10pm, took a cold shower, went to my favourite pub, the Brauhaus, to have a breakfast/late-night dinner before taking the tram to the factory. This worked for me somehow, but a basic condition of being tired all the time would accompany me throughout those weeks.

There were only a handful of guys who did this job on a temporary basis like me. The other men were spending their lives there. I didn't speak much to the German employees, who obviously knew I only did this as a holiday job and thus didn't regard me as one of them. I occasionally had a chat with the Turkish migrant workers, who were a lot more fun. Most of them were fathers who had to feed a wife and three or four children. They had been working there for many years. One night, I learned that not all of them were employed by the bread company but some were from the same agency as me. One of them, while complaining about general working conditions, referred to 'our hourly wage'. My jaw dropped, but I tried to hide my thoughts. I had negotiated 11,50 Deutsche Mark per hour, believing I would get less because of my inexperience in that factory. Then I learned that those bread-earners, who had been working with the company for ages, were on 8,30 Deutsche Mark. It did make me feel sick and a little guilty, but there was nothing I could do about it. I just saw it through and decided not to set foot in a temporary job agency ever again.

Around that time, I was about to make my first personal acquaintance with the British upper class, an experience that had still been missing in my grasping of British society as a whole. After Marmite, there would certainly be nothing near to that for me to get used to!

I went to a party with a few mates where I gained the attention of a young lady. She was an Oxford student who had spent a year abroad as a teacher near Heidelberg. My language skills, and thereby the ability to crack jokes in her native language to make her laugh, certainly gave me the edge over my adversaries in courting her. When she told me her name, I knew I was in for something unknown and rather rare.

After a short time spent intensifying our level of intimacy, Fleur asked me, 'Carsten, why don't you try to speak like me?' I couldn't detect any difference between her and my enunciation, parlance or diction, neither had I ever been made aware by any English native-speaking person that my vocabulary lacked a certain degree of style before.

'Carsten, you could pronounce the words you use more distinctly, couldn't you.' *Bloody hell*, I thought, maybe Fräulein Zaruba in second-class singing lesson had a point and was right after all. My conversations with Fleur felt like role play in which I took up the subordinated role of Eliza Doolittle while she was confident in acting as patronising Professor Higgins. I would have thought that it was my job to teach her German, but she sensed some serious responsibility to teach me appropriate pronunciation, sophisticated vocabulary and courteous phrases.

One evening, when she wasn't staying at my place, the phone rang. 'Good evening, this is Fleur's father speaking. May I speak to my daughter please?' I conversed in a brief cultivated colloquy with an interlocuter whose voice I defined as a cross between Jacob Rees-Mogg and Prince Charles. I instantly realised where her pedagogic measures were rooted.

I never figured out whether one particular phrase was part of her education programme or, in a rare moment of thoughtlessness, she only thought aloud. In a random situation far from any kind of intimate encounter, she told me, 'You're my bit of rough!' I actually liked the thought of my toughness being the source of attraction, although wasn't sure that it was perhaps my lack of sophistication or lower socio-economic status in her view. Whatever, whenever, wherever, I did my very best to live up to my imposed purpose.

Fleur played tennis, hockey and had a soft spot for rowing (the sport, not the quarrelling, for which she was naturally gifted, too). She also liked cricket, of course, but not in the sense of playing, following a team or watching on TV. It was more this overlying atmosphere of an outdoor get-together that tickled her fancy.

'Oh, it's so lovely and wonderful, Carsten, meeting people, sitting outside in the sunshine, eating strawberries with cream, drinking a glass of champagne.'

Bloody hell, I thought, before beads of perspiration forced their way out of my forehead's pores. I realised to my relief there was no cricket club anywhere near! I refrained from telling her that I would much rather have some fish and chips wrapped up in a newspaper, with vinegar dripping out, and a pint outside the Kop before a match.

'Bloody boring if you ask me!' I remarked.

'Carsten, how can you say something like that? You don't even know!' I tried to explain that everyone is entitled to like any sports, but I personally just couldn't warm to it. 'You don't understand!' was the end to the conversation. It would be the ending of many more to follow.

Meanwhile, Liverpool were top of the league and going for the double yet again in the 1989/90 season. An FA Cup semi-final against Crystal Palace was coming up. What better access to video footage could I have dreamed of than having a young English lady lying next to me in bed every night?

'Fleur, your parents do have a video recorder, don't they?' I had been briefed that her father was a CEO, a chairman in the cultural field, as well as president of various sports institutions. He even visited Downing Street to discuss budgets for one of his areas of responsibility with the prime minister over dinner. I had come to the conclusion before that he might not share the same interests with me, but, nevertheless, I didn't see any problem in asking for a favour. She looked at me quizzically, not saying a word as if she sensed what was dawning on her.

'Couldn't your parents record some live matches for me and send them over?' I suggested. 'I'm afraid they don't watch football,' was the shortest of superficial answers, which demonstratively withdrew any *raison d'être* for any further potential queries.

'Oh no, they don't have to watch it themselves, just press the record button. Or, if they record *Match of the Day*, they wouldn't have to wait for the Liverpool match, but just record the whole programme through.' After seconds of silence, I added, 'I mean, I'll pay for it, of course!'

She didn't look me straight in the eye as she said hesitantly, 'It has nothing to do with money.' Her aghast expression and derogatory tone unambiguously implied that I had just crossed a certain line and caused a kind of vicarious embarrassment. I felt as if I had just asked Her Majesty the Queen herself to join me in the pub for a few pints. Observing a reluctance while waiting for an answer, I reassured her I would pay for the rounds. Fleur wouldn't tell me directly that watching football is for riff-raff, but still wanted to make sure I unmistakeably comprehended that she wouldn't ever discommode her parents with my inferior concerns. I had to realise that I may penetrate her, but never her parents' life, even if only for some videotaping of Liverpool matches.

One Saturday evening, the overriding news on German media was riots on Trafalgar Square in London. Thatcher's 'Poll Tax' was about to be introduced and protests got out of hand. In Sunday's newspapers, I studied the sports section before reading thoroughly about the latest Tory politics to conceive an opinion. Fleur and I were sitting in the car later that afternoon and, actually, until then, having a good time.

The riots were mentioned on the radio and I rather casually mentioned, 'It's all bollocks, isn't it!'

'What are you talking about?' she responded.

'This new Thatcher thing. It's not fair, is it? A single flat-rate tax per head!' Never ever was a conversation blighted so quickly.

'We both don't understand enough to assess the whole situation,' she replied but she clearly meant to say, 'You don't understand enough to assess the whole situation! And anyway, why don't you just shut up and stop criticising our country's prime minister and her politics, which she's entirely entitled to exercise, however she wishes!'

I did have a reasoned opinion, though. Compared to Fleur, I occupied myself with the subject and invested time in reading articles in what even she would call quality newspapers to form a personal opinion. But I just couldn't be bothered to undergo another moody evening, so I just kept it to myself.

In an attempt to start an appeasing chat I mentioned the Oxford–Cambridge boat race that took place that same weekend. It had been shown delayed in full length on German TV and I couldn't understand why I always had to pray to watch some Liverpool highlights while some students paddling on the Thames was of general interest to the German public.

'Your boys' boat race was on this weekend,' I said. She didn't say anything, so I assumed something was building up in her. Perhaps I then uttered my following remarks in a too unimpressed way. 'It's funny, isn't it?'

What are you talking about now?' she responded in a rather irritated way.

'I mean, there are some young lads nobody knows doing a boat race and it's televised all around the world.' This time the silence was of a different kind. Something had been bottling up for some time with the urge to come out quickly. If you've ever shaken a bottle of Diet Coke before opening it, you'll have observed that all the bubbles float to the surface at once and there's a bit of a shower, which leaves a manageable mess. But if you dare sink a Mentos into an already open Diet Coke bottle, the outcome is rather intense. The mint provides a rough surface that allows the bonds between the carbon dioxide gas and water to break more easily, helping to create carbon dioxide bubbles. Because Mentos are rather dense, they sink rapidly through the liquid, causing a very fast and rather extreme eruption.

I wasn't even aware that I was capable of causing a Mentos effect. As my comments seemingly appeared rather dense on the surface, too, they sank rapidly through her otherwise noble composure, causing a short but intensive explosion: 'We're the most important people in Britain!'

My unsuspecting, naive, but innocent remark on a miniscule, negligible, insignificant subject turned out to be an affront to the whole British establishment. I wanted to burst out laughing, but in that moment was more engaged in analysing the mindset of the woman I spent every day with. There seemed to be no ifs, buts or maybes, let alone an okay, I can see your point. No matter what, nobody is ever entitled to argue, criticise, ignore, let alone make fun of or take the piss out of the Conservative party, the Tory prime minister, the royal family, the House of Lords with their many unelected hereditary peers, or even students paddling boats on a river, let alone strawberries with cream! And if you do, we, the most important people in Britain, tell you that you're wrong and you don't understand anyway. We don't even listen to your arguments as we don't care about their solidity. And it doesn't matter under any circumstances, one way or the other, as you don't belong to us anyway.

There was no point and I couldn't be bothered to debate. I refrained from asking her about her specific contribution to and personal importance to British society achieved so far in her young life. She was going back home soon anyway and so was Thatcher, too. On 22 November, the day Thatcher was forced to resign, a group of friends got tickets for a Pogues concert in the Stadthalle Ludwigshafen across the Rhine, the venue where I had seen Frankie Goes to Hollywood a few years earlier. An absolutely pissed Shane MacGowan came on stage and welcomed a packed hall: 'The bitch is gone, we're free!' What a great concert and night it turned out to be!

After my social service ended, I enrolled in business studies, media science and English language and literature at university. The real essential science of life, though, was presented to me when I discovered educational text sources of the highest quality. A new age broke in which I would be taught how to think, act and be a proper Red! I devoured every single edition of my newly acquired fanzine's subscription *Through the Wind and Rain* by Steve Kelly. The fanzine appeased my hunger for Kopites' opinions and beliefs on a regular basis. In particular, the exemplary, purely impartial and totally unbiased views about our neighbours in the wooden hut across the park and the inhabitants of a repugnant hole down the M62 served me very well in my further sophisticated education. In later years, the red brainwashing by John Pearman's *Red All Over the Land*, Dave

Usher's *The Liverpool Way*, Chris McLoughlin's *The Kop Magazine* and Gareth Roberts's *Well Red* played no minor part in my development in becoming an open-minded, cosmopolitan, balanced and fair-minded contemporary of the football world that surrounded Liverpool Football Club.

Live football in the early 1990s, however, was reduced to rare pre-season friendlies in Germany. There was a dull 0-0 draw with Bayer Leverkusen at the Ulrich-Haberland-Stadion. A few seasons later I went to the old Bökelberg in Mönchengladbach and stood on the terrace where the travelling Kop had watched Scouse captain Tommy Smith lift our first European trophy in the 1973 UEFA Cup Final. This latest encounter against our dear old rivals Borussia included a young lad called Robbie Fowler. He wasn't on the scoresheet, but a 1-0 victory allowed me to witness my first-ever Liverpool victory – in my tenth match! Hoodoo, jinx? I certainly got that monkey off my back that night!

In between studying Liverpool fanzines and attending university courses, I worked most of my time. I continued working part-time at the home for the mentally ill where I did around five night-shifts a month and took up another part-time job in a computer games shop where I hung out a couple of times a week. As I couldn't be bothered anymore to stand at an assembly line endlessly or carry crates all day long during semester breaks, I was always on the lookout for some coveted jobs to cash in properly.

The university had a noticeboard where they published job vacancies. A TV production company was looking for cable pullers for one of the big German *Schlager* music shows with compere Dieter Thomas Heck, which was going to be broadcast live from the Stadthalle Ludwigshafen. It was almost a full week's work from Tuesday to the live show on Sunday evening. There were around ten of us who got the job, which basically consisted of hanging around and waiting for something to happen.

Just before rehearsals started on the Wednesday and we were waiting for instructions, one of the people in charge pointed at me and said, 'We need someone to handle the microphone. You, come with me.' I learned that I wouldn't be pulling any cables but would be handing over the microphone to the artistes walking on to the stage and receiving it back when they left. None of them needed a microphone, though, as it was all playback anyway. However, it was fun to observe the arrogant or likeable behaviour of Germany's finest 'superstars'. The likes of Roland Kaiser, Bernd Clüver, Die Flippers, Bernhard Brink, Ireen Sheer, Karel Gott, Jürgen Marcus and others were the music genre's equivalent of the UK's Engelbert or Tony Christie.

The whole day I dealt with the challenge of remembering which artiste wanted to receive the microphone in their right hand or their left hand. Only by sticking to this individual accustomed procedure were they able to perform their lip movements over three full minutes. In between rehearsals, we hung around in the canteen most of the time. Backstage, some artistes without make-up and with their hair undone could easily have been mistaken for some of the lads who stood at the assembly line at night in that bread factory. One artiste in his late fifties was accompanied by a lady in her late twenties. Wondering what hourly compensation she was on when escorting her daddy, I overheard him introducing her as his wife.

A working day would last up to 12 hours for the remainder of the week and it was by far the easiest money I had ever earned until then and since. This is how TV works? I couldn't believe my luck to profit personally from the big, inexhaustible TV licence fee pot. And to top it all off, the icing on the cake was our invitation to the after-show party, where we raided the buffet and kept the bar busy all night. Unfortunately, this job was only a one-off opportunity as they picked different venues all over the country for their coming shows.

I needed more regular sources of income, though. In winter, from November to April, I took up a job with a private snow-clearing service company. A boyhood dream came true. You could steer a big wheel with a snow plough in front of you and a flashing beacon on top. Fun was guaranteed, too. In heavy winters, both co-driver and driver had to get out to shovel the tight spaces where the vehicle couldn't reach. Some nights the snow had already frozen into ice, and if you didn't pay attention you were lying on your back in no time.

The best part though was the guaranteed income. We were paid 500 Deutsche Mark each month over six months, no matter whether it snowed or not. The probability that it might snow in November, March or April was close to zero anyway. Most of the winters I had 3,000 Deutsche Mark in my bank account for which I maybe had to work seven, eight, some winters maximum 15 times. The main advantage was it wouldn't interfere with your daily routine as your knocking-off time was around 9am and you could still spend the whole day as planned. The main disadvantage only occurred if you went on a night out to town or a students' party without

Once a year granny as Santa could exact vengeance big time on me for terrorising her with playing loud music and ruining her flowerbeds. No wonder I was in awe when I saw Liverpool in their all-red kit for the first time!

Even The Sweet's frontman Brian Connolly never ever looked that hard. For a proper teenage rampage you just needed a proper haircut!

Fräulein Zaruba's measures to subjugate me to her austere discipline brought my teenage rampage to a temporary interruption! Just for the record, my mum bought me that blue jumper, not me, honest!

22 April 1981: European Cup semi-final, second leg – Bayern Munich v Liverpool. The first time I saw the Reds, in white, live. Ray Kennedy meets Paul Breitner who accused Liverpool of 'lacking imagination' in a pre-match interview. Bayern officials certainly did not lack imagination as they distributed leaflets advertising travel arrangements for the final in Paris before the match. Liverpool's captain's goal in a 1-1 draw saw the Reds go through on the away goals rule.

The 'JOEY ATE THE FROGS LEGS' banner in Rome certainly inspired me to make my own.

18 August 1984: Charity Shield – Liverpool v Everton. All of a sudden I stood on the terrace at Wembley. 100,000 Reds and Blues mixing together in both ends joining in 'Merseyside, Merseyside, Merseyside' and 'Are you watching Manchester?' The travelling Kop proudly presented a Roma flag they brought as a souvenir from yet another European Cup win the previous May.

Mum: 'Where's that sheet I put in your wardrobe?' Me: 'On the wall!' Mum: 'On the wall?' Me: 'On the wall! Looks great, doesn't it?' Mum: '……'

If I had known that the Scouse casuals only wore trabs with three stripes back then, I certainly would have swerved that swoosh. My mum wouldn't have allowed me to shoplift them in style though, but made me pay for them at the checkout.

9 February 1986: Liverpool v Manchester United. My first time at Anfield and I had to stand side by side with Mancs in the away end! Not only could I not join in 'You'll Never Walk Alone', but also couldn't celebrate when John Wark scored for the Reds a few yards away from me.

Saturday's weekly ritual before BBC's medium wave second half live commentary: Newspaper, tea and a sound Scouse playlist to warm up.

The official club news provided me with long-desired insight information. The fanzines fed me with the Scouse spirit and a proper brainwashing.

23 July 1987: A few moments before Kenny's boys of '88 with Aldridge, Barnes and Beardsley played together for the very first time in the Olympic Stadium Munich!

A 7 foot tall tower of a man suddenly stood in front of me outside Anfield and signed my match ticket: Ron Yeats

16 May 2001: UEFA Cup Final – Liverpool v Deportivo Alaves. God lifting the UEFA Cup after a 5-4 golden own goal victory in extra time. The most exciting, greatest ever European football final that could certainly never be bettered.

Touching the sign for the first time.

24 May 2005: 'Oh Istanbul Is Wonderful! It's full of mosques, kebabs and Scousers!' Taksim Square was home for the partying Reds the night before and after the European Cup Final in Istanbul in 2005.

25 May 2005: European Cup Final – AC Milan v Liverpool. 0-3 down at half-time, Gerrard, Smicer, Alonso made it 3-3 within six minutes. Extra time … Shevchenko … Dudek … penalties … Shevchenko … Dudek… 'In Istanbul we won it five times!' Back to Taksim Square!

23 May 2007: European Cup Final – AC Milan v Liverpool. Police at multiple ticket checkpoints before the final in Athens made sure not one Liverpool supporter would enter the stadium without a valid ticket! Not one would bunk in!

Participating in THE KOP magazine's photo challenge amongst Mancs and Mercenaries on Red Square before their European Cup Final … and making a Manc participate.

Conquering Europe in pre-season friendlies in some known and some not so known places.

CLUB NOTES   SPORT   send notes to sport@donegalpost.

dh Ruadh

. underage and or hurling fix-
es involving
h Ruadh were cancelled
week due to the sudden
sing of former under-
manager Peter O'Keefe.
er had a great passion
the game of hurling an
ched many underage
h Ruadh teams. He was
involved in the man-
ment of many underage
egal teams. In this role
rove up and down the
ity bringing Aodh Ruadh
vers to county training
matches. He will be
y missed by all in Aodh
dh. Our thoughts and
ers are with his wife Ro-
en and children Peadar,
ve and current under 16
h Ruadh hurler donal.
heis Dé go raibh a anam
al.
dh Ruadh opened their
) minor championship
paign with a hard-
ed
2 to 0-8 victory over Four
sters. The second leg will
place in Tir Chonaill
on Wednesday, August
at 7pm. The winners of

The numbers draw
4,13,14,15.The jack
stands at 2,800 Euro
The July draw for
Club was held las
night at the excueti
ing and the followi
the winners,1st pr
Euro Mary Mc Gett
5 prizes of 100 Eu
to Mary Doherty,
Bonner,Tony Thomp
Hegarty and James I
The club presen
Gallen this Saturday
the Highlands Hotel
are 25 Euro and are
in the Highlands Ho
Glincheys.
The club are ho
Kids Summer Camp
Mon 16th and Fri 20
gust.For more info
contact Martin Res
Wade,Anthony Th
or Muriel Hegarty.

Naomh Mhuire

THE numbers
drawn in the
weekly lotto were
14 and 23. There
outright winner. T
tion prizes went to
Greene (Gracie) F
Neil P. Boyle, M

J.P. and me staging a protest GILLETT & HICKS OUT NOW before a pre-season friendly in Mönchengladbach. Not only did it generate attention abroad, but also international media coverage by the Donegal Post. *Our protest eventually led to the leaving of the owners and paved the way for a new era and the first league title after 30 years under Jürgen Klopp. Both of us are fully aware and proud of our place in Liverpool Football Club's history. Just for the record, J.P. bought that half-and-half scarf, not me, honest!*

Bumping into David Fairclough Claire Rourke before a pre-season friendly in Switzerland.

Meeting Gerry Marsden backstage after a concert.

The German invasion of the Kop. Stefan, Thorsten and Andreas insist: Not Casuals, We Are The Men In Black!

The battle cry in Shevchenko Park before the European Cup Final in Kiev.

1 June 2019: European Cup Final – Liverpool v Tottenham Hotspur. Tens of thousands of Reds partied on Plaza de Felipe II all day before the final in Madrid. The Anfield Wrap, rapping John Barnes, Jamie Webster and many more heated up the mood in the greatest ever party!

Letting everyone know what we are on the way to Wembley.

being aware of the weather forecast. It might happen that you returned home and hit the sack absolutely, let me put it mildly, knackered, at around 2am and then the phone rang at 3am to inform you that an operation somewhere out of town was due.

In the summer, I found an annual job at the Formula One German Grand Prix in Hockenheim, where I did the dishwashing in the VIP area. It was a full week's work from Tuesday to the following Monday, during which we were working on 12-hour shifts. The first three days we cleaned crockery, cutlery, glasses and all kinds of kitchen utensils that arrived from the previous Grand Prix somewhere in the world. On the Friday, the first day of free practice, it got busy as hordes of waiting staff and chefs arrived. The VIP tent was absolutely empty, and on the Saturday for the qualifying few guests turned up either. However, each day, lunch, dinner and cakes were prepared as if guests turned up in full numbers, although only a handful were present. Innumerable huge trollies carrying plates of freshly cooked cuisine returned untouched in masses and the food found its way to the bins. Some plates were saved by the chefs and handed out to hungry service staff. They all knew each other as they kept travelling to the races together. As dishwashers, who were only temporarily hired locally, our standing was really low down the pecking order. I mean, really low. Whereas the attractive ladies and male models, who were carefully selected to serve the rich and beautiful VIPs, were treated with lunch and dinner, our sort was happy to snatch a dessert. Some guys depended on the money as this would be their only cash-in-hand income besides their dole. One guy did three 12-hour shifts back to back, working 36 hours running. When we turned up on the last day he looked like the walking dead. The stimulants he kept taking made him stay awake somehow, though.

The Monday after the race, after all the chefs, waiting staff and most of the management had gone, we tidied up the place and got everything in order for transporting to the next Grand Prix.

'Didn't you bring your bag?' I was asked by one of the guys who had worked there the previous year.

'What for?' I asked. With a shake of the head he turned away. I soon conceived the motto of the day: 'What you see is what you get,' meaning: 'Take everything useful as long as you don't get caught.' Some of the veteran guys brought huge rucksacks and crammed them with two-litre bottles of the finest of red wines that entertained Ferrari's top management and Michael Schumacher's family, which they had stashed away in their hidey-holes over the weekend.

I met my mate Thorsten there for the first time. He was another student who, during semester breaks, even travelled with the company to other sports events, such as ATP tennis tournaments. He keeps telling me today that he got his first proper kitchen appliances from one such working weekend. By the mid-1990s, I decided to call it a day with the wild circus life of jobbing and take more serious student employment in marketing.

'Carsten, a new Irish pub opened in Heidelberg!' The thought of a real pub in my town like I knew them from Britain made me shiver with excitement. There was a chance they would have satellite or cable TV or maybe BBC, ITV, or in later years BSkyB reception. Naivety, driven by desperate hope, characterised my world of thought. Despite the experience of disappointment before, I kept visiting new places to check them out but it was always the same old story again and again. The only Irish element about this new pub was the Guinness sign outside and the Guinness beer inside. Some others even had green paint outside or inside or even outside and inside to give them an Irish touch. Some even had a dartboard or a pool table, while others a painted shamrock on the wall. The pure Irishness of the places could even be heard as they were playing The Dubliners and The Pogues. This is where the dream ended. Every time! Whenever I approached the landlord or the staff and started to speak in English, they would only reply in a language that revealed they weren't even Irish. The German-looking German speaking German behind the bar didn't even try to make an effort to speak with an Irish accent.

My mate Georg, who I got to know in one of my courses at university, had returned from his year abroad in Birmingham, where he read business studies at Aston University. During the previous year, we planned that I would visit him and I chose the FA Cup Final weekend 1996 when the Reds played the Mancs. As late as the mid-1990s, none of the German TV broadcasting companies bothered to televise the FA Cup Final live. The biggest domestic cup competition in world football was shown all around the globe, but not in my country! We wanted to watch it in a pub, but on the day Georg decided to drive up to Liverpool. We thought there might be a giant screen put up somewhere in the city centre.

When we arrived in Liverpool we learned that there would be no such public screening and we would be better off in a pub. As we didn't want to miss any of the build-up, we decided to park the car as soon as we spotted a pub with a Liverpool flag, scarf or anything red and white in sight. In some quiet street on a hill we spotted such a red-decorated place. When we entered the pub it was like one of those western movies. The regular crowd were sitting at the tables. Anyone who ever entered this place had been living within walking distance for decades and had known each other since nursery school. When two tall foreign-looking fellas entered through the saloon's swing door, the world inside the pub came to a standstill. The piano man interrupted his playing, the barman stopped filling the pint, women and children disappeared quickly through the back door. Nobody moved, nobody spoke, but all eyes were on us. Soon, one of the bad guys would challenge us to a duel. Where's the sheriff? Oh, he's sitting there playing cards with the other locals. He would get up any second with his hand on his revolver asking us to leave his town immediately.

I looked at the TV screen and realised that the locals didn't know what had hit them. First they saw the heirs of Ron Yeats, Tommy Smith and Graeme Souness in white suits doing their pre-match walkabout, then two strangers had invaded their territory.

'Can we watch the Liverpool match here?' I asked in a very submissive tone. The landlady responded with the broadest smile. She pointed to the stools in front of the bar, providing us with a perfect view of the TV screen. No one who walked up to the bar to get their drinks returned to their seats without giving us a smile. Everyone who entered the pub looked at us, wondering who we were, but not one of them didn't say 'hello'. One elderly gentleman walked through the door and, without asking around, came straight to us and said, 'You left your car's lights on.' He automatically knew that a car he had never seen before with a German number plate must belong to the only strangers who had ever entered this place.

Georg and I were always served first with our lager requests and even served cheese sandwiches on the house. The rough saloon atmosphere would only re-emerge temporarily when the Manc manager appeared on TV for an interview. The landlady immediately switched off the sound and shouted at the screen, 'Shot yer fockhin' gob, will yer!' Lord, I felt at home! We lost the match by a single goal to a team that had a giant transatlantic sailing ship on their badge despite the fact that its inland canal city inhabitants never ever got a sniff of salt water all their lives. The outcome of the match left a gutted feeling, but what I kept in mind was the cordial encounter with the Scousers and watching the match together in the pub. People around every corner seemed to smile and say, 'We don't care what your name is boy, we'll never turn you away.'

Back in Germany, Georg started work for a global software company near Heidelberg, where many employees came from all over the world. There was quite a considerable number of English and Irish expats, who spent their nightlife in nearby Heidelberg, some ten miles away from Mannheim.

One day during the close season in the summer, he told me about an Irish pub he had heard of from one of the British guys he worked with. He heard that live football matches were being shown there as well. I just couldn't be bothered. I was fed up with building up my hopes only for my dreams to be tossed and blown again. I didn't have the guts to believe the news, so I asked him to pass on the question of whether those people had actually seen a full live match on the Sky Sports football channel. He rang me up a few days later and confirmed that this would be the case.

My mind listened, but my heart, soul and stomach didn't know how to handle this information. The new season would soon start and Liverpool's first home match against Arsenal was going to be screened live on BSkyB on a Monday night. I searched for the telephone number of O'Reilly's pub and called them in the afternoon on the day of the match. 'Yeah, it's on,' was the simple response.

Speechlessness on my part was followed by a hesitant and more explicit repetition of my question. 'You mean, you do have British Sky Broadcasting and you do show the full Liverpool match live tonight on your TV in your pub, right?'

'Yeah, sure.' The lady's Irish accent increased the Irish pub's authenticity.

'Oh, thank you! I'll come, I'll be there ...' I stuttered as if I feared they would close the pub if not enough people turned up by early evening.

'Great, we're here, bye!' the lovely lady responded.

I drove to Heidelberg in disbelief, which vanished quickly when I walked inside. The place had typical pub furniture and served Guinness as well as English draught beer. On a table I spotted a plate with fish and chips next to some English newspapers. The pub seemed to be full of British people. I looked around and there it was, a big TV screen. Some soap was on, but no one was watching. I prayed that I would overhear one of the actresses saying that she fancied a cuppa or was just about to put the kettle on. Cup of tea wasn't the topic, but I realised it was definitely English TV.

I walked up to the bar, pointed at the TV and uttered rather timidly, 'Liverpool?'

'Yeah, it's gonna be on in a minute.'

To this day, I've never forgotten that feeling I sensed in these particular moments. The blood flow in my veins accelerated with each step. I floated on cloud nine towards paradise. It felt like coming home from a long journey full of austerity and hardship, when Sienna Miller would open the door and welcome me with a deep, wet kiss. The bar lady took the remote control and switched the channels. Sienna lasciviously drops her clothing in front of me and walks in her black lingerie to the bedroom. Looking at the screen, I just caught a glimpse of Liverpool's and Arsenal's crests. Kate Beckinsale walks out of the kitchen with a drink in her hand, licks her glass and whispers, 'Have a sip from my glass, sweetie, and follow Sienna. I'll join you two in a minute.'

A voice on the TV said, 'We'll be right back for kick-off in a short moment,' before the programme went into a commercial break. Even the sweet tune of the advertising jingles triggered my fantasy. The smooth sound was like the ringing doorbell to which Kate responds, 'Carsten, would you like to answer the door, please? That must be Margot! We invited her around, too. I hope you don't mind?!' The commercial break ended and the presenter and pundits resumed their pre-match talk in the studio inside Anfield. I open the door and Margot Robbie greets me with an innocent smile. She passes me by, waves playfully with a massage oil bottle in her hand and gives me a naughty look. The match commentator took over from the studio and the camera showed the Redmen on the pitch! Sienna, Kate and

Margot all snuggled into each other on my bed. The match kicked off. Sienna, Kate and Margot beckoned me over: 'Come on boy, we're ready to goooo.'

Two goals from Steve McManaman without reply from the Londoners made the night all the sweeter. On Monday, 19 August 1996, 9pm Central European Summer Time at O'Reilly's Irish pub, Brückenkopfstrasse 1 in Heidelberg, the gate to the Garden of Eden was opened for me! I finally felt at home!

CHAPTER EIGHT

Priorities

THE CHARACTER Dorothy in my favourite British sitcom at the time, *Men Behaving Badly*, once commented while her boyfriend Gary was watching football: 'Why do all Italian footballers look like models and all English footballers as if they just got out of prison?' The Liverpool team in the following 1996/97 season certainly looked more like Italian models, played the most entertaining, exciting football, but for their casualness and blunders, some should have been sent to prison.

Heidelberg became my second home. I soon found out that another proper Irish pub, Napper Tandy's, in Heidelberg's Old Town showed live matches from England, too. They had a massive separate TV back room and would turn up the sound when an important match was on or if enough viewers gathered to watch any match. Every single Liverpool match was an important match and me, myself and I were always a sufficient gathering in order to turn the sound up anyway. The staff soon got acquainted with me. The staff very soon got acquainted with me and my association with

NOT GERMAN, I'M SCOUSE

Liverpool. I was a regular for every single Reds match and after a while they automatically switched on the TV as soon as they spotted me entering the pub. They even changed channels to Sky or Channel 5 on UEFA Cup nights when the Reds were on, irrespective of other guests already watching some other programme. Germans sitting in the pub following Bundesliga football were left wondering why they couldn't watch Bayern Munich or Borussia Dortmund when they were kindly asked to take their drinks and move to the front room with the much smaller TV screen and quieter sound. They looked even more astonished when my pint was served at the table, although I had only just sat down seconds before and didn't even have to order it in the first place.

That season, Liverpool had their first proper fight for the title for years. I was finally able to witness the Merseyside derby, the encounters with the Mancs and especially matches you wouldn't expect to become such a thriller as they turned out to be. 'When Liverpool met Newcastle last year it ended 4-3. You won't see this happening tonight!' the commentator remarked. I couldn't see it live last time around, certainly nothing similar will happen tonight again! The previous season's fixture had been referred to as the greatest ever Premier League match. Now, King Kenny returned to Anfield as Newcastle manager and it was a strange sight to see him take a seat on the opposition's bench. McManaman, Berger and Fowler ensured the most comfortable half-time score in the most superior way I had witnessed all season. The Geordies got one back with some 20 minutes to go before they scored another one three minutes from stoppage time. I was in a bad mood as we should have finished the match off much earlier and not led by just a single goal. A minute later I was hoping we would win by a one-goal margin, when Newcastle equalised in the 88th minute. Within the last seconds of the match Mr Robert Bernard Fowler from Toxteth scored another to repeat the 4-3 result from the year before.

On the flipside, I also had to endure painful defeats. A comfortable 2-0 half-time lead at Stamford Bridge in the fourth round of the FA Cup was surrendered by conceding four Chelsea goals in the second half without reply. A lack of goalkeeping concentration brought a 3-1 home defeat to the Mancs and our surrender in the title race.

Access to live TV matches also brought a new experience with very strange kick-off times that I needed to get used to. Watching a football match in a pub 12 miles away at 12.15pm – I had the privilege of having kick-off an hour later than the 11.15am UK time due to the time difference – meant I had to be up and ready by 10.30am. This endeavour was sometimes quite challenging for a student who had enjoyed a typical Friday night out. I would have to get up, ignore the hangover with a throbbing head and a sick stomach, put on my jeans and shirt, grab my money and keys and move myself out of the flat. In such a state, the one-mile walk to the main station at fast pace would regularly worsen my condition, especially when I overslept. Sometimes, I managed to jog to make up for lost time and gained important spare seconds to buy a coffee, orange juice and a sandwich on the way. Most of the time, though, the clock wouldn't allow it and the first nourishment I could enjoy was the first pint of lager in the pub. I would always be sitting on the train with my lungs gasping and my body sweating.

Getting to early morning kick-offs on time was one challenge, but getting back home after midweek evening matches was another. This was especially the case when Liverpool's participation in the UEFA Cup at the end of the 1990s was broadcast by Channel 5. Sometimes, I opted for staying on after the final whistle to listen to the post-match interviews instead of heading straight to the station. The local public transport's connection time schedule wasn't adjusted to Liverpool's midweek European nights. This sheer ignorance of the local authorities led to the sole alternative of having to run my guts out to catch the last train home or call a taxi. My first-hand practical experience of running just after being on the booze meant I often opted for the comfortable seat in the cab. The 80 Deutsche Mark fare to get home was more or less unbudgeted in a student's life, but worth it every time!

The choice of acquaintance with members of the opposite gender could turn out to be a benefit if the lady's residence geographically matched the locations of pubs of your personal preference. As it happened, I fell madly in love with a beautiful medical student in Heidelberg. Adriana lived in one of the many student homes close to the Old Town. At an early stage of our relationship, I somehow had to break my Liverpool time system to her, an explanation process that required sensitive prudence and vigilance for any girlfriend in my life. I could find the odd excuse for needing my own time for weekday evenings; however, asking for a few hours on my own on a Saturday or Sunday demanded some serious justification.

'You're trying to say you can't spend Sunday afternoon with me because you would rather sit in a pub, drink your beer and watch your football match?'

'It's not just football, it's Liverpool,' I remarked.

'Well, they do play football, don't they?' she argued objectively.

'Yes,' I answered soberly before adding emotionally, 'but it's Liverpool and I've been waiting all my life to watch them live!' Unaware and unintentionally, I had provided a stage to discuss the fundamental priorities of my new life.

'Oh, so you haven't been waiting all your life for me and for spending time with me?' I couldn't retort sensibly for an appropriate vindication.

'Look, yes, but we can also go out afterwards.' I tried to ease the situation, but the stage was still hers.

'Is it a final?' The interrogation continued in a rather provocative tone.

'Er, no. It's just a normal match.'

'Who are they playing again? Who? Middelsbowou? Tottingham? Wimbledon? Don't they play tennis?' It was quite a task and took some bravery to answer these direct questions with a direct 'yes'.

'Yes!' I replied directly. I made sure this was quickly followed by an assurance that I would make up for it. I didn't know how, though, as I still had to make amends for the weekend before, and the one before that.

Sometimes I planned and behaved too casually. I thought it would be a clever idea not to mention a match at all when she didn't plan to see me anyway.

'Fullum?' she asked. 'Why are they playing on a Tuesday night?' She knew that it was no UEFA Cup week when matches were played on a Tuesday. I managed to argue plausibly about the importance of every single league fixture. I had succeeded in convincing her about the relevance of European encounters.

Even an away tie in Kosice or at Celta Vigo was a high-profile match as qualification for the next round was at stake. She had even developed a kind of understanding for the FA Cup as the final would take place at Wembley, but beyond that there wasn't so much room for yet another all-important competition.

'Never heard of them!' Her tone became a tiny bit aggressive. It was Fulham at home in the League Cup and I hadn't found time to justify my absence in advance. We had seen each other all weekend and I figured that I would spend Tuesday on my own anyway. So what would have been the point of telling her I was going to watch Liverpool when I might just as well have been spending the evening alone at home anyway? 'Anyway' as in 'any' 'way'!

'Where are they in the league?' she asked. I was clutching at straws. I saw my chance here to answer her direct question literally.

'They are top of the league.' It was true. They were top of their league and emphasising that fact might convince her of the importance of the match. She would understand and realise that going to the pictures was always possible a couple of days later. This would ease the situation and get me off the hook. So I thought. I underestimated the knowledge she had attained while being with me.

'Top? I thought Manchester United were top!' she argued.

'Well, Man United are actually top of the Premier League,' I explained. Confusion was increased.

'And in what league do they play if not in the Premier League?' she interrogated.

'They play under the Premier League, sweetie.'

'What? They are in the Second Division?'

For a split second I thought to leave it at that. More detailed explanation would aggravate the complication of the conversation. I always hated the modern renaming of the old divisions. The old 'First Division' was the new 'Premier League', the old 'Second Division' was the new 'First Division', and so on. But in that particular moment I thanked the English Football Association and Sky. I was just about to confirm that Fulham were in the 'Second Division' when my bad conscience crept in. I loved her and I never told her anything but the truth. In this case I knew I would give her the wrong answer if I confirmed her thoughts, so I attempted to enlighten her.

'Well, it's called the "Second Division."'

'What? What do you mean? Are you having me on?'

'Well no, they actually play in the Third Division, which is now called the Second Division because the Second Division is now the First Division and the First Division is now the Premier League.' I knew I was telling the truth, but it still felt weird because it sounded weird.

'You're not trying to say that you decline going out with me on Tuesday because your Livvapuul is playing a Third Division team in a competition that's called the Worthington Cup and they can't win without you?' In that moment, I was glad the League Cup was called that. The name sounded much more worthy than Littlewoods Cup or Rumbelows Cup. I would have been in even deeper trouble if I had to explain that the coveted trophy they were playing for was the Coca Cola Cup or Milk Cup.

'Well, but Keegan is coming home. He's their manager,' I explained.

'Who the devil is Keegan?'

'He used to play for us under Shankly and Paisley.' The many names got her confused and I tried to avoid giving her the impression that I wanted to give her lame excuses. By being totally honest about strange facts I became entangled in a web of truths and was still peculiarly caught in my own trap. Then I had a cunning idea that would make her understand.

'The final will take them to Wembley!' That was a mistake! I had jumped out of the frying pan into the fire.

'Wembley?' she asked bewildered. 'But you said the FA Cup is so special because the final is at Wembley! Are you saying there's another cup competition where the final is played at Wembley?' Not only had I failed to deliver a point pro the League Cup, but in the very same breath also devalued my argument for needing time to watch the FA Cup! A very frosty evening followed. Not so much at Anfield on the Tuesday night when we won 3-1. I'm convinced to this day that the Reds hadn't won without me!

Being an intelligent young lady she quickly concluded that if she couldn't beat the enemy, she would just join them. 'Oh, they're playing Manchester United at the weekend? I'll come to watch with you!' Before the hammer could drop to the floor after hitting me on the head, she added, 'I like them. They are always winning things, aren't they?' I looked at her in silence, seriously thinking I had made a mistake in my choice of girlfriend. I convinced her it was better not to join me this time as I had arranged to go with a group of lads anyway. The pub would be full of blokes drinking and using swearwords all the time. She understood that.

'But Carsten, you're not the same, are you? You're not sitting in a pub drinking pints, one after another, and swearing at the TV screen?'

'No love, I don't do that. Of course not. Not me. You know me. We're playing the fucking Mancs, but I would never swear!'

Later that season, it was derby day and we were playing Everton at Goodison. I ran out of arguments for why she should stay away. Admittedly, I even liked her being with me to share my love ... my love for Liverpool that was. I was in Napper Tandy's early to get a good spot and enjoy all the pre-match build-up.

She decided to go shopping with a friend first before joining me to watch the match. We had come to a stage in our relationship when a man starts to be himself in certain manly situations. Lager was flowing and I was, as everyone else around me, cursing at the ref and the Bluenoses. At every attack, missed chance, defended shot, corner, foul, I moaned.

After a while I noticed that Adriana wasn't following the match but was looking at me. I looked at her and asked, 'What?'

She leaned towards me and whispered in my ear, 'Can I tell you something?' I just prayed it wouldn't be another fundamental debate on the principles of my behaviour in the middle of the Merseyside derby! 'Are you always like this?' she asked.

'What do you mean? It's the Merseyside derby! I haven't sworn or drunk too much yet, have I?'

'No, it's not that!' she remarked hesitantly.

'What is it then?'

With a very worrying facial expression she explained, 'If I just sat next to you with my eyes closed, ignored everybody and everything around me and only listened to the sound you're making, I wouldn't be able to tell the difference between you watching Liverpool or making love to me!'

I took it as a compliment, just grinned and watched on. It was apparent that the consequent question, which of the two was more satisfying for me, was most certainly to follow. She refrained from asking, though! I would never assume that she might have forgotten about the situation afterwards, but much more likely just dreaded the answer. Anyway, I never insisted on wearing my Liverpool kit while making love to her and chanting, 'Oh when the Reds go marching in.' Honest!

Heidelberg and its pubs were generally full of British people. They worked in large numbers in one of the global companies nearby, studied at the world-renowned university, served in the British Army or just visited the city as tourists. It was always good fun when England were playing. As far as the international tournaments were concerned, I still watched and followed the English team. In the 1980s and early 1990s, the players in the national team were likeable or not so likeable, but always harmless chaps from Derby County, Newcastle United, Aston Villa, Tottenham Hotspur, and yes, even Everton. You could support England without having a strange feeling in your guts.

The late 1990s saw not only the resurgence of the Mancs in the league, but their players, combined with Arsenal's contingent, also began to increase in number in the English national team. If Liverpool had still been the dominant force in domestic club football, I most probably wouldn't have felt weird about following England. Whereas I had nothing to be happy about with Liverpool, I couldn't really celebrate an England victory anymore with players in the team who I otherwise despised week in, week out. But there were more reasons that influenced my way of thinking in the summer of the World Cup in France in 1998.

Napper Tandy's was completely crowded an hour before kick-off for England's matches against Tunisia, Romania, Colombia and Argentina. The chanting, celebrating and dancing on the tables was like being on the terrace in the England end. Before the round of 16 knockout match against Argentina, expectation and atmosphere were boiling. Liverpool's teenager Michael Owen scored one of the most memorable goals. At half-time, some guys I had occasionally chatted to before passed around a copy of that 'newspaper' by Rupert Murdoch, the one in which former editor Kelvin MacKenzie had decided to print 'THE TRUTH' on its front page a couple of days after Hillsborough. It depicted a funny instruction of how England fans should pray for victory that evening.

An awkward feeling crept inside me. I had often spotted England fans on TV wearing hats depicting the St George's cross and the logo of that 'newspaper', which were obviously handed out as freebies on a massive scale. It had always disgusted me that brainless, ignorant football fans even provided their heads as free advertising boards for that rag, but this was different. It was my first personal confrontation with readers of that rag since Hillsborough. I had to react somehow, although I knew it would be difficult to get my message across in an overcrowded pub at half-time in an Eng-er-land World Cup match.

'Hey mate, I know for you it's just fun, but you shouldn't buy that shitty newspaper,' I told one of them.

'Why?' was his half-drunken response.

'It's because of all those lies they wrote about Liverpool supporters after Hillsborough,' I attempted to enlighten them. They only looked confused and obviously didn't even know about the 'article' on Hillsborough. And even if they did, they wouldn't have cared.

One of them tried to give me a friendly answer by saying, 'It's just a newspaper mate. They always write stupid things.' I was aware that I couldn't rationally expect the millions who opt for buying this kind of shit every single day to know and understand Liverpool's view, but neither could I just accept this ignorance. This incident would stick in my mind long after England had been kicked out of the World Cup. Subconsciously, I sensed a rift between my Liverpool spirit and followers of the England team in general. These and other different incidents accumulated over a period of time and culminated in the consequence that I couldn't care for the English national team anymore at all! Out of this ignorance and indifference I perceived a gaping distance towards all those little Englanders.

One day, I drove by Mannheim main station and spotted a big renovation taking place in one of the nightlife's dives in this area. It was more of a reconstruction as the entire interior was being taken out and the exterior was to get a completely new facade. A few days later, I noticed the window frames were painted green. A few more days on, there was a Guinness sign installed. Another couple of days later, you could read Murphy's Law above the entrance. The name says it all, I joked to myself! Anything that can go wrong will go wrong?

Certainly not! A proper pub only a ten-minute walk away from where I lived was a sign that everything was going in the right direction.

On opening day, I entered the place and spotted the TV screen. I asked the staff whether they also showed English football. 'Oh yes, sure, we show every single match from England that's televised live.' I spent that night sound asleep with the sweetest of dreams. This was the most Irish of all Irish pubs there could be. The place was run by an Irishman, attracted all Irish people from the area, played Irish folk music and offered an Irish menu, including Irish Sunday roast. You left the place and all your eyes could see was a blurred layer of green, white and orange. You left the place and all you heard was ringing in your ears of the never-ending, resonating fiddling sound of an Irish violin. I had always liked the Irish. In fact, I can claim that I've never ever come across an Irish person who I haven't found likeable, a stark contrast to some Englishmen I've encountered in my life. The Irish were now my gateway to Liverpool, so close to my home. I loved all Irish in all their Irishness!

Soon I figured out what it's like when the Irish love their Irishness. One afternoon, when I entered an already packed pub looking forward to watching the Reds, I was told it wouldn't be on. 'What you mean, not on?'

'Naah, sorry, it's rugby today.' It was five minutes before kick-off and too late for any alternative measures. With a lump in my throat I walked quickly to the station to catch the next train to Heidelberg. I had to learn to overcome the cultural barrier and come to terms with the experience that every country has its own understanding of national sport. The English had their men in dentists' outfits to play what they call cricket and the Irish had their grown men who liked to touch one another and roll on top of each other on the floor in public in what they called rugby. From then on, I regularly checked the Six Nations fixture list to avoid the pain again.

I felt quite safe for Liverpool's next live match. When I walked into the pub, a few people already sat around the screen. There was already a football match on. Taking a closer look I witnessed to my surprise that the players were taking the ball into their hands whenever they felt like it. They ran with it and then bounced it on the floor like in basketball and then ran with it again. I realised it must have been the *Benny Hill* show, just not accompanied by the *Benny Hill* theme, but with live commentary. Still, funny!

I asked politely whether the Liverpool match would be on. 'Oh sorry, you have to wait until the Gaelic football is over,' the waitress informed me.

'The wha … ?' Now it was time for action. I confronted the guys who were obviously watching the Irish version of *Benny Hill* with the question: 'Are you watching this?' They looked bemused and nodded. 'When will this be over?' I asked. One of the guys replied that it had just started.

'It's our national sport, ye know!' Another walk to the station, another ride to Heidelberg followed. I was fed up with missing most of the Reds' first halves on a regular basis.

On another afternoon when a train journey to Heidelberg was required again and I realised I had to wait 40 minutes for the next one to arrive, I just jumped on a train in the opposite direction. I had found out that there was an O'Reilly's Irish pub in Frankfurt just outside the main station. They had around ten screens on which every single televised match was shown. Therefore I travelled 45 miles to Frankfurt to watch the Reds and then back again. This couldn't be a long-term solution, though.

Next time, I had the cunning idea of going to the pub the night before a match and asking the barman whether there would be any rugby or Gaelic football on the following day.

'No, not tomorrow.'

'So, I can watch Liverpool tomorrow?'

'Yeah sure. I'll put it on for yer.'

It was a beautiful sunny afternoon and, due to the great weather, an almost empty pub awaited me. Almost. One single bloke was sitting at the bar with his eyes on the TV set watching some live sport, broadcast by RTÉ, TG4, TV3, Setanta or whatever. The barman from the night before who had promised to choose my channel wasn't on duty. Of course! The waitress gave me a smile, but I could tell from her eyes that yet another disappointment loomed on the horizon.

In a demonstratively self-confident tone, I asked, 'Could you please switch the channels? Liverpool will be on in a minute!' The guy behind the bar told me I would have to ask the gentleman who was here before me.

'I wanna see the hurling,' he told me before I could even start to enter serious negotiations. You just couldn't make it up!

'Ah, don't tell me. It's your national sport, right?!' I said in a rather provocative manner. The guy just ignored my comment and watched on. If they had shown 15 grown men on each team trying to compete against each other in Mrs Kastner's crocheting lesson live on TV it would have made the same sense to me. I felt like I was on *Candid Camera*, but this farce was for real.

On afternoons like that, they wouldn't even contemplate changing channels briefly just to check the Liverpool score for me. On days when Liverpool were actually shown and any Séan, Conor or Oisin came in and asked for a quick glance at a different channel because they put money on some horse called 'Paddy', the remote control was used in no time without even consulting me about whether I was bothered or not.

'I need to know how the race went. It's our national sport, horse racing, you know!'

What would come next that I wouldn't see coming? Something would keep me from watching the entire 90 minutes in peace. Irish beef carriage steeplechase? Irish sack race? Irish egg-and-spoon race? Irish test fishing series? Johnny Logan returning to the Eurovision Song Contest for Ireland and singing in an afternoon preliminary knockout round against Azerbaijan?

Around the turn of the millennium, over 20 years after being born a Red, a new German pay TV channel, Premiere, began to broadcast all live matches from England. Apart from watching Saturdays' three o'clock kick-offs live, it included the option to enjoy the original English commentary as well. I could finally watch Liverpool at home with no interference from hangovers, train timetables, unreliable barkeepers or innumerable national sports from other countries.

CHAPTER NINE

On the March with the Red Army Again

WHEN THE Beatles' new best of compilation CD, *1*, hit the top of the charts in autumn 2000, it sparked Reds' imagination. Memories from 1964 were awakened when Liverpool had won their first league title after the dark ages just in the same season that Merseybeat ruled the charts. In my philosophy, there was a spiritual connection between Scouse music and Scouse football success. Something big was about to happen that season. I read in a newspaper that some bookmaker had offered odds of 1,000-1 for Liverpool to win the cup treble of League Cup, FA Cup and UEFA Cup. I imagined what I would get for a fiver or a tenner, but never bothered to actually place a bet. Even my power of fantasy wouldn't take me that far.

A visit to Anfield was long overdue and now I felt the time was right. I had started a regular job with an IT company and earned good money. After working part-time as a student for a couple of years, my boss had offered me a permanent job when I finished my studies. I established and ran the marketing department quite successfully at the time. For a long-term career in that industry, though, at a certain stage I had to realise that my technical competence was comparable to a vegan's expertise working for the local butcher.

After spending some time on the telephone, I managed to obtain tickets for the Kop for back-to-back home matches over a few days. It was Olympiakos in the UEFA Cup on the Thursday, followed by Ipswich Town in the league on the Sunday. After dropping my bag at the B&B, I put on my 60s long-sleeve replica home jersey, which Ron Yeats wore when he lifted the league trophy in 1964 and the FA Cup the first time a year later, and headed straight to Anfield to collect my tickets. An inner unrest wouldn't leave me during the whole journey until I held my tickets in my hands. Before the pub crawl in The Albert and The Park on Walton Breck Road, I took a seat in Linda's Cafe. Sipping my tea with milk while reading the *Liverpool Echo*, and enjoying a pre-match meal of fish and chips, seemed the perfect preparation for the big night ahead.

An hour before kick-off, I took a walk around the ground. Outside the main stand I spotted a ticket collection counter for VIPs. A 7ft-tall-looking man in his black winter coat walked inside. Within a split second I realised that I had seen this man in interviews on videos a long time before. I quickly got my ticket and pen out to be prepared for when I addressed him. When he left the office, I quickly approached him.

'Excuse me, Mr Yeats. May I have your autograph, please?' I've never been a collector of signatures in my life. Never! But this was one of Bill Shankly's early signings and our captain who led the Reds from the dark ages of the Second Division back to the top flight and to the first league title as well as our first FA Cup trophy.

'No problem, son, no problem!' he said while signing my match ticket. I can't recall to this day why I had a pen on me at that moment. There are people who may never leave the house without their mobile phone, watch or a pen. Well, I'm the kind of person who never ever leaves the house with a pen. Never! I mean never ever! He smiled at me and handed over my signed ticket, and also the mysterious pen.

I looked up to him and replied, 'Thank you,' with a smile. He vanished as quickly into the crowd as he had appeared before. It was the briefest of all encounters but it was perfect. I would have given away my ticket for an evening with him. I would have loved to listen to this man's stories all night long. And I would have loved to tell him that he had always been wrong about claiming he's only 6ft 3.5in and that Shanks had always been right that he actually was 7ft tall!

The happiness I felt couldn't be surpassed, not even by the comfortable 2-0 victory to see us through to the next round. After the match it was straight back to The Albert to strain my already hoarse voice before I was off for a very long night in Mathew Street, Slater Street, Fleet Street and Concert Square. The impressions of the city, individual encounters with Scousers in the pubs and overall emotions were just overpowering. And I had only arrived in the city some eight hours earlier and had three full days ahead of me.

During daytime, the Friday and the Saturday were devoted to the typical day trippers' tourist attractions. I took a ferry 'cross the Mersey, then went on a Magical Mystery Tour before I headed to Anfield for a stadium tour. At night,

I served as a funny tourist attraction to the locals. As it was December, it was cold. As it was cold, I wore appropriate clothes to keep me warm while outside. The Scouse lads and lasses weren't interested in temperatures whatsoever. Whereas on the streets of Liverpool, men just wore long-sleeved shirts, and women were just covered by blouses and short skirts without even a hint of tights, I wore a 'spot the German in the crowd' long winter coat. It turned out to be the most perfect trip and even the 1-0 home defeat to Ipswich on the Sunday couldn't tarnish my weekend.

A penalty shoot-out victory over First Division team Birmingham City in the League Cup Final and a 2-1 win against Arsenal in the FA Cup Final brought two trophies back to Anfield. The road to the UEFA Cup Final was anything but easy. By beating Roma and Barcelona we eliminated most serious contenders for the trophy on the way. Liverpool were back on the big stage. The Mighty Reds had reached their first European final since Brussels 16 years earlier. They would meet Spanish team Deportivo Alavés in Dortmund.

The Westfalenstadion's massive capacity of over 70,000 enabled me to apply easily for a ticket at Borussia Dortmund's ticket office, which was handling the ticket distribution for the neutral section, I thought. Tanja, the lady I was dating at the time, was roped in to help when obtaining a ticket proved trickier than expected.

'Carsten, but I've a job to do too,' she responded when she realised that any attempt to get hold of the ticket office wasn't a one-off. She worked in a bank and dialled the ticket office number during work at various times but couldn't get through. I was impeded as I was in meetings all day.

'Tanja, you know it's for a good cause!' She also had access to her own fax machine, and I didn't, which was necessary as Borussia Dortmund required a confirmation of personal contact and bank details by fax. At some point, she couldn't hide her activities from her colleagues anymore. Bankers in her department were occupied with market trends, shares, interest rates, but most certainly not tickets for an English–Spanish football match.

'It'll be doomsday for my little boy if I don't succeed in getting him his tickets,' she explained to them. Neither did they know me, nor did they have any affinities with Liverpool Football Club, but after a few days they were mentally entangled into the whole project and shared the thrill. A few days later, Tanja got confirmation and, when positive news spread in her office, the whole floor breathed a huge sigh of relief simultaneously. Stock Exchange business in Mannheim could finally resume again!

The anticipated walkover on our way to our treble lasted until half-time. Markus Babbel, Steven Gerrard and Gary McAllister put us 3-1 up. Alavés managed to score a second then equalise early in the second half. Substitute Robbie Fowler put Liverpool 4-3 up, but another late equaliser meant Liverpool had to go into extra time. Another penalty shoot-out loomed, but Delfi Geli's golden own goal sealed victory for the Reds. Liverpool had won the cup treble in the most exciting European final there had ever been. There was no way this could ever be surpassed in the future! I was wondering that night whether someone had put a bet on at the 1,000-1 odds back in autumn, and how much?

As I had forgotten to put a couple of spare grand on the cup treble bet, I didn't become a millionaire. As a consequence,

I fatefully had to pursue having a steady job. I quit the IT industry for the aforementioned reasons and joined the live entertainment business. It was a pretty demanding and hectic job that meant I had to travel all around the big cities in Germany. Even on normal office days, you never really got home early. Leaving your desk before 6pm actually never really happened, not even on Fridays. If you accumulated a certain amount of overtime hours, you could apply to take half a day off.

One Friday, I was taking the afternoon off as I was going to see Oasis in concert in Frankfurt. It was the first time in over one and a half years I left the office early. I went to town to buy some new CDs and then walked home by around half past five. When I opened my letterbox, I discovered an envelope with my address written in strangely familiar-looking handwriting. It was my own! The British stamps were puzzling, the red postmark reading LIVERPOOL dumbfounding. I opened it straight away and withdrew contents that put me in a state of shock. In my hand I held a ticket for Liverpool FC v Manchester United at Anfield the following Sunday, kick-off 12.15am, Main Stand.

Out of the blue I had been handed one of the most precious tickets I could ever have dreamed of. A million thoughts crossed my mind – who, how and why? From a far distant memory, bits of details came flooding back. One late night during the close season in the summer, I got home late from a night out in town. I was in a good mood, put The Farm, The La's and The Lightning Seeds on and poured myself a drink. Maybe one drink led to another, maybe! I can't recall what prompted me to do what I had never

ever contemplated doing before in the whole of my entire life. I wrote a begging letter to Liverpool Football Club. I sat down and wrote to the club asking politely for just one single ticket for the match against Manchester United anywhere in the ground. Suddenly I remembered that I even enriched the letter with pathetic, heartbreaking, pitiful content such as 'being a German in a far foreign land and no season ticket holder and not being in possession of the sufficient amount of ticket stubs in order to qualify and therefore my dreams will forever be tossed and blown as I'll never ever in this life have the opportunity to visit my Reds in an encounter of this magnitude … blah blah blah'. I enclosed an addressed envelope with an international reply coupon and my credit card details and sent it off the next day. Within 24 hours I had completely forgotten about the whole operation.

Standing in front of the letterbox, I had to come to terms with the hard facts of life. Kick-off was just over 40 hours away! Now the biggest challenge wasn't the match ticket anymore but the fact that I didn't know how to get myself from Mannheim to Liverpool in the remaining time available. Travelling on matchday was out of the question due to the early kick-off time. I had no option but to get it sorted for the next day. It was the flight that worried me most as accommodation wouldn't be a problem for sure.

I ran out to the street and to the nearest travel agency to book myself a flight. Yes, there were already online flight booking websites at the beginning of the millennium, but I had no nerves to gamble on whether in the early years of the World Wide Web my search results would load properly and hold for the duration of my payment process. In different circumstances, if the long-haired brunette loaded face and neck but got stuck by endless buffering just underneath her shoulder blades, you could still rely mentally on your real-life blond neighbour with a catching smile or the waitress with that mellifluous voice to serve your imagination. In a situation when a Liverpool match against the Mancs was at stake, there were no such options!

'I need a flight from Frankfurt to Manchester tomorrow and back on Sunday evening.' The lady searched the system and shook her head. I was contemplating travelling to Switzerland or France by train and then taking a flight from there.

'Sorry, the only possible connection that's available is with British Airways from Frankfurt to Manchester Saturday late afternoon and the return flight on Monday late afternoon.' Right, there was at least a possible connection.

'Thanks, I'll be right back!' Now I had the task of ringing my office to arrange a day off on Monday.

There was a company rule that you couldn't take time off in lieu and another day off back to back. The fact that at the start of December we were in the middle of our Christmas business didn't really soothe my nerves. While I ran back home across the street, I decided to deal with that later. I would have to sort accommodation first. Now I did search the World Wide Web for any telephone numbers offering a bed in Liverpool. The only offers, though, were a couple of five-star hotels in Liverpool's city centre. For the price of the two nights I would have had to fork out for, I could have easily bought my own B&B on Walton Breck Road.

I decided to ring the Liverpool Tourist Information Centre. It was ten to six and I realised I would have to call the office first to get the day off. Waiting for my call to be answered, I prayed that they hadn't left the office early. I also had to get to the cash machine to withdraw some money before I returned to the travel agency. Forget that! Shit, where was my credit card?

'Hey, it's me, Carsten. I know it sounds funny but I have to take Monday off. I have to fly to Liverpool because I got a ticket for a football match on Sunday. I didn't know this before. I just received the ticket when I got home. And now I have to book a flight, but I can only return on Monday late afternoon. I'll even take today's afternoon off as a normal vacation day retrospectively in order not to breach the company's rules not to have a holiday after I took the afternoon off in lieu the day before. I mean, I'll even take the whole day today off retrospectively. You understand? Could you please just confirm that it's okay?'

It took some five seconds before I could hear a response on the other end: 'Whaaaaaaat?' It did work out for me!

'Sorry, Liverpool is fully booked as we have an international students' day over the weekend. And besides, there's a football match going on, which usually draws many people from outside Merseyside to the city who seek accommodation,' the lady from the Tourist Office confirmed. I took a deep breath. I took a very, very deep breath. The lady in the travel agency had promised to keep the flight reservation until closing time, for which I had less than 15 minutes remaining. Eventually, I found a place for two nights outside Liverpool. I rang them and settled the details. I was going to sacrifice a Saturday night out in the most beautiful, most stunning, most sexy city in the world and would have to make do with some accommodation in the demons' cave. I had just booked a room in a Protestant Church home somewhere near the centre of Manchester.

I ran back to the travel agency and confirmed my booking by 6.28pm. Alright! Organised! Finished! Done! Ready! Now I had to speed to the station to catch the train to Frankfurt. Oasis were waiting for me.

My Saturday nightlife experience the following evening was briefer than the shortest defecation had ever lasted in the whole of my entire life, a process unfailingly more pleasurable and entertaining than my night out in Manchester. In some place I had one pint that I didn't even finish, strolled back to my accommodation and had an early night.

The match turned out to be one best to forget. Jerzy Dudek conceded twice and didn't look too fortunate in the whole act. Liverpool not only lost the match 2-1 but also more of their eight-point cushion at the top of the league that had kept them ahead of the Mancs a few weeks before. The match was part of a run of 12 in which the Reds failed to win in the league. Another title chase was over. After the match I stayed as long as possible in The Albert. I didn't feel like going into town as I was too devastated. Neither did I fancy spending any more time in the area of my accommodation than I had to.

When I finally arrived there in the early evening, all the pubs were full of people I intended to avoid. I felt sick. I was overrun by a culture shock. I had just returned from the pool of life, the centre of the world's most creative and intelligent supporters, who never stop inventing new love songs. Now I was surrounded by life's most lowbrow and boring fan base, who were repetitively singing about ... Liverpool. It conveyed a perfect depth analysis into the wobbly organs underneath their skullcaps. Apart from bawling about Liverpool, their repertoire didn't consist of any real qualitative content about their own club. The occasional reference to their current manager or players did occur, but sentences either lacked any kind of structure or were just very short. It appeared as if the arty vocalists weren't so much concerned about praising their own history, but were more obsessed with Liverpool.

One rendition stood out due to its repetitive application. Whenever they intoned their hymn, they all had this similar bizarre grin on their faces, which gave them a joint physiognomy as if they were all related to one another and their club was followed by one big family. Their native town was adored to be oh so wonderful. I became curious to learn more about the reasons behind their worship. The explanation wasn't long in coming.

'Oh, Manchester is wonderful,' because it was, and presumably always would be, and now I quote, 'full of tits, fanny and United.' A thorough analysis of the connotation provided the inevitable conclusion that those inhabitants expressed an underlying subjective perception and harsh self-reflection that they were all tits and pussies. Such a critical, open and honest self-awareness is rare but, admittedly, speaks for their character. I liked the tune, though. An inner voice told me that better lyrics, much better lyrics, could be added to it. I finished my pint and sadly went to my parish room. Certainly better nights were to follow someday.

By 2004 I lived in Lindenhof, an area that was predominantly occupied by born and bred local residents of a rather elderly age. People led a quiet life. The only noise you were accustomed to was the occasional and very rare baby cry from a pram mother's push through the street or from ships passing by on the Rhine. It was a very conservative vicinity where pensioners enjoyed their retirement. Sometimes these pensioners appeared not to enjoy their spare time as much as they were supposed to. Some kept a wary eye on proceedings going on in a law-abiding manner. The monitoring of appropriate parking on the street, the unlawful crossing of somebody's lawn or using the bottle bank after sunset seemed to be their main occupation. In some cases I couldn't figure out whether this could be attributed to lack of alternative hobbies or to their German law and order education in the 1930s. People tended to go to bed at a reasonably early time.

In the first couple of weeks after moving in, I rolled down the shutters before switching on the TV for a European Cup (now called the Champions League) live match. This was just a precautionary measure to avoid neighbours hearing me in case I got carried away. After scraping through the qualifying round against Grazer AK in August, the Reds were drawn in a group with Monaco, Deportivo La Coruña and Olympiakos. The final fixture brought the Greeks to Anfield in early December. Only a win by two clear goals would get us through to the knockout stages of the competition.

Rivaldo's first-half goal saw our chances of progression slipping out of reach. When we failed to get one back before half-time, hopes vanished completely. There would have to be three Liverpool goals in the remaining 45 minutes. Where would they be coming from, Djimi Traoré? Probably not! He was subbed at the interval for Florent Sinama-Pongolle. He meant business and it took him just two minutes to equalise and put us only two goals behind. In the 78th minute, Milan Baros was replaced by another youngster, Neil Mellor. He didn't keep us waiting long either as he also scored within two minutes of coming on.

Naaah, it's not gonna happen, is it? I had read so many stories and watched video highlights of European nights and comebacks in decisive matches at Anfield, such as David Fairclough and the third goal against Saint-Étienne in 1977, or Mark Walters and the third goal against Auxerre in 1991, which I followed live on a crappy radio medium wave reception. But that night in December 2004 was real. I didn't have to read about it afterwards anymore. My eyes were at Anfield. When the ball fell to Stevie G with four minutes remaining and he hit it into the net, the roar that erupted in my living room must have startled my entire neighbourhood just as the Kop did to all residents on Walton Breck Road.

'YYYEEEAAAASSS!!!' The most sensual, intimate and ecstatic moment I've ever shared with any Liverpool player in my life followed. My face was pressed against the TV screen and Stevie G melted in between my kissing lips, while the Kop was going wild in the background by the time 'you beautyyyyy!' was screamed out on the live commentary. Coming from behind like that and scoring three goals in the second half in the European Cup would surely never be surpassed. Something special was on. It had to be.

In my job I had a few cooperation projects with some Bundesliga football clubs over the course of summer 2004. The negotiations either took place in their conference rooms or in one of their VIP lounges inside the stadium with a perfect view of the pitch. This kind of surrounding gave them, as they probably assumed, a psychological advantage in the negotiating process. In the case of Werder Bremen, the meeting took place in the board's conference room. The club had just won the league and cup double a few months before and they displayed both trophies in the room. There were also meetings held at Borussia Dortmund, 1. FC Cologne, VfL Bochum and MSV Duisburg.

Another club I visited was Bayer Leverkusen. The two marketing managers took me to one of their VIP lounges behind the goal. I mentioned, of course, that I stood on the old terrace when Liverpool played there for a pre-season friendly in 1991. The meeting went really well and we stayed in touch over the following months. Every time I spoke to one of the ladies on the phone, we were joking about Liverpool and Bayer Leverkusen and that both teams might meet one day in a European encounter.

When the draw was announced for the round of 16, I kept updating the UEFA website, waiting for Liverpool's opponents. Bayer Leverkusen! There was no way the Reds would play in Germany in the European Cup and I wouldn't be in the stadium. I rang the marketing lady straight away, but couldn't get through to her as she was on holiday. Well, there's no holiday for anybody when it comes to Liverpool. I checked her business card that she had given me and, to my relief, realised I was in possession of her personal mobile number.

'Hi, it's Carsten Nippert.'

'Oh, Herr Nippert, I was just thinking about you. We're on the way to our skiing holiday and we just passed by Mannheim on the motorway.' *Holy crap, she's thinking of me*, I thought. 'Heard about the draw?' I asked.

'No, Herr Nippert, we've been trying to get hold of that news on the radio, but no radio station would say anything.'

'Guess who,' I replied.

'What?' she asked.

'You may guess only one time who you've just drawn,' I said. After a pause, she just uttered a simple 'no', which was responded to by my simple 'yes'.

'It's not Liverpool.'

'It is!'

'And now you want tickets for the match?' Women can sometimes be quite straightforward!

I formulated my request rather meticulously: 'Well, I would like to kindly ask you to possibly open the opportunity to me to be entitled to buy, at the full price of course, one single ticket for any seat inside the ground.'

She quickly remarked, 'Herr Nippert, I'll see what I can do. I'll call you back in a minute.' When the phone rang a few minutes later, I picked up the phone nervously. 'You'll get your ticket. I just rang my colleagues. I can't tell you what ticket it will be as I have to sort that out after my return, but I just made sure you have your ticket,' she explained.

'Yeeesssss, sorted!' I was guaranteed my seat in the European Cup return leg at Leverkusen long before ticket-selling arrangements were announced. Merry Christmas!

When I hadn't received any further information by the beginning of February, I rang her. She wasn't in the office for a couple of days and one of her colleagues answered the phone. After introducing myself, I explained, 'I only called because, so far, I haven't received an invoice for my ticket against Liverpool that your colleague has reserved for me. I would just like to make sure I transfer the money in time.'

'So I've heard,' was the not so amused reaction from the gentleman. It was evident that he knew he was talking to a Liverpool supporter. His displeased voice gave vent to an utter incomprehension of how his colleague could give away one seat for one of the most important matches in their club's history to a supporter of the opposition. I received the ticket and the invoice the following week. My seat was in the main stand. *Oh, she meant well, didn't she?* I thought when I opened the envelope. I couldn't figure out where exactly I would sit, but I didn't care anyway as long as I was inside the stadium. The first leg at Anfield turned out to be a comfortable 3-1 win.

I took two days off work and travelled to Cologne where I would stay the night. The travelling Reds had already taken over the Alter Markt, and the Irish pub The Corkonian was already packed by midday. The atmosphere inside had already hit peak level. Red banners covered the entire space available on the walls. On the big screen the Olympiakos match was shown again. Everyone was just glued to the screen and the singing kept going as if it was live coverage. Emotions were no different to that night back in December. Everyone suffered when we failed to score, everyone screamed when Sinama-Pongolle and Mellor hit the back of the net. All hell broke loose when Gerrard scored that third goal. At around 5pm beverages were sold out to the great relief of the waiting police outside, who wanted to escort us to Leverkusen in time.

At the ground there was no chance to get into the away end in the corner of the stadium. The stewards employed on the day were too professional to be fooled. 'No, sorry sir, your seat is in the main stand. It's only a bit further down this way.' It was no party time, but parting time with my Red soulmates. I would be on my own, but was still excited about what kind of fun I was to expect. Would one single Red among a thousand locals be running the gauntlet or would he be the annoying cat among the pigeons? Walking up the steps, I realised my seat wasn't only in the main stand, but also right next to the press box, which was just behind the club's VIP section. More and more people were taking their seats as the ground filled, honourable ladies in fur coats and gentlemen wearing elegant hats. I felt less than a cat among the pigeons, but rather like the grey stray cat among the white swans. And the match hadn't even kicked off.

Two elderly gentlemen walked up the stairs and stopped at my row. They greeted me with a smile and a handshake and said, 'So we're seatmates for the evening? You've got the ticket of our friend.' I learned that they were a group of three who attended every single Leverkusen match, but this time their mate couldn't make it. They had no other person interested in the ticket, so they had offered it to the club to put on general sale. I let them believe that I was lucky in the general sale. They assured me that we were going to have a good time together.

'Well, maybe you'll think differently when I tell you that I'm a Liverpool supporter.' Silence followed.

'Ah, it doesn't matter. We're all having a good time here.'

'You better wait until the Reds come out,' I joked.

The travelling Kop created an atmosphere straight away. The home fans, who are not really known in Germany for being a massively vocal support, were very impressively at full voice to cheer on their team for an unlikely comeback. Their faintest hope for such a sensation disappeared, though, when Luis Garcia scored after 28 minutes to put Liverpool 4-1 up on aggregate. The crowd were silenced and the whole stadium came to a complete standstill, apart from the celebrating away end obviously. Looking around, I could spot people jumping up in various parts of the ground. In fact, there were four different sections making up the 'away end'. There was the official standing area in the right corner and the official away seating area a couple of rows in the main stand next to it. Then there was a big gap occupied by locals only, not all in fur coats, and then there was me.

To my left across the aisle, some more Liverpool supporters were positioned in a rather unusual place. At the very back of the press box, there were two young women and a guy jumping up and down with their Liverpool scarves stretched in the air. They must have sneaked in with an officially accredited journalist. The three were looking over to me and we were saluting each other with clenched fists. For them and for me it was very obvious that we were sitting in seats where we officially shouldn't be. For all the rest of the home supporters around us it was very obvious that there were people who were sitting in seats where they officially shouldn't be. It made the celebration even more exciting. We kept looking over and even from the distance encouraged each other to keep the party going in our part of the ground.

When Garcia scored another one four minutes later, we were 5-1 up on aggregate by half-time. After Milan Baros joined the scoresheet after 67 minutes, there was no holding back. Standing and singing alone in Bayer Leverkusen's main stand made me an odd, but quite entertaining attraction. The locals around me wouldn't dare ask me to sit down. Some were no longer watching the match, but were amused by my and the press box fellow Reds' party.

Being 3-0 down, 6-1 on aggregate, with over 20 minutes to go, some locals left the stadium. A few upper-class fur coat ladies in my row kindly asked me to let them pass by. They were smiling at me and I couldn't resist responding to them in a friendly manner. 'You're leaving? No, don't go. You'll miss more goals.' I tried to encourage them to stay. This not only amused them, but also made some other people sitting around me laugh out loud. They were just being kicked out of Europe and were laughing at getting the piss taken out of them.

Two minutes from time, Leverkusen got their consolation goal at last. This wouldn't really be worth mentioning at all if that moment hadn't been the birth of a new enrichment in Liverpool's songbook repertoire. It had become a tradition in Germany to play a favourite tune after the home team scored a goal. Most of the time, it was a song from the charts not linked with the club at all. Some clubs chose a funny tune and some chose a catchy one to encourage the crowd to join in the singing and clapping. Either way, it was stage-managed cringy crap that hadn't been adopted outside this country, fortunately. It typified one of the many virtues this country has always been famous for. Germans can't help organising even the smallest details to perfection.

Travelling Kopites had to wait a few seconds to find out what Bayer Leverkusen's tune was. Probably the stadium announcer wasn't in the right frame of mind to celebrate that goal, but his German sense of duty got the better of him to see through the pre-determined procedure. He was a bit slow to react to the goal and pressed the CD player's button some 20 seconds late. Once it played, he pumped up the volume for Status Quo's 'Rocking All Over the World'. Reds on the terrace didn't have to listen too long before joining in. 'And I like it, I like it, I like it, I like it, I li-li-like it, li-li-like, here we go-o, rocking all over the world!' Leverkusen were just about to be kicked out of Europe and they were claiming to rock the world. The away support knew that they were still rocking on in Europe and took up the song until the final whistle.

The quarter-final provided an encounter with Juventus, the first time we had met our opponents from our last European Cup Final. A 2-1 win in the home leg was enough to qualify for the next round. For the semi-final one might have wished to avoid being paired with a team that had already beaten us three times that season. After a brave scoreless draw at the ground of the soon-to-be-crowned champions of England in the first leg, Chelsea faced champions of a different kind in the return leg under the floodlights at Anfield. European Cup matches were, especially at this stage, nerve-wracking, cardiac-rhythm-ruining stuff. I didn't need any further disturbances, distractions or annoying comments by other people in the pub and decided to watch at home.

Milan Baros was fouled by goalkeeper Petr Cech, but there was no time to scream for a penalty and a red card. Luis Garcia was in the middle of the action and kicked the ball towards the goal. Seconds felt like ages. The Chelsea defence tried to clear the ball, but the Spaniard was already running off with a smile. He looked back as if he wasn't sure whether the goal would stand and then celebrated in full swing. 1-0 up! The tension and strain wouldn't cease for the remainder of the match.

My mind wandered 16 years back when we were playing Arsenal at home in the last match of the 1988/89 season. We only had to not concede a goal in the final minutes and we would have been crowned champions. The screams I heard over an abysmal medium wave reception led me to believe the Reds had won their 18th league title after the final whistle had been blown only to realise it was the away end's Michael Thomas goal celebration.

There was no way we could keep this lead up forever, could we? There wouldn't be too much added time as no interruptions caused any delays in the second half. The fourth official held his board up to signal there were six additional minutes to be played. Six minutes! Even the commentator asked, 'Where did they come from?' I didn't want to watch, I didn't want to leave the room either. When Eiður Guðjohnsen received the ball in the box in the dying minutes, I knew, I was convinced, I couldn't be persuaded into believing anything else but that this would be the 'Michael Thomas moment' of modern times. There was no way he would miss. He missed! I couldn't move anymore. I couldn't say anything. I couldn't sense anything. I was empty. I just wanted it to end. Moments later, an exhausted scream followed the final whistle. Standing in the middle of my living room staring at the screen, tears shot into my eyes. When 'You'll Never Walk Alone' was intoned, I saw a banner on the Kop: 'MAKE US DREAM'. We were on the march with Rafa's Army, we were all going to Istanbul!

CHAPTER TEN

Oh, Istanbul is Wonderful

I NEVER stood a chance of obtaining a ticket for the European Cup Final through official sources. Demand would definitely exceed supply multiple times and even regulars wouldn't be sorted automatically. A colleague of mine from the travel department assured me that getting a hotel in Istanbul would be no problem whatsoever. 'I've got a few good connections, Carsten. Don't worry!' A few days later when I asked about finalising the hotel booking, I came to realise that these connections were actually not so good anymore. The cheapest available room was €600 for the night of the final! This was six hundred Euros for sleeping in one bed for one night! It did include breakfast, though. I refrained from confirming the bargain straight away and decided to look for alternative quotations. Moreover, I was fully determined to arrive a day before the final to enjoy the entire build-up to the big day.

I searched the internet for ticket agencies and found offers at four-figure prices apiece. I was willing to make a huge financial sacrifice to get to Istanbul, but it had to remain within a realistic framework. I was wondering how they were in a position to offer tickets of that calibre in the first place? As long as any of them would sort me out, I didn't care. Some suppliers even offered all-inclusive packages, some at a rate for which they should have been sent to prison for extortion.

One company appeared to be denying itself the maximising of a potential profit margin, so I took a closer look at their offer and entered the negotiation. The package consisted of one match ticket, a return flight and two nights' accommodation in a hotel, including breakfast! It also included a pre-arranged sightseeing trip around Istanbul and an expert evening on the eve of the final. They had invited a former Bundesliga manager to join the group to give his preparatory opinion on the two teams. *Fuck that*! I thought, *I'm not attending that crap*! Further negotiation allowed me to withdraw from the sightseeing and the expert dinner. Thus, I haggled the price down and paid them €1,700 for the whole trip. That deal also included the luxurious freedom and joy of looking forward to the final totally relaxed with some ten days to go. I was going to Istanbul! Now I could concentrate on some rather serious matters.

From the night of my rebirth on 25 May 1977 and ever after Liverpool's first European Cup Final, dark-red banners with big white letters had always had a fascinating effect on my mind, my soul and my psyche. Since the days when I was a little boy, I not only dreamed of being right in the middle of Liverpool's European Cup Finals, but also of being a part of the Red Army's creativity that made these special nights so unique. I decided against a banner production by a manufacturing company as the best banners I had seen on the Kop and at finals always looked handmade. So, a few days later I found myself in the cloth section in a department store, where I mingled with housewives arguing with their husbands or teenage kids about how to decorate their bedrooms.

The last time I had been to a place like this was in primary school with my mum when I needed to buy some stuff for art classes. I could see Mrs Kastner coming around the corner yelling at me and pulling me by my ears. When I woke to reality again, I spotted the perfect material. The most beautiful dark-red cloth on one single roll smiled at me from between the many different colourful patterns. I sensed that it felt uncomfortable among all the other less worthy colours and was signalling a telepathic cry for help towards me. It had been lying there unnoticed and unappreciated for its whole life. Its real value, destined purpose and upcoming greatness had finally been recognised. Now came the moment of salvation.

A middle-aged woman approached the roll, my roll, dangerously close. Just to make sure I could rescue it from potentially being abducted, I obtruded myself upon the lady and barged in between her and the cloth of my desire. My body leaned forward, my fingers pressed into the cotton, my hand grabbed it tightly and pulled it until I held it safely in my arms. The lady gave me an irritated look but actually wouldn't start a fight. Some expert shoptalk with the sales assistant followed about the ideal affixing of letters on to the material. A visit to the paint shop provided me with the purest of whites for the letters and the most beautifully matching yellow for the Liver bird. All the important ingredients had been secured. Now I just needed to create a good slogan and I would be ready for Istanbul.

My intention was to produce a poem that was unambiguously connected with that particular season. I remembered the mother of all Liverpool banners from the European Cup Final in Rome in 1977, which related to the Reds' matches against Saint-Étienne, FC Zürich and Borussia Mönchengladbach: 'Joey Ate the Frogs Legs, Made the Swiss Roll, Now He's Munching Gladbach'. This brilliant idea could never be matched, but maybe I could think of something different.

The self-proclaimed 'Special One' manager, armed with a Russian billionaire's roubles, his mercenaries on the pitch as well as his plastic fans, who seemed to have mushroomed in masses overnight, would have to get a mention.

A change of name of the old First Division to the FA Premier League and a sale of TV rights to a pay TV channel appeared to have initiated a new time reckoning in 1992. Over 100 years seemed to have lost their meaning overnight. Whenever a Manc crossed my path and imposed a conversation on me, I was always presented the 'fact' that I couldn't argue with the fact that we had 18 league titles and four European Cups, only with zero Premier League titles and zero Champions League trophies. My calculation was obsolete and Liverpool's history had been deleted. If you can't beat imbecility, join it. I always replied with the fact that in terms of winning the Canon League, as the First Division was branded between 1983 and 1986, and the Barclays League, as it was named from 1987 to 1992, Liverpool beat them 2-0. That didn't count, though. When that lot got their hands on the Champions League trophy in 1999, all of a sudden they were leading 1-0 against us. Listening to those pathetic arguments from little, neglected runts who desperately sought attention and recognition was so boring and tiring. 'Yes, you're the greatest. No, you may not be forgotten anymore! Yes, everybody respects you, only you!' The Mancs would most certainly get some recognition on my banner too.

Our little neighbours actually managed to finish the season above us in fourth place in the league. It was their greatest achievement for a long time and relegated us to the UEFA Cup spots. In nearly two decades, Blues had very little reason not to be bitter but they still kept finding reasons to release DVD after DVD. The *Great Escapes* commemorates the final fixtures of the 1994 and 1998 seasons in which Everton escaped relegation in the final matches of the season against mighty Wimbledon and Coventry, respectively. For their 2002/03 season's review, they opted for the title *The Magnificent 7th*. You just couldn't make it up. When you thought it couldn't get any better, Evertonians even improved on that by naming their 2004/05 DVD review *Champions League … We're Havin' a Laugh*. After the Reds on Merseyside kept laughing at the Blues for years, now was the time for the Evertonians to convulse in laughter. Surely! The Bluenoses would most certainly qualify for a top spot on my banner!

Mercenaries, Mancs, Bitters, something was still missing to make the haters complete. Ah, got it! To top it all off, the London-based media would have to be considered, too! It had been quite obvious that they wished for nothing more than a long-lasting, successful team from the capital. For a long time, London's press had clung to Arsène Wenger, who they hoped would be their hero to not only bring domestic honours to London but also put the city on Europe's map. When they realised the Frenchman wasn't up to accomplishing the mission, they turned to the Portuguese self-proclaimed 'Special One' as their saviour. They wouldn't rely on his managerial abilities alone, though, but made the biggest of efforts to have a journalistic impact on their new darling's fortune. On multiple occasions they even tried to 'write' Steven Gerrard to Chelsea.

My poem was about picking all of them up from their parties, making them sit in class and sober up, reminding them and teaching them a lesson that we're Liverpool Football Club and still record holders of league titles as well as European Cups! Two beautiful yellow Liver birds stood opposite each other in the bottom corners of the flag. In the centre, I positioned a yellow number 18 and a self-confident number 5. The finished lyrics in pure white above read:

> No Small Toffees For Feast Tonight
> Kopites Party With Turkish Delight.
> Jose, Sir Alex, London Press,
> All Choking On Sweet Success.
> Money, Not Love, Is Your Drive
> But Tell Us … Can You Count To 5?

My flight's departure was scheduled from Düsseldorf airport late on Tuesday morning. I was desperate to make sure I arrived there in plenty of time and not get stuck anywhere on the way. Many stories were doing the rounds on the internet forums that travelling Reds couldn't get any flights to Istanbul. Some had decided upon rather adventurous means of transportation. Four Scousers hired a taxi from Liverpool to Istanbul and back. Others planned to fly to Turkey's bordering countries to take the bus to Istanbul on the day of the final. If I missed my flight, I would be stranded. I decided to travel up to Cologne the night before and stay in the same hotel as on my trip to Leverkusen a couple of months before. It had to be a good omen and it wasn't to be the only one.

When news broke that we were to play the final in our red jerseys, although we were drawn as the away team, and therefore Milan were to play in white, online forums went mad. We had always won our European finals playing in all red against opponents in white. Borussia Mönchengladbach in the UEFA Cup in 1973 and European Cup in 1977, Bruges in the UEFA Cup in 1976 and European Cup in 1978, Real Madrid in the European Cup in 1981 and AS Roma in the European Cup in 1984. The omens wouldn't stop there. In 1977, the year of our first European Cup triumph, the final was also played on 25 May. In addition to that, our greatest victories were always achieved in Europe's flashiest capitals such as Rome, London and Paris. Now it was Istanbul.

Furthermore, the first time we won the UEFA Cup in 1973, we won the European Cup four years later. Four years before 2005, we had won our last UEFA Cup in 2001. In 1981, we finished fifth in the league, reached the League Cup Final and won the European Cup. The very same applied to the season that had just concluded. Every manager since Bill Shankly had won a trophy in their first full season in charge. Bob Paisley won the Charity Shield in 1974, Joe Fagan won the treble in 1984, Kenny Dalglish won the double in 1986, Graeme Souness lifted the FA Cup in 1992, Roy Evans landed the League Cup in 1995 and Gérard Houllier, err, won the Carlsberg Trophy in 1998 with a little help from joint manager Roy Evans. It just had to be Rafa's turn to continue this rule!

More and more links to past occurrences became apparent that just couldn't be argued away. Not only had our own history played an influence on our fate, but also the ill health of the head of the Roman Catholic Church and even the love life of members of the royal family. When we won the European Cup in 1978, it was the last time a pope passed away. Now, John Paul II had died. When we won back our European crown in 1981, it was the year when Prince Charles got married the first time. In 2005, he had married Camilla. The same applied to Ken and Deirdre from *Coronation Street*, who got married in 1981 and again in 2005. For those still unimpressed and unconvinced, they should be reminded that in those very same years Wales won the Rugby Grand Slam; a new *Dr Who* was presented in 2005, just as in several years when we won the European Cup before; in 1977, the first *Star Wars* movie came to the cinemas and the recent episode was released in 2005. And! Whenever I had attended a match in the knockout stages of a European competition, as in 1981 and 2001, we went on to win it! The trophy was already ours. We only had to make sure we made the journey to Turkey.

At Cologne main station on Tuesday morning, I bumped into Reds who were on their way to Cologne airport. They told me that one of their mates, who had booked an earlier flight in the morning, had missed his departure time. As he couldn't get a replacement flight, he was trying to get a train connection to Istanbul. An uneasy feeling and inner tension that a similar fate might befall me would only ease when I finally arrived at Düsseldorf airport.

At the check-in counter I was amazed by how many Turkish families filled the queues, although it wasn't even summer holidays. Most of them were carrying trolleys with luggage that was obviously way above the allowed maximum weight per person. The family in front of me looked surprised when they learned that they had been declined from taking that much on their journey unless they paid the extra fee. They turned to me politely and asked whether I would be kind enough to claim some of their luggage was mine. In any other situation I would have been willing to offer my support. The sheer thought, though, of a minimal chance of having to explain the contents of 'my luggage' that I knew nothing about to some customs officer at my arrival quickly convinced me to decline in a very friendly manner. Their most innocent appearance, free from all suspicion of being involved in smuggling or drug-dealing, didn't alter my decision. The airline must have made a fortune on that flight from all those extra fees they were entitled to charge.

At the check-in, at the security checkpoint and later on my way to the lounge, I didn't spot any Red colours. In the lounge, I was one of the first passengers to take my seat. Gradually more and more people entered and filled the rows around me. There were families who had been relieved of their heavy luggage as well as their cash, businessmen with a serious demeanour operating their mobile phones and laptops, and men on their own or in groups of two or more in normal casual gear.

Whenever you encounter strangers, you usually don't greet them with a 'hi', 'hello' or 'good morning'. You may conform to etiquette by acknowledging a manageable number of people when entering a doctor's waiting room or a hotel lift but in airport lounges I had never had such an experience. A couple of lads in jeans and shirts took their seats in the middle of other passengers. Two of them looked over to me, we exchanged brief glances, they nodded towards me and I replied. Another guy in casual gear sat down two rows opposite to me at the far end and looked around. Our eyes met and we acknowledged each other. This went on and on. We didn't know each other, where we were coming from or what language we spoke, but we definitely knew exactly where we were going.

The Reds in that lounge, who all wore anything but red, distinguished themselves from the rest of the crowd and recognised their peers naturally. Everyone had the same expression on his face: calm, determined and confident. 'We're back' was the joint thought. I was wondering how many Reds in this moment were gathering in how many airport lounges all over Europe to fly into Istanbul to meet up. All strength and support was required and therefore all Reds were following the call to summon them for a joint operation. We had been on a mission impossible for months and we were going to accomplish it by all means in the greatest oriental metropolis. Over 40,000 sisters and brothers were on the march with Rafa's Army; we were all going to Istanbul. And we were going to really shake them up, when we bring back what belongs to us and take back our ancestral place in history!

My personal calmness, determination and confidence vanished soon after I entered the plane. The combination of a claustrophobic disposition, a body of 6ft 2in, a window seat and a flight of over three hours, during which I had no extra leg room, made the journey really unenjoyable. A noisy hustle and bustle surrounded me that I had never encountered on a flight before. Armies of mothers were changing nappies in the toilets while leaving the doors open to discuss their respective technical skills with mothers in the queue behind. I always had a very reliable bladder, which never confronted me with a strong desire for a urinary urgency. Just by observing these congestions in overcrowded aisles before each washroom made me pray not to feel the need to pee any moment soon, though.

Hand baggage turned out to be picnic baskets. Sandwiches, vegetables and fruits were passed back and forth above my head. The movement of goods overburdened all involved hands available and I expected my head any time to serve as a temporary tray. The boisterous gesticulation and loud articulation, which I perceived as aggressive shouting, combined with screaming babies, compounded the intimidation. I shrank into my seat. Anxiously, I was waiting to make the acquaintance of what I expected to be XXL oversized seatmates, who would block my escape route to the exit door. I thanked all gods, especially mine and Allah, that two totally calm and relaxed Turkish businessmen were seated next to me. I refrained, despite feeling as if I wanted to, from resting my head on his shoulder to signal how much he radiated comfort and safety.

In Istanbul, I took the shuttle bus to get into the city centre and then a taxi to my hotel, both means of transport with sufficient legroom in front and space around me. Innumerable Liverpool banners were hanging out of the windows. It was Reds territory already. At the Grand Anka hotel, I just checked in, dropped off my bag, went back out again and caught another taxi to meet the guy from the agency at his hotel to collect my match ticket.

Just hand me over the bloody ticket, I thought, when I met him in the lobby and we had a bit of small talk. In his profession he was obviously accustomed to conversing in a fancy language with his corporate clients who hop from one exclusive event to another. He even invited me for a drink at the bar to have an 'entertaining chat' and to 'introduce me to the importance of the final'. *Are you taking the piss out of me, mate?* I thought. *Introduce me?* All I had on my mind was to get to the city centre as soon as possible to mingle with the partying Reds.

'Oh, that's really very kind of you! I really do appreciate that! But I'm meeting friends in the city centre and I'm late already.' He passed me an envelope that contained my ticket and emphasised that his seat would be next to mine, so I would be in good company. In my mind I envisioned him sitting next to me during the match and entertaining me with a running commentary: 'The final is quite important for Liverpool who actually haven't won the European Cup for over 20 years. In fact, they also haven't won the league since 1990, would you believe it? They used to be great in the 1970s and 80s, but that's a long time ago, you know. Quite an interesting piece of football trivia is that the football anthem "You'll Never Walk Alone" is sung at Anfield at every home match. And you probably don't know this fact, but Steven Gerrard, their number 8 and captain, and Jamie Carragher, their number 23, are actually from Liverpool.' The elderly gentleman next to me at Leverkusen sprang to mind, who promised we would have a good time together and then, once the match kicked off and he made intensive acquaintance with my characteristics, went noticeably silent towards me. I grabbed the ticket, thanked him for all his kind support and left.

Another taxi, another driver, another direction followed. 'Irish pub, please!' The gentleman replied a couple of sentences in his native language, which due to my lack of Turkish I couldn't comprehend in its entirety. I just wanted to start off the evening somewhere safe, where I could join a group and then see where the evening would take us. There were obviously already a lot of Reds in town, but I had no clue where any particular meeting point would be. I trusted the driver to know where to take me. The least situation I fancied was to be stranded somewhere in the middle of nowhere with no Liverpool supporters in sight.

All of a sudden, he stopped at what appeared to be a massive square with the world's biggest advertising screen I had ever seen. While cars behind us kept honking, he pointed, alternating between my door and the other side of the road. His gesture unambiguously indicated he wanted me to leave through that door and walk across that road. I insisted, 'No, please, Irish pub!' He kept pointing to the direction where I couldn't recognise anything at all. Looking through the cars speeding in both directions, I only saw silhouettes of trees in the darkness.

When the traffic noise dropped around us due to a red light, I heard drum beats from afar. The sound actually came from that area he was pointing to. Scousers sing and clap, but drums? Drums were a well-known component of Turkish fan culture. I guessed it might be a group of Galatasaray or Fenerbahçe or Beşiktaş fans gathering in the city centre to mark their territory. For one last time I mentioned the more common phrase 'bar', but he wouldn't listen. I decided not to enter a contest in eloquence in a language I hadn't mastered. I paid, thanked him and left the taxi through the exact door he pointed to in order to walk into the exact direction he instructed me to.

Shit! I stood in front of a massive main road with hundreds of cars, vans and buses flying by. To cross that road alive I would have needed to have started playing skill-based computer games at an early age. I mean very early age! Only those gaining maximum points at the highest game level would be able to survive that challenge unscathed. In a hesitant 'Mr Bean' walking style I manoeuvred through the vehicles until I finally arrived on the other side. Alive! The drum beats got louder and gradually I recognised the size of the crowd. Eventually, I spotted something red. It was a Liverpool banner. I saw one, then two and then I knew I was home. I realised I had arrived at the headquarters of the Red Army for that night. My driving guide knew exactly what I wanted all along. Now I comprehended that his indifferent facial expression towards anything I uttered wasn't down to sheer ignorance but an overriding care. What a nice guy!

The open-air party centred outside McDonald's on Taksim Square, and this particular location would be my spot for the rest of the night. Reds were not only occupying the entire area between the restaurants and shops, but also the roofs above, where banners were on display en masse. In any of the many kiosks in the side streets, liquid catering in the form of Efes lager cans was also provided in huge supply and, surprisingly, for reasonable prices. Turkish police handled the big crowd and entire situation very professionally and perfectly well at all times. They showed presence but always kept a distance. When some small local youngsters attempted to stir up a provocation, the police immediately intervened, picked them out and let the Reds continue with their party.

It was a beautiful, warm spring evening and an indescribably euphoric atmosphere. The nonstop Reds' singing session included all-time greatest hits and also some new favourite songs. In between 'Five Times', 'Luis Garcia', 'A Team of Carraghers' and 'Fields of Anfield Road', the relentless beating of the drum to the 'La Bamba' tune for Rafa Benítez seemed to last for hours. If the drummer felt a touch of fatigue and had a break, it was taken up again a couple of minutes later by somebody starting to clap. In rare moments when we took a deep breath before the full repertoire was taken up again, the time was bridged with yet another rendition of Johnny Cash's trumpet theme tune 'Ring of Fire'. One particular song that had been newly created for the special occasion became an integral part of our songbook that night. It was a tune I had heard in different and less pleasant circumstances before, but only now was it being provided with quality lyrics and content: 'Oh, Istanbul is wonderful, oh, Istanbul is wonderful. It's full of mosques, kebabs and Scousers. Oh, Istanbul is wonderful!'

Hoarse, exhausted and tired at around 2am, the area emptied gradually and I caught a taxi. The party, though, wouldn't even stop on the ride back to the hotel. We passed several red banners hanging out of hotel windows and red shirts on their way back to their accommodation. Whenever Reds spotted each other sitting in another taxi or in a bar outside, the windows were wound down and songs started anew. A short 'Ring of Fire' tune was followed by 'Li-ver-pool, Li-ver-pool, Li-ver-pool' and 'Five Times'. Once we stopped in front of the red traffic lights, more Reds in cabs arrived on either side. The signature tune of the night rang out again and everyone joined in, wanting to outdo one another: 'De de de de der deerrrr.' Some lads sitting in a bar jumped from their seats, stretched their arms in the air and responded. Other Reds suddenly appeared at a hotel window far upstairs and joined in.

My taxi driver ignored the green light and stayed on the spot until our jointly intoned chorus of 'in Istanbul, we'll win it five times!' was finished appropriately. Whenever new Reds appeared in the streets he drove slower, expecting the singing to take up again. He certainly did enjoy the whole atmosphere! It all felt crazy, it all felt unreal, it all just felt perfectly great! And this was just the night before! It was difficult to estimate how many Reds were in town already, but they were virtually everywhere. At the same time, not a single Milan fan or any black-and-red colour could be seen anywhere all night. You couldn't help but feel that the Red Army had already conquered and taken over Istanbul. The trophy was already ours. We only had to wait for final day to arrive.

Back at the hotel, I was running on empty and all I longed for was my bed. My adrenaline level had a clear veto on this decision, though, and just didn't want this night to end. Not yet! Down the street I saw a small bar still open. *Just one more Efes for a good night's sleep*, I thought. Just one. I passed by four guys sitting around a table. One of them wore a white shirt with a black-and-white photo of Shankly and Paisley. I presumed that they must be real Reds as that kind of clobber was certainly only available locally and definitely not through the official online merchandise channels. I said hello and they invited me to join them.

John, Brian, another John and Ian were Scousers and had been Kop season ticket holders for decades. At first I feared the Efes was having an effect on my eyesight as I saw one of them twice. John and Brian were the most identical twin brothers there had ever been in the history of all identical twin brothers in this universe. As kids they had once met Bill Shankly after his retirement from Liverpool FC. He regularly went to a cafe opposite the Alder Hey Children's Hospital in West Derby. John and Brian attended Cardinal Allen Grammar School, now known as Cardinal Heenen Catholic High School, which a certain Steven George Gerrard attended years later, too. They knew about Shanks's habit and waited for him to have their Shankly book signed by the man himself. They narrated many more personal stories about Liverpool until even my adrenaline, my strength and my eyelids were on the same lowest level. We said goodbye, wished each other a great day and best of luck for the following night.

We, my bed and I, said hello at around 4am and all I wished myself was that I wouldn't suffer from too bad a hangover when I woke up again. Dreams were already running through my head before I entered the slow-wave sleep phase. The trophy was already mine. I only had to wake up one more time.

When my eyes opened up again six hours later, my head felt funny and my stomach was in desperate need of some proper breakfast! I rushed down, hoping they would still serve some food. To my delight they did. Loads of cheese sandwiches and litres of black coffee should kick-start my day. Through my still almost closed eyelids, my pupils spotted a guy at the buffet filling sausages into a fez, the traditional

Turkish hat. The process of thinking about plans for the day was still too strenuous, so I opted for observing that lad to see what he was going to do next instead. I wondered why he didn't use a plate and fill it with just about enough content that fits the predetermined space to allay his hunger sufficiently for a short moment before returning to the buffet for another course of sausages. Chewing on my sandwich, I tried to analyse his value creation process, but couldn't find any comprehensible solution. I convinced myself that it was my own constitution that was failing me in not being able to understand the underlying details of his sophisticated system. When our eyes met, we realised we had met before. He was one of the guys from the early morning session across the road a few hours before. We didn't know that we were staying in the same hotel. A taciturn, sleepy, brief chat followed: 'The rest of the lads couldn't make it downstairs, so I'm getting as much food upstairs as possible,' Ian said. They were going to spend the day with a trip to the coast before returning to the city for the match. I couldn't wait to get back to Taksim Square as soon as possible.

It was a warm and sunny day. On the drive to the city centre in the bright sunlight, the beauty of Istanbul and the sea fully unfolded. Reds in yellow cabs were all heading in the same direction. Implementing communicative skills was a rather challenging task. Apart from 'Taksim Square', the use of the English language towards the driver was an endeavour that immediately proved to be futile. My second attempt was directed at him in my native lingo. I hoped that he might have spent some time in Germany, a likelihood that wasn't too remote as Turkish people make up the largest number of immigrant workers in my country. But this attempt was also in vain. When he realised I did intend to enter a conversation with him, he started like a waterfall in Turkish and wouldn't stop. When I make use of the term 'waterfall', I don't refer to the likes of the Turkish Manavgat, but rather the power and quantity of Niagara Falls.

The way the water pours its way down the cliffs also applied to his style of manoeuvring us through the streets of Istanbul. His either confident or oblivious handling of lines, lights and traffic rules in general made me question whether he was in possession of a valid driving licence, let alone a passenger transport certificate, or perhaps he had obtained these certified documents as part of an all-inclusive package when he bought his taxi. Looking around it appeared as if all drivers had purchased that same package from that same vendor.

Looking out of the window on my right, I saw myself in the mirror before I realised it wasn't me, but another Liverpool supporter sitting in another taxi's back seat with the same intimidated facial expression, staring at me. Looking ahead, I was continuously pushing my imaginary brake in order to not end up in the taxi's boot in front of me. The gentleman to my left was unimpressed and talked to me relentlessly. My physiognomy indicated that I wasn't really getting the gist. But this didn't deter him from continuing his monologue. His voice became louder and his gesticulations more hectic. The sentiment grew inside me that he was shouting at me. I nodded approvingly at whatever he uttered, just to not let matters escalate. Was it about the traffic? Was it about politics? Was it about me being a Liverpool supporter? I sank in my seat and felt totally lost.

Suddenly, a rare smile sneaked through his facial expression. I felt relief. Everything was alright. I joined him and a monologue turned into a conversation, which in detail consisted of two separate monologues. I tried hard to pick up any word from him I could make any sense of and then integrate it in a response. So we continued philosophising about Galatasaray, Fenerbahçe and Beşiktaş until the end of the journey, each of us in his own language, of course. It was great fun, especially when we both started to laugh for some reason, but never about the same content and never at the same time. When we reached Taksim Square, I gave him a good tip, shook his hand and wished him well. His thumbs-up gesture at the end convinced me of his loyal allegiance later that day in front of his TV.

The square was already dressed in red and the singing in full swing. Reds' unique creativity and Scouse witty ingenuity was immortalised on the best day of all our lives by phrases and choice of clothing that will always stick in my memory for the rest of my life:

GLAZER'S DOLLARS OR ROMAN'S ROUBLES?
RAFA, JUST 5 EUROS POR FAVOR!

ROMAN'S TAXES PAY MY GIRO

LUIS SANK LEVER' AT THE BAY
STUCK IT IN THE OLD LADY
MADE THE RENT BOYS PAY
NOW GONNA STUFF AC IN TURKEY

MY WIFE THINKS I'M WORKING
AND SO DOES THE GAFFER
BUT I'M IN ISTANBUL
WITH STEVIE AND RAFA

NOT GERMAN, I'M SCOUSE

MOSES SAID COME FORTH
RAFA SAID NO
WE WILL WIN THE CUP INSTEAD

HE PUT NEDVED TO BED
AND KEPT EIDUR DOWN
NOW SHEVCHENKO CAN'T SLEEP
COS CARRA'S IN TOWN

FOR THOSE OF YOU WATCHING IN
BLUE AND WHITE,
THIS IS WHAT A EUROPEAN CUP LOOKS LIKE

1. CARRA 2. CARRA 3. CARRA 4. CARRA 5.
CARRA 6. CARRA
7. CARRA 8. CARRA 9. CARRA 10.
CARRA 11. CARRA
WE ALL DREAM OF A TEAM OF CARRAGHERS

RAFA IS THE BOSPHERUS

YOUR DREAMS ARE OUR REALITY

4 MINS FROM GREEK TRAGEDY
4 MORE THAN THE HUN
4 GIVE, NOT 4GET – JUVE
4 INCHES OVER THE LINE
4 EUROPEAN CUPS
4 IS GOOD BUT 5 IS 4 KEEPS

THEM SCOUSERS AGAIN

First stop was the kiosk, when one guy passed by wearing a white suit. That looked funny but I couldn't make any sense of it. Then a second one walked by with the same suit, then a third, then a fourth, then a fifth. Five Reds dressed as Spice Boys wearing cream-coloured suits, which looked just as good as the Armani ones worn by the players before the 1996 'White Suits' FA Cup Final. The whole afternoon was like attending a comedy festival. You just have to walk through the crowd and observe, read and listen to the various acts. Taksim Square was high-quality live entertainment at its best.

The square emptied at around 5pm. A couple of Reds, who I had spent all afternoon with, and I made our way to the pick-up point where shuttle buses would take us to the Ataturk Stadium. It would take a considerable amount of time to get to the stadium, we had been warned all afternoon. Whatever that meant! We sat down on the stairs at the square, waiting to be picked up. It was the first moment all day that I sensed a kind of quietness. Next moment, one guy climbed up a 60ft-high flagpole in no time. At the very top, he clenched his fist up in the air to symbolise Liverpool were on top of the world. The singing got going again. There was just no chance to rest for a split second. Another guy appeared at the end of the stairs with a replica European Cup, which he stretched into the air in front of waiting Reds. The crowd went wild and the full repertoire of songs started anew. The trophy was already ours. We only had to wait for the shuttle bus to arrive.

On the bus, it was eventually time to relax after hours of standing in the sun and singing our lungs out. Everyone felt exhausted. I closed my eyes for a moment and tried to calm down. I leaned my head on the window and started to reminisce about the previous unbelievable, indescribable, crazy 24 hours that had passed. The trip to the stadium would be the last calm before the storm. I wanted to recharge my batteries. I wanted to be fit for tonight. Then the loudest imaginable 'de de de de de der der derrrrrr' was screamed out behind me by one lad, whose batteries needed no recharging apparently. The whole bus was wide awake again and got going endlessly! There was just no escape!

Everyone would have loved to have fallen into a burning ring of fire if it meant getting anywhere near the point of our desired destination soon. But the journey went on and on, and on and on, and on and on. We were no longer in Istanbul but somewhere in the countryside. Streets were lined with locals, who predominantly showed their support for the Reds. The areas became poorer the longer the journey lasted. After a while you saw big housing blocks with nothing else around but wasteland. The many smiling faces and waving hands towards us all along the way to the Ataturk Stadium implied that we had made their day. Some of them showed their allegiance by having 'Liverpool' drawn on a simple piece of paper. It was a great feeling to receive such support and we tried to respond in non-verbal communication to them, which caused some laughs on both sides on many occasions. All the locals were on our side. The trophy was already ours. We only had to arrive at the stadium.

After sitting on the bus for nearly two hours with still no stadium in sight, we arrived at the end of a traffic jam in the middle of a lunar landscape. Slow-motion velocity enabled us to observe funny goings-on around us. Consumption of Efes all afternoon caused some lads to answer the call of nature on the way. As a consequence, it also meant several additional hold-ups. Vehicles had to wait for those in need to return to their respective buses or taxis to continue the journey.

Taxis passed by with Reds not only sitting in the passenger or back seats, but in open boots, on roofs or bonnets. Some Reds hired local lads, who drove them on the back of their motorbikes. When we spotted the stadium from a very far distance, people started getting off the buses and made their way on foot. Over the final miles we had to overcome small hills, big holes, and stones everywhere. You seriously had to mind your step. When we eventually arrived outside the stadium, the party went on.

The ticket checkpoints couldn't be called anything other than a farce. You could easily tell that untrained stewards were employed only for that particular match. They wouldn't have stopped you if you just walked by without showing your ticket at all. *Interesting*, I thought, *I'll keep that in mind*! I walked up to my seat in the middle tier of the main stand on the far left, west, block 301, row 58, seat 506. I fixed my banner in the very best of neighbouring company:

WELCOME TO HELL
MY ARSE IF YOU
THINK THIS IS HELL TRY THE
GRAFTON
ON A FRIDAY NIGHT

FORM IS TEMPORARY
CLASS IS PERMANENT

Looking down, I noticed that there were no gates or checkpoints segregating the main stand and the scoreboard stand behind the goal, where the Liverpool supporters stood. I walked down again and took my place right in the middle behind the goal. Looking around the arena, it appeared as if three-quarters of the Ataturk Stadium was occupied by Reds. Our dominance inside the stadium was very obvious when our players ran on to the pitch for their warm-up to 'You'll Never Walk Alone' and over 40,000 Liverpool supporters, with banners and scarves all around, formed waves of one big red sea. Ataturk Stadium was ours. The trophy was already ours. We only needed the match to kick off.

Kick-off! Milan were awarded a free kick. All of a sudden, players in white were running to the sidelines in celebration and a massive roar echoed from the opposite end. We had just conceded a goal within the first minute. Earth's movement came to a standstill.

Within a split second, Reds who had been so full of confidence and drunk with joy sobered up. We were woken by reality. The trophy wasn't ours yet! It was the very first time I realised that there was actually still an opponent to overcome. The scoreboard read: MALDINI 1'. The guy had played his debut for AC Milan before my first European Cup Final 20 years before. It was only one goal though. There would be enough time to level the score. I was even glad that it happened early in the match and not late in the second half.

Late in the first half, Luis Garcia had a shot on goal blocked by Alessandro Nesta, who was on the floor in the Milan penalty area. The ball rolled against his hand and Liverpool's shout for a penalty was turned down. Play went on and the Italians countered. Andriy Shevchenko passed the ball across the edge of the six-yard box to Hernán Crespo, who tapped in from six yards. The scoreboard read: MALDINI 1' CRESPO 39'. Liverpool were all at sea on the pitch and we were in a state of shock off it. A few minutes later, just before the half-time whistle, a long ball from midfield was played to Crespo, who lifted the ball over our goalie Jerzy Dudek. The scoreboard read: MALDINI 1' CRESPO 39' 44'. We were being outclassed by Milan's domination. Fortunately, it was half-time and the slaughtering took a break.

Shattered. Devastated. Gutted. Rock bottom. My stomach felt sick, my heart broken. I tried to put my mind at rest, but too many emotions ran through my brain. I recalled the past six months, the comeback against Olympiakos, the walkover contest with Leverkusen, the brilliant performances against Juventus, the 180 + 6 minutes against Chelsea, the omens, the banners, the party of the previous 24 hours on Taksim Square, the journey on the bus, the smiling locals wishing us well. Probably even the little kids lining the streets driving up here might have changed colours and were cheering on AC Milan by now.

Apart from the fact that the final was being lost, fear inside grew that it might continue this way in the second half. Getting beaten is one thing, losing the final without having a go is another matter. There had been high-scoring 4-0 results in European Cup finals before, both of them with AC Milan on the winning side. There had also been a 7-3 in the competition's history when Real Madrid beat Eintracht Frankfurt in 1960. Would there be a new scoring record? My biggest fear was becoming the laughing stock of Europe. Istanbul was supposed to be the catalyst for our return to the big stage. Now it seemed as if it was to become the platform of the biggest knockback. Frustration, anger, sadness, mingled with tiredness. Within 45 minutes, Reds had dropped from the highest feeling a Red could sense to a freefall down to the roughest rock bottom. One guy a few rows in front of me started to sing very slowly on his own, '4-3 … we're gonna win 4-3.' Hardly anyone joined in. I always believe, always, but that was just too far away. I tried to console myself that we would score at least one goal. Maybe we could achieve a 3-1 defeat, maybe 4-2. I was solely focused on losing with dignity. I wouldn't let the result ruin the entire Istanbul experience anyway.

A few minutes before the players returned, our anthem was intoned somewhere inside the stadium. Within a few moments, all Reds, every single one inside the stadium, joined in the most serious 'You'll Never Walk Alone'.

In the second half, Jerzy Dudek prevented Liverpool from going four down by producing a fine diving save from Shevchenko's free kick. I just hoped that time would pass without conceding another, and pass and pass. When John Arne Riise on the left was given sufficient space to cross the ball into the penalty area, I just saw bodies jumping up in the air, heading for it. I didn't recognise who hit it, but the ball was directed further right towards the Milan goal until its movement came to a sudden halt and dropped. By the reaction of the Liverpool players and the roar from around the stadium I realised we had actually just scored. I didn't really sense any joy, but only a kind of relief that we had managed to break them down and score. People around me were still paralysed. The scoreboard told us: GERRARD 54'.

I tried not to build my hopes up again only to experience another freefall. Certainly Milan would score another soon anyway.

Liverpool were again on the left wing, where Milan left enough open space, and the ball was passed smoothly to

Vladimir Smicer. *Pass it on, don't shoot*! I thought. He did shoot and the ball rolled on and on. It felt like ages. Someone would intervene, definitely. Dida, the Milan goalie, dived for it but couldn't reach it. The ball stretched further and further. I saw it rolling between Dida's hand and the post. The net moved and a massive roar from the Red masses echoed around the stadium. Some people were jumping, some were screaming, some were just staring at the pitch. I didn't see a single face smiling. We were looking at each other, confused in disbelief. The scoreboard told us: GERRARD 54' SMICER 56'.

This had all happened too quickly to comprehend. I couldn't control my emotions and neither could I concentrate on the match. All of a sudden, Gerrard ran into the penalty area, fell, and the referee pointed to the spot. The atmosphere around me was indefinable. Nobody dared to believe that this was happening. Nobody dared to trust their hope. Nobody was capable of realising that we were seconds away from being level. We could start the game from scratch. The tension in the eyes indicated that everybody dreaded that roller coaster of torture we were riding would continue. We were going up and up and eventually would come down again. But this time, the wagon we were in was taking us further until it reached its peak.

It became unbearable to wait, it became unbearable to watch. Xabi Alonso ran up, shot, Dida saved. It was over. Okay, normality would be resumed and Milan would be on their way to victory. But Xabi followed up, got to the ball, put it over Dida and scored! The scenes and emotions that followed I had never witnessed before or since in my entire life. People were jumping on one another, lying in others' arms and falling on the floor. People's faces looked as if they were in agony, but it was sheer ecstasy. Emotionally, we had just been rocketed from hell to heaven within six minutes. I turned around to the scoreboard just to see the official confirmation that I wasn't hallucinating. I wasn't!

3-3

MALDINI 1' CRESPO 39' 44'

GERRARD 54' SMICER 56' ALONSO 60'

We were level with 30 minutes to go. Everyone around me watched the match in disbelief. Destiny wouldn't allow something like this to happen, would it? It's too unreal! Whenever Milan approached our goal, the tension inside caused me to hold my breath and I couldn't even move. Whenever Milan approached us anywhere on the pitch and Djimi Traoré was nearby, tension caused me to hold my breath and I couldn't even move, but at some stage in the second half the man who couldn't control his feet blocked a shot from Shevchenko a yard off our goal line. Alright, we had escaped yet again! From a corner Jaap Stam headed to Kaká, who headed just wide. Alright, we had escaped yet again! Time was running down. Eventually, the 90 minutes were over! It was time for a breather, but tension still gripped everyone. I still couldn't see any joy in faces, as disbelief was still in control. At half-time it was shock, now it was incredulity.

In the first half of extra time, a long cross into our box couldn't be cleared by Traoré. Milan's substitute Tomasson stood next to him in the perfect position but he hadn't expected to receive the ball and therefore missed.

In the second half of extra time, I was observing the clock more than what was going on on the pitch. Time was running down and I was calculating the number of potential attacks possible from AC Milan. Two, maybe three? The guy next to me didn't bother standing up anymore. He sat down all through the second half of extra time with his head in his hands. Maybe it was healthier if you couldn't see anything, but only relied on the noises around you.

Another attack started towards our goal on the left-hand side. The cross flew into our penalty area and reached Shevchenko, who headed it on target. Now, it's going to happen for them! This is it! Standing behind the goal you could see the ball going towards Dudek. Next moment I saw the ball come off our goalie's hands. It's not over! Shevchenko picked up the rebound, this time with a shot from only a yard out. It's a wide-open goal with only Dudek to overcome. The next thing I saw was the ball ricocheting off Dudek's hands and flying over the bar. Not sure whether I was about to have a heart attack or should be screaming, I buried my head in my hands. This was the moment when I was convinced that destiny had changed its direction for good and was on our side. The greatest sense of relief followed when I heard the final whistle.

Penalties! After all six goals had been scored at the Milan end, the chosen goal for the penalties to be taken was also their end. Not that I contemplated asking UEFA for compensation, but the Italians certainly got a lot more entertainment for their money than we got at our end.

AC Milan started. Before Serginho even ran up to shoot, Dudek was hopping on his line from left to right and back again with both arms waving about above his head. It certainly had an effect, as the Milan player shot over the bar. I couldn't believe that Dudek had copied Bruce Grobbelaar's antics from the penalty shoot-out from Liverpool's previous triumphant European Cup Final in Rome in 1984. It was the very first time in over 120 minutes that we had the advantage. Didi Hamann walked up and scored. We were leading! For the first time all night we were ahead.

A million thoughts crossed my mind but there was no time to think. Andrea Pirlo took a run-up, was put off by Dudek and his shot was saved. Djibril Cissé ran up, 2-0! People were screaming, with tears in their eyes. Jon Dahl Tomasson converted his penalty and kept Milan in the match. John Arne Riise was our third penalty taker. His low shot to Dida's right-hand corner was perfectly saved by the Milan keeper. I caught my breath. We wouldn't let it slip again, would we? Dudek continued his irritating movements, but couldn't put off Kaká, who scored for Milan. Vladimir Smicer stepped up and put us 3-2 up. Andriy Shevchenko and Steven Gerrard were the only takers left. If the Ukrainian scored, the Liverpool skipper could still win it for us. Shevchenko ran up, shot, and Jerzy Dudek saved. The last I saw was players in red running from the halfway line to Dudek. On the terrace the wildest of celebrations started. We were jumping all over each other. People were screaming, hyperventilating, others couldn't move. Then the most unreal scenario followed when Stevie lifted Ol' Big Ears. We had won it five times and would keep the cup forever.

After the lap of honour, when players had left the pitch and the stands started to clear, I looked up to my banner and saw it was gone. I walked up to check whether it was somewhere, but I saw nothing but empty seats. Someone had taken it! It was the most personal memento of the greatest two days of my club's history. I couldn't grasp what use it would be for any other person as they wouldn't have any personal attachment to it whatsoever.

To whom it may concern:
If you're in possession of my Istanbul banner and
read this, get in touch you ****!

The situation back in the car park was as chaotic as you would expect from a UEFA-organised event. There was a sufficient number of buses available. The only problem was that they were either already full, completely empty with no bus driver at all, or had no clear sign of their destination. Many Reds wanted to go to the airport as they were headed straight back to Liverpool. Others like me needed to get back into town, preferably Taksim Square. You definitely needed to make sure you got on the right bus as you wanted to avoid having to spend hours on the wrong one heading to the airport and being stranded miles away out of town. It happened a couple of times that we rushed into a newly arrived bus until it was full and only then learned it was the wrong one and had to get off again. Eventually the right bus arrived. I took a free spot at a sash window in an overcrowded bus that would only move a couple of yards every five minutes. Street sellers appeared around buses to offer a can of warm Efes for €12. Some lads on the coach were so desperate that they took the deal.

At around 3am we reached Taksim Square. The pub was already full of Reds but every single one was so knackered you wouldn't have believed we had just won the Champions

League. It was completely mute. Half an hour later, a group of Reds sitting at a table started singing, 'We won it at Wem-ber-lee, we won it in gay Paree, in '77 and '84 it was Rome, we won it five times, we won it five ti-i-imes, in Istanbul, we won it five times ...' They repeated it again, but now knocking their bottles and glasses in a corresponding rhythm on the tables. They repeated the verses over and over again until every single Red in that pub joined in. People stood on benches, stools and tables. Those who couldn't bang on the table used anything their hands could touch: the wooden ceiling, the windows, anything. After 20 repetitions, and I do understate numbers here certainly, the full repertoire got going again. It appeared as if only then everyone realised that we had won it five times, although temporarily undermined by one of the worst nightmares anyone could dread!

The party inside and outside the pub went on long after the break of dawn. People passing by on buses or walking to work looked bemused at singing Reds with mugs in their hands at that time of day. At around 7am, I had to sit down outside to relax for a while. I reminisced about what had started at exactly the same spot 36 hours before and what had followed since then. I still couldn't grasp the time in between, but I did realise that I still needed some very special souvenirs of my time in Istanbul. But what could they be? The paper sellers opened their stalls and I was wondering whether the newspapers would have already covered last night's match, which had only ended some six hours before. I went up and spotted six different daily newspapers, each of them showing Stevie lifting number five. Although I would never be able to read any of it, I decided to buy every single paper. For some reason, I bought every copy twice. Therefore, I'm in possession of two full sets of Turkish daily national newspapers from 26 May 2005.

To whom it may concern:
If you're in possession of my Istanbul banner and read this and are interested in one full set of Turkish newspapers
dated 26 May 2005,
get in touch you ******* ****!

At around 8am the pub staff decided to tell all remaining Reds that they had run out of Efes and kindly asked us to leave. It was time to get some sleep anyway. I took a taxi to my hotel and decided to get some breakfast straight away. Once I hit my bed, there would be no way I would get up on time. Entering the restaurant I was amazed that it was completely full. Full of Italians! I was the only Red amongst a Milanese-only breakfast area. Not even one Scouser could be spotted filling his fez with sausages. Still wearing my Liverpool jersey, I quickly attracted attention. Politely I asked, or rather gesticulated, whether I could use the one spare seat I had spotted at the very end of a table. Reluctantly, they nodded and let me have my breakfast. My neighbours were obviously not enjoying their early morning meal. While I was sipping my coffee I wondered what the likes of Senhor Mourinho, Mr Ferguson and the Cockney media pals were having for brekkie or whether they were refraining from any meal that morning as the previous night had caused them too much of an upset stomach. Would there be some sad Scousers back in Liverpool feeling blue and ordering the next round of bitter?

After I had landed back in Düsseldorf the following night and taken a late train connection to Cologne main station, where I waited for my connecting train to Mannheim, it was the very first time I could rest. I was sitting on a bench on the platform and there were hardly any other people to be seen anywhere around. It was a stark contrast to the previous 48 hours. From the busy, hectic streets of Istanbul with thousands of Liverpudlians singing, chanting and joking around me, I had been taken to this awkward silence that surrounded me right then. Despite a hangover, hoarse voice, tiredness and earworms, I missed Taksim Square already. I wanted European Cup finals every week. I had become addicted to the Reds' parties!

CHAPTER ELEVEN

Bunking In

I CONTEMPLATED going to Monaco for the European Super Cup Final at the end of August. Another European gathering in the heavenly setting of the French Riviera caused some thrill of anticipation. I booked a place in nearby Nice for a couple of nights and a flight. Tickets were on sale and availability wouldn't be a problem for such a match anyway. Even the final against Bayern Munich four years earlier had empty seats, as you could see on TV. Totally relaxed and confident, I checked the official UEFA ticket website one evening. Sold out! The Liverpool website couldn't help either. Searching the entire web, I had to face the reality that the match had actually sold out. I still travelled and tried to sort out a spare down in France. I spent the evenings in the Irish pub in the city centre, where loads of Reds got together. All enquiries for a ticket were in vain, though.

The already most enjoyable party atmosphere intensified when a local football team from Merseyside, whose name can't be detected by international opponents on any map, tried to get a sniff of our European royalty. A few days before our final, 'Champions-League-We're-Havin-a-Laugh' Everton had to play their return leg of the third qualifying round that would actually take them into the Champions League. If they qualified for it, they certainly would have been entitled to have a laugh. Everton lost the home leg against Spanish team Villarreal 2-1. The return leg was live on all the screens in the pub that night. The bitters lost the match 2-1 again and there would be no Champions League football at all.

Instead, Everton played in the first round of the UEFA Cup, the competition they were having a laugh in next. The mighty Dinamo Bucureşti, from the superpower that's the Romanian league, thrashed Everton 5-2 on aggregate and the Blues were out of Europe twice in a month! The next cup competition wasn't too far off for having a laugh, though. The League Cup third round produced a home tie against Middlesbrough. 'Carling Cup, we're havin' a laugh' lasted only one match as Everton's hopes were dashed by a 1-0 home defeat. Soon they would find out their opponents in the third round of the big one. 'FA Cup, we're havin' …'

On the day of the Super Cup Final, I had already given up hope of getting hold of a ticket. Lying on the beach reading a book, I decided to go for a last swim before getting ready to watch the match in the pub. Walking towards the water I spotted a couple wearing red Istanbul shirts. My inner voice told me to approach them just to say hello. Rather casually I dropped the question of whether they happened to have any spares. 'Oh yeah,' one replied, 'we've got a few.' He was from an official Liverpool supporters' club from somewhere up north in England and some of his members couldn't make the trip. Money was exchanged for a ticket and I was sorted.

The Red Army made its way to Nice main station to catch the train to Monaco. The journey must have been the most beautiful trip to a Liverpool match any Red on this planet ever experienced in their lives. The railway route along the coast ran between the mountains on the left and the cliffs on the right, overlooking the Mediterranean Sea from high up above at sunset. 'Five Times', 'Fields of Anfield Road', 'Luis Garcia' and 'Rafa's La Bamba' transferred the atmosphere from Taksim Square on to that train.

The only locals getting on or off the train were commuting housekeepers and cleaning ladies who worked in the millionaires' villas in the hills. At first they looked a bit bewildered, especially as one very emotional Red gave a rather attractive lady a five-finger salute. Being totally lost in sign language translation, she assumed she was subject to an indecent offer. Surrounded by jumping, screaming lads with open spilling cans in one hand and bags of more unopened lager in the other, she and the other ladies certainly felt intimidated at first. The guy realised what he had provoked unintentionally and his charming gesticulation convinced them of his good nature. Once she smiled, he wouldn't stop narrating in the broadest Scouse, not French, how he won it five times in Istanbul! When she got off the train, she turned around, gave a smile and a five-finger salute to the biggest cheer the train had ever witnessed. We tried to console the poor guy, who definitely would have given up his ticket to carry her bag home for her.

Once you arrive in Monaco, you realise you're in the tidiest, clinically cleanest place in the whole world. Even the smallest side street looked as if it had just been given a complete overhaul in the morning. The traffic islands' lawns could easily compete with Anfield's pitch at the beginning of a season. On the way to the stadium, where every ten yards you looked into a closed-circuit TV camera, all shops and restaurants were closed. Inside the stadium, the CSKA Moscow following accounted for more than two-thirds of the capacity. Only then I realised where all the tickets had gone. In the stand on the right next to ours, you could see many families and young couples who had obviously spent their summer holidays at the Côte d'Azur and most certainly had never visited a regular home fixture of their team before.

Moscow scored just before the half-hour mark, but Djibril Cissé, who had come on as a sub for John Arne Riise, equalised with eight minutes remaining. Cissé scored again in extra time before Luis Garcia made it 3-1 to bring yet another trophy home.

In defence of the European Cup, Liverpool walked comfortably through the group phase with three wins and three draws, but couldn't overcome Benfica in the first knockout round, losing 3-0 over two legs on aggregate. Another party in May, on the Champs-Élysées, had to be postponed.

Over the years I had turned into a Swiss pre-season friendlies regular, where Liverpool played many of their training camp preparation matches. I visited stadiums such as Zürich's Hardturm Stadium or St Gallen's AFG Arena, but the really adventurous trips took me to the likes of the Herti Allmend Stadium or St Leonard Stadium in the middle of nowhere. In the middle of the week I took half a day off work to drive some five hours to arrive just in time for kick-off to watch more or less our reserve team, and then another five hours back to return home long after midnight. On a trip to Grenchen, where the Reds played Lucerne, I bumped into David Fairclough, who after his Liverpool career played for Lucerne. He was working for LFC TV that day and took time to have a little chat with me. Meeting our Saint-Étienne hero was worth the trip alone!

Another unforgettable trip took me to see the Reds play Mainz at their ground. The Bundesliga outfit would serve as a proper rehearsal for the upcoming 2006/07 season. It was a sell-out crowd and many Scousers made the trip over. A certain Herr Jürgen Norbert Klopp was the manager of 1. FSV Mainz 05, and the club had won promotion with him for the very first time in their history a few years earlier. A 5-0 demolition made many shocked Reds stay on the terrace after the match, wondering what the season would bring.

In the European Cup, Liverpool kicked Barcelona and PSV Eindhoven out before they were drawn to play another semi-final against Chelsea. The omens were on again! Even before we played the first leg at Stamford Bridge, I searched the web for all sorts of ticket agents for the final. Another summer holiday would have to be sacrificed. Cheapest offers just for the ticket were at €1,000 minimum. I called a few German agencies and asked for a reservation, but they all wanted cash up front.

When it comes to Liverpool, I tend to lose any kind of connection to rational thinking, but I wouldn't go as far as committing financially to that amount before even knowing for sure we were going to Athens. It would be a smart move, though, to book a flight and hotel in advance before prices soared. I booked a Germanwings flight from Stuttgart to

Athens for €240 and got myself a hotel room for two nights in Piraeus for only €30 per night! The €300 for the whole trip was a brilliant deal if we were to bring number six home, and a considerable risk if we didn't make it to the final. Liverpool lost the first leg at Chelsea, but a Daniel Agger goal in the first half in the return leg put the teams level. The tie went to penalties, which Liverpool easily won as the Mercenaries lost their balls twice in front of goal. Another European Cup Final was coming up, our second in 24 months!

The celebration had to make way for rational thinking as panic set in. I needed to make sure I could get hold of my ticket before the outcome of the other semi-final the following evening. If Milan made it again, their fans would maximise their allocation, but wouldn't fight for further spares on the market. If the Mancs qualified, the overall quest for tickets would be a rather impossible task. The ticket agency I bought the Istanbul package from was my first port of call. My enquiry to purchase a ticket only was declined. I would have to buy the whole package, including flight and hotel. Any questions about the guarantee of the ticket were answered in an evasive way, which caused some suspicion. They couldn't tell me what category or in which end of the stadium the seats would be. Asking about delivery by post in advance or pick-up at the hotel in Athens couldn't be answered either.

I was asked to hold the line until I was put through to the boss. He waffled about me having to await the outcome of the second semi-final. What? I couldn't make any sense of it at all. I confronted him with the fact that he offered a specific product for a specific price on the one hand, but couldn't answer my specific questions on the other. If Milan were to succeed it would be no problem, he assured me. If it were to be an all-English final, demand on the ticket market would most certainly exceed supply. 'But if you pay now, we will guarantee you a ticket if we can get hold of one.' I couldn't deal with probabilities, including any ifs. I needed facts. 'Thank you! Goodbye,' was my reply.

I went straight back to the internet, where prices were continuously rising. I acted quickly and made a decision. After filling out my credit card details and accepting further costs of processing fee and postage, I hit the confirmation button. I had just purchased a single ticket of the lowest category 3 for the European Cup Final in Athens. An uneasiness infiltrated my happiness as I didn't intend to spend a fortune. Money can't buy me love, I thought. Thus, when I can spend time with my love, I shouldn't bother about the money it requires. What a feeling! I could sit back and relax while looking forward to the other semi-final decider that night. Milan kicked the Mancs out by three goals without reply and 5-2 on aggregate. It was Liverpool v Milan again!

The online ticketing agency left a very professional impression on me. They asked me to send them my mobile phone number as well as my hotel's address, telephone and fax number as they may receive tickets late and therefore would have to send mine out to Athens directly and be able to contact me locally.

I planned to leave on Monday night for Stuttgart airport to catch the flight very early on Tuesday morning. The whole day in the office I wasn't really able to concentrate as I was still not in possession of my ticket. At around 3pm, I was checking my private email account. I read the subject line of a new mail: 'Cancellation Order European

Cup Final'. I felt as if I had just been pushed off the top of a skyscraper.

> Dear Client, we're sorry to announce that we just got a final negative answer from Liverpool and AC Milan club providers regarding your tickets for the Champions League Final 2007 in Athens. These tickets had been promised to be delivered to us 7 days before the match. During all the last days we were delayed by the providers (promising that we will get the tickets). Due to this problem, we're sorry to announce that your order is cancelled, and we have already started the refund process to all our clients. Based on our terms and conditions, in case of cancellation or undelivered tickets for any reason, we're refunding the same amount as paid to us by the clients. All refunds will be direct to the same credit cards, as we charge you. Best regards.

I would have thought that in a situation like this I would be panic-stricken, but I kept calm as I knew it was too late to pursue any alternatives now. The argument that they had received a final negative answer from the clubs sounded very dodgy, but in that very moment I couldn't care whether there was something suspicious behind this or not. Ticket availability in Athens would be close to zero. On the internet forums I had already read many stories of many season ticket holders who had been denied tickets despite qualifying for them.

Disappointment couldn't have been greater but I somehow sensed joy for another European Cup trip. The airport was empty at the check-in counters at around 4am. Some 50 Liverpool supporters were sitting in a bistro. When I dared approach them for spares, the only replies were: 'Yer havin' a laugh mate!' 'Don't take the piss so early in the morning,' 'Hahaha.' This was only one flight from Stuttgart to Athens and nobody seemed to be in possession of a valid ticket. I wondered how many more Liverpool supporters on other flights via Frankfurt, Munich, Cologne, Düsseldorf, Hamburg, Berlin ... the Netherlands, Belgium, France, Norway, Sweden, Austria, Switzerland, let alone from Liverpool directly were ticketless. The ticket fiasco I had read about was worse than I feared.

In Athens, my first action was to walk straight up to the ancient sights to get the cultural part out of the way. After visiting the Acropolis, the serious programme commenced by midday. In a bar full of Reds, a young couple sat next to me and we started talking. They weren't from Liverpool and appeared somehow to be no real supporters. However, he was in possession of one ticket and they were looking for another one. The guy knew someone at UEFA and might be sorted with another spare late Wednesday afternoon. If he got it, they would go to see the match together. If he didn't, they would sell their ticket to me as he wouldn't leave his girlfriend by herself. Very good decision, I thought. Never ever leave your girlfriend alone! This must be a proper Red, I thought. He travels to a European Cup Final with a ticket in his pocket, takes his ticketless girl with him to look for another ticket and if he fails he gives up his own ticket. Lady Luck, this time embodied by a ticketless girlfriend, strikes again, I thought. We exchanged our mobile numbers and I went to Syntagma Square!

The party was already in full swing, although in general a little subdued because of the high number of ticketless Reds. A group of lads passed by whose faces looked somehow familiar, but I couldn't place at first. Memories of Istanbul flashed through my mind, when I realised it was that lad who stuffed all those sausages into that fez at the breakfast buffet. It was the four Scousers from Istanbul again who I had met in the bar early morning before the final in Istanbul. They had made a brilliant banner and contributed fittingly to the creativity that was on display on the day: 'AKOPALOTATHIS'. They also had their tickets for the final. They wouldn't tell me what kind of creativity they had applied in that respect, but all four were luckily sorted!

The party on Syntagma Square on the Tuesday lasted long after midnight and took up Wednesday morning again. I was desperately waiting for that phone call. At half past five I received a text message that informed me that they couldn't get a second ticket, but had also met another guy who had offered them €1,300 for the one they had. They would sell to him as they couldn't miss the chance of making so much money. Subconsciously, I had feared all along they would want to profit on their asset instead of selling for face value. A deep disappointment was accompanied by tiredness and a conviction to give up at last. I decided not to travel to the stadium to try my luck there. If I failed, I wouldn't get back in time to watch the match somewhere in the city centre. The last thing I wanted was to miss out on the match entirely.

By around 6pm the crowd had gradually cleared the square. Standing on the steps with the Greek parliament behind me, I observed a group of lads from a distance exchanging bank notes. Lacklustre but curious I walked over and saw a pile of match tickets in one of the guy's hands. I couldn't make any sense of it. For one last time I asked the question: 'Any spares?'

'Yeah, course! They're fakes, though, you know!' he very frankly told me with a smile. 'It's only 50 Euros if you wanna try. It's better than nothing.' The ticket he handed me looked genuine, absolutely legitimate, apart from the unforgeable glittering silver Champions League logo. The copy machine had produced a print in a kind of orange that could easily be recognised as not a genuine ticket. My mind drifted away and while he was dealing with the other guys, I was weighing up the pros and cons. What alternative did I have?

I remembered an old video recording of the 1986 all-Merseyside FA Cup Final against Everton. The original BBC footage showed the entrance of the Liverpool end from a helicopter's camera. A few moments before the singing of 'Abide with Me' outside an already packed Wembley, a crowd of Liverpool supporters were still trying to find their way in. Some were climbing up the wall. One guy hung on one of the window frames and swung Tarzan-like over to another window where a mate grabbed him and pulled him inside the interior of the stadium. Later on, during the match, the camera spotted another Red on Wembley's roof. He was sitting on his own watching the match comfortably with his legs dangling over the edge. I had never felt comfortable with climbing, nor would I ever feel happy with sitting on a rooftop.

In that moment I remembered the ticket checkpoint in Istanbul, where I certainly would have been able to squeeze through without a ticket. I might have gone through by just holding up something that looked vaguely like a ticket or even without showing anything at all. Maybe some untrained student part-time stewards would be deployed again that night.

'Fifty Euros you said?' I asked, while handing over the money.

'Yeah, mate, 50. You know, you might not make it, but you never know. It's just a try. All the best of luck to you!' I sat down and took a deep breath before I headed with the Reds to the Olympic Stadium.

After getting off the train at the metro stop, the whole crowd was held back at the exit by riot police. They were forming a close line and wouldn't allow anyone to leave the station for about half an hour. I stood in the first row directly in front of a policeman. The crowd behind me grew bigger by the minute as more trains were arriving from the city centre. I kept my 'ticket' safely hidden in my trouser pocket. When the police decided to open their line to let us through, they shouted, 'Tickets, show us your tickets, only with tickets!' My attempt to walk through without producing my ticket was met with a stern look. 'No ticket, no go through!' he said.

I estimated it too dangerous to present it right in front of him so I claimed my ticket was with a mate of mine who is already further up the way and I was going to collect it later.

'No ticket, you don't go through.'

'But I've got a ticket!' I assured him.

'Call him to get here!' he stubbornly replied. I realised there was no way he would let me pass. Keeping a low profile would be a better option. I got it out, left it folded with the orange logo on the inside and pointed it quickly to him. When he saw it I quickly returned it into my pocket as if I wanted to keep it safe. 'See, see. You have it!' he grumbled.

For a split second I feared he would pick me out because I had lied to him. He wouldn't, though, as it probably would have meant too much hassle for just one guy as there were too many people he had to look after at the same time.

I walked on slowly. There were supporters everywhere but the stadium was nowhere to be seen. I just followed the crowd for a couple of minutes until we arrived at what appeared to be another ticket checkpoint. The stadium was still nowhere to be seen. Several parallel gates lined up were supposed to provide control of the queues. When reaching the end of the queue, I realised that the entrance was tiny. There were stewards on the left and right side to inspect supporters as well as an additional semicircle of riot police standing further behind to form another line of control. A rather tough proposition lay ahead of any ticketless suspect. For only €50 I was experiencing a new thrilling genre of live entertainment, which I wouldn't forget too soon.

'No way will I get through!' I started to say to myself. They were really checking, person by person. I observed the stewards and the police and tried to read the situation and grasp their approach. How did they check the tickets? Who did they control more intensely? Was there conspicuous behaviour by some supporters that led to another inspection? I needed to learn by observing and I needed to learn fast. The next thing I witnessed was a father being frogmarched off by police in a not-so-friendly manner with his little son walking behind them. *Okay, that's it!* I thought. Panic grew inside me that I might miss the match altogether if they took me away. They wouldn't lock me up in a room with a TV, would they?

Only then did I realise what I had started. *What the fuck*

are you doing here, Carsten? I thought. *I'm a law-abiding citizen, have a job, pay my taxes and have my life under control as long as Liverpool don't interfere.* As I hadn't been previously convicted, I did have a clean record. In a few seconds it would be my turn. I kept watching the behaviour of the police who I would face as my second hurdle as soon as I had overcome the stewards. I noticed that some supporters, who had already passed the stewards and then also the second barrier of policemen, were again confronted by more stewards standing even further behind. It was just crazy!

A very unpleasant feeling was running through my body, but I kept my cool. Well, I pretended at least. A strategic plan was needed. This dark orange logo on my ticket was so unglittering dark and so unsilverlike orange that I would be arrested and deported to a proper prison for the poor effort itself. Before the police took out the handcuffs they would all be rolling on the floor pissing themselves at my amateurish, ragged attempt, though. I folded my ticket a couple of times with the logo on the inside. I made sure that it could easily be identified as an official match ticket. Attack is the best defence. I held it up head high but very close to me. I deliberately walked through the checkpoint with enough people around me as a human shield. My mimic and gestures suggested that the pushing of the crowd made me feel uncomfortable and therefore I couldn't show the ticket properly. I focused on the stewards by looking straight into their eyes and pointing my ticket to them. Thereby I indicated that I was willing to show my ticket and had no reason to sneak through. Meeting their eyes I entered a kind of communication with them, gaining their approval that I could pass. Having overcome the stewards I walked calmly past the police. People around me were checked by the second line of stewards and some were taken away. I walked slowly and confidently on and on.

I was safe. Right, now there had to be only one more checkpoint at the stadium. There had to be. Another couple of minutes' walk remained. In Istanbul no one had a clue of how long the bus journey to the stadium would be, but when you arrived at the ground you knew you were finally there. In Athens you arrived at the gate and didn't know how far you were away from the stadium, or just the next checkpoint. All of a sudden, a loud scream came from afar. Two men were running as fast as they could with one guy behind the other shouting: 'Stop him, fucking stop him. He got my tickets, my tickets, stop him!' I've never witnessed anyone running so fast and within seconds they virtually vanished over the horizon. I walked on when I spotted a crying woman surrounded by people explaining that one guy came up to ask what their tickets looked like as he wasn't sure whether he had bought genuine ones or fakes on the black market. They showed him, he took it and ran off. Words will never suffice to express my thoughts on how someone can bring themself to do that to another Red. What a terrible thing to happen! What an unthinkable thing to do!

A few minutes' walk later, I eventually reached the stadium. It was checkpoint time again and the third stage-managed play-acting performance was required. The focusing on the stewards' eyes had worked once, so I would stick to that strategy. But now I could tell from a distance that the entrance was even narrower. I waited for a little while until a group of people walked through. I forced my way into the middle of the group, thus being able to feign being pushed by the crowd around me and thereby not being able to show my ticket properly. It had become a routine. A bit of pushing, a bit of meeting the eyes and I was through again. By that time my confidence had grown so strong that I didn't even fear the line of stewards any more. I walked very slowly and unsuspiciously further, until I was underneath the terrace of the Liverpool end.

One more checkpoint! I noticed that there were only two stewards and no policemen assisting them at all. I waited again until some Liverpool supporters approached the entrance. I decided to stay away though, as there weren't enough to distract the stewards. I waited another couple of minutes until a big enough crowd was nearing the entrance. I mingled in between them to make sure I was right in the middle with at least two people on the left and two on the right. The game was on again. Ticket folded, ticket held up in the air, stewards' eyes focused on, ticket presented to stewards, staying right in the middle, pushing, pushing, pushing a bit more until I was through. I started to walk quickly, then faster, and then I ran as fast as I could until I reached the interior of the stadium. I was in!

The match was one we should have won. Filippo Inzaghi scored twice at the end of each half before Dirk Kuyt got one back a minute before the end. After the match, I went straight back to Piraeus. I was disappointed, tired and couldn't be bothered to hang around town. Leaning on the window, I had to laugh about the whole process I was going through to watch the Reds. Was it all worth it despite the defeat? Definitely! Did I ever doubt what I was doing? No! Would I ever doubt it? Never! What I didn't know was that after my return home I would find out that I had been cheated by a fake online ticket agency from Barcelona. It was one of those companies that were founded only to be declared officially bankrupt and vanish a few weeks later. A solicitor I contacted advised me to write the money off as a court case would be very expensive and couldn't be justified for such a small amount.

When I arrived at the metro stop in Piraeus, some lads got off with me. They looked familiar. It was them Scousers again that I had met in Istanbul and the day before on Syntagma Square. All good things come in threes. We looked out for a bar where we could still enjoy our drinks when the sun rose on the horizon. We have stayed in touch ever since. John, Brian and John have sorted me out on many occasions to be able to sit with them on the Kop. I often wonder how many times they must have cursed the moment they met me for my unbearable craving for recognition.

'Yes, Carsten, you're an adopted Scouser! Yes, yes.'

'Dee do da dou, dontee dou.'

'Very good, Carsten, yes, yes!'

CHAPTER TWELVE

You'll Never Walk Alone

THE MOST emotional and memorable performance of our hymn was certainly at Wembley before the 1989 FA Cup Final a few weeks after Hillsborough. Gerry Marsden's live act embraced the whole of Merseyside at a time when people in grief weren't aware of what kind of long, hard fight for justice lay ahead. Over 20 years later, justice still hadn't been achieved and relatives of the 97 felt that they had walked alone. The virtue and the spirit of our anthem came to life when an online petition to 10 Downing Street took off. On the Reds online forum Red and White Kop, I learned that over 100,000 signatures were required to be able to call on the government to publish cabinet papers about the disaster. Like many other non-UK residents, I was disappointed that I couldn't take part.

If the people in power suppress the truth, you have to go certain ways to make them live up to the truth!

On the petition site I found further information about the requirements. Name, address and email were required to prove that signatures were genuine. Authorities would have to employ quite a few people on a full-time basis to check the authenticity of every single signature.

Unlike the Dark Net, where dodgy people can swap illegitimate purposes, the World Wide Web serves a platform where communities can exchange positive ideas, awaken creativity or remember old mutual friends. Or all of these at the same time!

Many UK as well as non-UK passport holders in the forum remembered that we all had many long-forgotten, good old mates with a permanent residency in the UK who would most certainly support the idea. My mates' names sprang to mind immediately: James, Peter, Dave, Tony, Mike, Robert, John and some 20 others. Then I remembered their surnames: Smith, Miller, White, Black, Brown, Jones, Williams and some 20 others. Yellow Pages helped me find them homes all across the country in streets with corresponding postcodes. Unfortunately, James, Peter, Dave, Tony, Mike, Robert, John and the other 20 didn't have an email account, so I went out of my way to be helpful and provided them with accounts with a domestic co.uk domain.

'What's the point?' Former Prime Minister Tony Blair had questioned the reopening of the case. Another Prime Minister, David Cameron, was made to stand in the House of Commons and apologise to the suffering families in front of the whole nation. In the biggest cover-up in the history of not so great Britain, police statements were altered and comments removed that were unfavourable to the police. Worst of all, Liverpool supporters could potentially have been saved. As a consequence, the verdicts of accidental death were quashed. The 97 Liverpool supporters were unlawfully killed due to grossly negligent failures by the police to fulfil their duty of care to the fans. The inquest also found that the design of the stadium contributed to the crush and that supporters weren't to blame for the dangerous conditions.

'Oh, get on with it!' would be the typical reaction by Little Englanders, who had been fed like gullible parrots by the Scouse-criticising media since the early 1980s. Just because the rest of the country wouldn't have fought for justice in court 27 years after a tragedy, does not mean that the people of Liverpool orientate themselves towards that behavioural benchmark. The 'tragedy-loving, whinging' Scousers let their own values show through. Liverpool isn't the 'self-pity city', but the 'solidarity city'. Nobody had been held accountable for Hillsborough. Whereas others would have left it, Scousers wouldn't accept that. They knew the truth. They didn't wait for the truth, which they had already known for decades, but they waited for the establishment to be forced to face up to the truth. Families who had campaigned for decades and fought for 'the truth' finally got it! For many years they must have felt as if they walked alone and were fighting an enduring, lonesome battle against the establishment and the media. However, those in a superior position had taken on the wrong city, had taken on the wrong mothers and had taken on the wrong supporters. Justice had officially been done!

A certain 'newspaper' that claimed to report about the truth in 1989 is still being boycotted on Merseyside to this day. Sales have dropped by 80 per cent from 55,000 per day before Hillsborough. 'Don't Buy the S**' campaigns first aimed at decreasing purchases, then also the supply of it by retailers. Nearly every taxi in Liverpool has 'Total Eclipse of the S**' and 'Not Welcome in Our City' emblazoned on the side. The 'newspaper's' owners are estimated to have lost £15 million per month since April 1989.

I still hadn't seen Gerry live on stage and I wanted to change that. I checked his website to see whether he still went on tour in Germany. Hamburg would have been a nice place to see him, but it was mainly UK venues that were listed. I tried to combine a Liverpool home match with a concert nearby the night before or after, but I soon realised it wouldn't work out. There were tickets on sale for Porthcawl, Billingham, Tamworth, Bromsgrove. If you had told me those were brands of Marmite, I would have believed it. Never before had I exercised such an excessive overuse of Google maps. I searched all kinds of UK airports near to a concert's venue and checked whether any flight carrier from anywhere in Germany flew to the respective destinations. 'Harpenden? Where the ... Oh!' I realised that the venue was only a couple of miles and a ten-minute taxi drive away from Luton Airport. I booked my ticket for Harpenden Public Halls for a Saturday-night concert.

When the big day arrived, I was in the best of moods. The Reds had beaten Arsenal 5-1 at home and were on course for a title fight. I wore my best shirt for that very special occasion, my long-sleeve home jersey that the Reds wore in the 1963/64 season. When I entered the venue I soon realised I was by far the only guest under the age of 60. It was an all-seated concert and I sat right on the inside in the middle aisle. A few minutes past eight o'clock Gerry came on stage. I had never been nervous at a concert and never thought I would be, but this was a goosebumps moment. Apart from his greatest hits, his repertoire consisted also of American chart toppers from the 60s era. In between every single song he cracked a joke and told an anecdote from the past. It was live entertainment at its best! After a few songs he pointed to me and commented, 'I know this jersey very well.'

The concert flew by and culminated in the introduction of his final song. 'The next and last song is the one you've all been waiting for. When you walk ... ' No one sat on their seats anymore as everybody stood up and waved their arms above their heads. After a very long finale, he left the stage and the lights went on.

In the lounge I stayed on for a while and chatted to a few people who had been to his concerts before. One of Gerry's crew members appeared to collect the merchandise that was on sale. I told him that I was from Germany and had come over only to see Gerry live in concert. He was delighted to hear that and advised me to go around the building to wait backstage in the car park. It was early February and it got colder with every second. Minutes later, Gerry came around the corner. He approached me directly with a broad smile on his face and gave me a hug. He started chatting to me straight away and asked me whereabouts in Germany I was from. We talked for a few minutes and he spoke about his time in Hamburg in the 1960s and about other places in Germany. We took some photos and he even joined in giving the five times salute. When he walked off he looked around and said, 'I'm off to my hotel to watch *Match of the Day* now.' Then he drove off. And I needed a drink. In fact, I needed a few.

The most beautiful song had initially brought me to the most wonderful football club in this universe and beyond.

I had heard our anthem the very first time on a Pink Floyd LP decades before. That night I finally lived to see this wonderful artiste and gentleman, who had brought the song into Reds' lives over 50 years before, perform it live.

CHAPTER THIRTEEN

World Order Restored

'HAVE YOU actually ever been to Anfield at all?' Glory has always attracted its hunters, but the hype in Germany that has been triggered since Jürgen Klopp was unveiled as the new manager of Liverpool Football Club is unprecedented. Many followers of his previous clubs would naturally show interest wherever he went next. Even general football fans who don't really follow any football team find this cult figure at this cult club too much of a fairytale combination and want to be part of it.

One typical incident occurred on a flight before the final match of the 2018/19 season against Wolverhampton Wanderers with the title still at stake. I had booked my trip without a match ticket months before, just to be in the city if it might happen. I overheard quite a few German people mentioning they were making the trip over to Liverpool for the match. One woman of around 60 years of age said that she and her husband had decided to visit Anfield again. They had been there the year before and had now picked the Wolves match for another trip. She had gone to her local travel agency somewhere in Germany and booked a Don't-Worry-Be-Happy-All-Inclusive-Weekend.

The match had sold out of tickets and city break packages months before. I wondered where that travel agent in Germany could get hold of two tickets for possibly the most important league fixture in decades. And where did the others … ? Never mind!

'Oh, we always liked Jürgen Klopp and we wanted to hear "You'll Never Walk Alone", you know, the song they're always singing, live once.'

Well, for those two reasons alone I backpedalled mentally and convinced myself there wouldn't be two more deserving spectators in the ground the following day. In my imagination, I saw them wearing half-and-half scarves while flicking through *The S***. In my fantasy, Purple Aki would come along and feel the husband's muscles to deter them from setting foot on Liverpudlian soil ever again!

Harmless, innocent people, who have done nothing wrong, are most certainly entitled to visit any sporting event they wish. However, these event hoppers with no heart and soul attached to the club, willing to pay cash just for this one-off day-trip, are the ones who shut out genuine Reds. Even worse, on a larger scale in terms of European Cup finals, they boost the already crazy price spiral even further upwards. The amount of money they feel it's right to spend on a once-in-a-lifetime event trip exceeds the financial capacity of most real supporters and especially regular match-goers. In moments like these, the amount of vomit I sense to relieve myself of would exceed the maximum possible capacity of my stomach!

In other moments, I'm grateful my stomach wasn't there to witness it at all. John and Brian once observed one guy getting out of a taxi outside the Kop wearing a Manc jersey. He must have come straight from the early Saturday match in Manchester. He took his jersey off, put his Liverpool top on and walked towards the entrance of the stadium. I wonder whether Purple Aki can be hired for spontaneously selected target persons.

The total of 'Liverpool's number one fans' in this country that has mushroomed over recent seasons exceeds any capacity of imagination, too. Never have I considered myself as a number one of anything and I wonder how these people of this new 'Liverpool Family' generation even classify themselves as such. Whenever I bump into a member of that species, the narrative of having been a diehard Red all his life is unexceptionally always followed by the query of whether I have actually ever visited Liverpool's home ground myself. Wherever you go, the latest merchandise on chest, neck, head and every other thinkable bodily part that can cover something red serves as genuine proof of their lifelong-diehard-blood-red-or-dead-ness. The interrogation of my personal classification is accompanied by an overflow of red testosterone gushing up from their three red testicles producing red sperm. When a typical number one fan realises after a brief cringy Q&A session who they are talking to and their hormone level normalises again, one question unfailingly follows: 'Anyway, what's your German team?'

The man who I had wished would one day become Liverpool manager, Jürgen Klopp, wouldn't take long to bring European nights back to Anfield. At the beginning of the 2017/18 season, the Reds were paired with German team Hoffenheim in the qualifying round, a match we reached from Mannheim by local train. If only I had known before how many spares for the away end were available, I would have saved a lot of money on some online ticket platform. After eliminating Hoffenheim, Liverpool went on to Maribor, Moscow and Seville, then to Porto where we twatted them 5-0. The quarter-final first leg brought the soon-to-be-crowned league champions to Anfield. If they considered the power of Anfield on a European night a pure myth, they were taught a lesson or two they wouldn't forget. As soon as we beat City in the quarter-final, I started to make arrangements for the trip to Ukraine. The last time I had booked flight, hotel and even ticket for a European final before the semi-final, I was there but the Reds just didn't turn up!

In 2008, I had been sorted and ready to go to the final in Moscow! I had participated in various Champions League sponsors' and other organisations' raffles. When I was drawn to be entitled to buy a ticket, I arranged travel and accommodation straight away. However, this time Liverpool couldn't get past Chelsea in the semis, so they were to play the Mancs in the final. I still travelled to Moscow to do some sightseeing. There was no way I would be attending the match myself though, to watch either the plague or cholera lift our trophy. I passed my ticket on, for face value of course, to the only genuine Manc supporter I knew, Del, the Irish chef of Murphy's Law.

The night before the final I went to a bar where many international guests gathered. I talked to a guy who introduced himself as a bar owner from the Netherlands. As he was one of a Champions League sponsor's best beer retailers, he had been invited to Moscow, including flight, two nights in a five-star hotel, VIP treatment all day and a match ticket. Bluntly, he told me he took the whole outing as a fun trip and would sell on his match ticket for around €1,500 as he wasn't interested in the match anyway. I wonder whether Purple Aki can be hired for coming on European tours.

When I met up with Del next day, the first thing that happened to us was to be set up in a scam, including a guy dropping a bundle of dollar notes, a bogus policeman appearing out of nowhere and some ten witnesses. It all happened so quickly. We had less time to think clearly about the situation than John Arne Riise had to ponder whether just to kick the ball anywhere into the stands or head it directly into our own net in the last minute of the first semi-final. The compassionate gang members showed mercy towards me though, as they didn't relieve me of any content of my wallet. They must have figured I had been punished enough, being surrounded by Mancs and Cockneys. Probably they just intended to distract me from their dealings with Del, who was ripped off to the tune of a couple of hundred Euros.

However, even Russian criminals couldn't prevent me from sticking to the deal I had negotiated with Del before. While I was in Moscow and Liverpool weren't joining me, then at least I wanted to have some fun on my own. The *Kop Magazine*'s editor Chris McLoughlin introduced the 'SUMMER CHALLENGE 5' after Istanbul. Reds travelling the world should send their photos in with a *Kop Magazine* in one hand and giving the five times salute with the other. It was such a huge success that the challenge went beyond the summer and readers kept sending in their pictures over the years. On Moscow's Red Square with Mancs and

Mercenaries all around us, I asked Del to take a photo of me with the *Kop Magazine* and giving a five times salute in front of St Basil's Cathedral. Then I reminded him of our deal. We exchanged camera for magazine and he posed the same way. Rather anxiously in his Manc jersey, he looked around to check that no one was looking at him, smiled but declined to do the salute. He still made it into the magazine as 'the most ridiculous Kop Summer Challenge 5 photo we've ever had – a Manc clutching *The Kop* in the middle of Red Square!'

This time, preparations for the trip to Kiev proved to be another challenging task. Prices for direct flights and accommodation were astronomical. I soon realised that the city picked for the final wasn't fit for the world's biggest football encounter in terms of beds or for seats on planes. '2,985 people are looking at this room at the moment' and it was up to €800. I decided to sacrifice the party on the night before the final and just arrive on the day. Memories of Istanbul and Athens had proved that no bed was needed after the final anyway. Direct connections from Frankfurt to Kiev weren't available and the alternative to sleep rough for a couple of nights wasn't really an option. I would have to use any European airport to get me to Ukraine's capital. My reluctance to depart from Stuttgart, the jinxed airport I had used before our defeat in the final in Athens, had to be ignored.

Stuttgart airport would be the first stop after a one-and-a-half-hour drive after leaving the house at 2am Saturday morning. At 6am I would get on a one-and-a-half-hour flight to Amsterdam, in the opposite direction to my final destination. There I had a three-hour stopover and then another three-hour flight from the Netherlands to Ukraine. The return flight at 6.55am Sunday morning would take me to Vienna, where I would have a five-hour stopover before another flight of over an hour to Stuttgart, from where another one-and-a-half-hour car journey would bring me home. Knowing that I had never managed to have a kip on a plane as I just can't fall asleep while sitting, I realised I would be some 38 hours on a non-stop trip without sleep.

My plan turned out to be wise though. Hotels started to cancel bookings that had already been confirmed, only to put them on sale again for multiple times the original price. Many Ukrainian locals found out about that rather inhospitable behaviour and offered private accommodation to meet the demand. My Irish mate and lifelong Red J.P. got sorted with a room and went on a 35-hour one-way bus trip and stayed for a whole week.

Excitement was mixed with tiredness when chasing a ticket again. While there had been only a few resellers ten years before, a whole new market had established itself with people making a living out of buying and selling tickets for highly rated sports events. Out of a multitude of ticket agents I picked a local one, whom I could track down, check the validity of the company and confront them face to face if they tried to cheat me. After a bit of haggling and deciding I wasn't going on a summer holiday anyway, I agreed terms and conditions for the European Cup Final against Real Madrid. John, Brian and John were only partly lucky in the ballot. One confirmation mail got stuck in the spams and, when they found out days later, it was too late for them to arrange any accommodation and flight. They decided to stay at home and passed on their ticket.

I find it generally a rather challenging task to fall asleep in the late afternoon or early evening. This condition doesn't improve when you're buzzing for a European Cup Final trip ahead. I had a normal working day on Friday, left the office early and decided to go straight to a beer garden near my home. Two or three wheat beers in the sunshine would make me tired and all I would have to do is go home by 8pm, set the alarm, lie down, fall asleep and get up at around 1am. This was my brainchild's master plan that I cunningly thought through! The plan worked out until some details began to crack.

Tension grew inside me when I took a trip down memory lane, to my first European Cup Final, then Istanbul and Athens. By the time I was scheduled to go home, the planned third and final pint had already been history for some time. To make matters even more complicated, tiredness was nowhere near. Around 9.30pm, with my drinking and sleeping schedule completely fucked up, I eventually felt a sense of fatigue and went home. The last time I checked the clock it was after 11pm. When I woke some 90 minutes later I was not only totally knackered, but I still had some residual ethanol in my blood, and worse, in my head. I felt as I should have after the match, but not 20 hours before kick-off.

Sitting in a café at the airport, I tried to get my brain's synapses going by downing a couple of espressos. There was quite a large number of Reds waiting for their connecting flights, but not one of them would accompany me to fly in the opposite direction to Amsterdam. In the departure lounge, I felt all eyes on me and my red shirt. I could tell people were whispering and wondering whether they should tell me I was going to be on the wrong plane. The feeling of being subject to some incorrect programming of my personal matrix simulation intensified when I entered the plane consisting of only a single floor and only one aisle. The steward inspected my boarding card, looked at me and pointed to the direction I was supposed to walk, even though the only alternative directions I could have taken were the cockpit, the coffee kitchen or the toilet.

I looked at him quizzically, wondering about the necessity of his directional information, before he repeated his sign language and added, 'This way, please, sir!' I convinced myself that he must have encountered some Evertonians on their European holiday maiden flights, who had asked him whether they could sit upstairs for a better view as they usually do on the Arriva buses. One passenger on the plane remarked seriously, 'Are you sure you're on the right plane?' I nodded tiredly. 'Will you make it on time to your final?' Don't tempt fate, I thought!

Nervousness and fear faded when I landed at Amsterdam airport, where I joined up with hundreds of Reds waiting for our flight to Kiev. I finally felt back in reality when I heard the announcement 'boarding completed' and some lads struck up a familiar tune: 'We conquered all of Europe ...'

Exhaustion disappeared when I reached Shevchenko Square. The party was already in full swing. Banners were decorating trees, bushes and walls all around. The Istanbul feeling was back! The lads from *The Anfield Wrap*, *Redmen TV*, The La's John Power and The Farm's Peter Hooton fuelled the mood until it reached boiling point when Jamie Webster entered the stage.

The atmosphere and singing on Taksim Square and Syntagma Square couldn't be bettered, but to have a BOSS

Night concert in Kiev was of a different quality. The vast repertoire lasted longer than the booze supply, which ran out when the sun was still very much right above us. As mobile connection didn't work, I couldn't get hold of J.P. all afternoon. When we eventually bumped into each other I saw a beaming smile. He had got a spare on the black market and it was no fake either!

Before kick-off, the choral duet of Dua Lipa and the travelling Reds inflamed the atmosphere. 'One Kiss' was still ringing in my ears, when Sergio Ramos's dirty tricks ended our dream. The disappointment that followed all night was the biggest I had ever witnessed, far worse than Athens.

The worst bit after a defeat in a final is killing the time, when you yearn to get home as soon as possible. But misery can be topped when you sit in Vienna airport's bar, where they put on a news channel that shows nothing else but the goals of the night before. I felt gutted and wondered how many years it would be before we had a chance to have another go at Ol' Big Ears. Despite the dejection, sadness and frustration of the evening, the party, humour and joy of the afternoon would stick in my memory. Tens of thousands of travelling Reds had set another unreachable party benchmark somewhere in a remote region on the edge of Europe. To say it in Jamie Webster's words, it was certainly no pointless 30-hour bender, but a weekend in paradise. One banner that day summed it up quite appropriately: 'IF I HADN'T SEEN SUCH RICHES I COULD LIVE WITH BEING POOR'. Only Reds really know how great life is. If you never experience our greatness in life, you don't know how shite life can be.

* * *

'Always Look on the Bright Side of Life' wasn't played too often in the Irish pub O'Reilly's in Heidelberg. It was quite obvious, though, that it was especially played for me one night. The Spanish bartender thought it funny to play it straight after the final whistle after Liverpool had been beaten 3-0 by Barcelona at the Camp Nou the following season in the European Cup. Every single Spaniard in the area gathered for that massive semi-final encounter. Even the Spanish bartender, who was a Real Madrid fan and had been taking the piss all year for beating us in the previous final, wanted Barcelona to win. 'It's a Spanish team and you got to stick together in Europe!' Sometimes, life is just incomprehensible!

Hubris has the potential to make the extent of the dramatic hero's fall all the sweeter for the antagonists. Same place six days later, any fantasy of a comeback was delusional. It was Anfield though! Fantasy became reality when ball boy Oakley Cannonier assisted Trent Alexander-Arnold in taking his corner quickly, which led to the much-anticipated fourth goal. No Monty Python songs were played after the match in the pub that night. Bring on yer Barcelona, yer Messi, yer biting Suarez and yer back pain Coutinho, who the fuck are you trying to kid?! It was Tuesday night and the Reds made Barca look like shite.

If emails had sound, you would have heard loud laughter in the reply I received from the ticket agent the next morning. I enquired about buying my Madrid ticket from the same vendor for the same price I had purchased the one for Kiev a year earlier. When I rang him up personally I was told that prices had gone up. He asked for €2,700 for the cheapest available ticket! I tried to teach him some maths by calculating for him that his offer was over 100 per cent up on our previous deal. He explained that he as a trader was offered the tickets for €2,000 for the cheapest category, and therefore his offer of €2,700 would be a good deal for me. Some corrupt UEFA officials with access to match tickets serve a secondary market and seemed to make a nice little earner on the side. I checked the internet and realised that this was the best price available. The cheapest tickets on offer were €3,000. I decided straight away not to enter the race for the ticket anymore but to just enjoy the whole run-up in the weeks ahead, and most of all, the Reds' party. I was going to Madrid anyway!

I stuck to my proven Kiev schedule to get tired early in the beer garden, get some sleep before getting up at 1am, drive to the airport, fly into Madrid early morning, stay up all day and night and take the early Sunday morning flight back. The difference, though, was that I had no stopover in Reykjavík or Helsinki this time, but a direct flight from Frankfurt. For further details of how my sleep preparation schedule worked out, just re-read the passage about the evening before Kiev.

After arrival at Madrid's airport, a local TV team stood on the escalator in front of me. *C'mon, have a go*! I thought. 'Tienes billetes?' I asked. They turned around, wondering whether that poor sod in front of them couldn't even afford the money for a public transport ticket into the city centre. I added 'Billetes por la match?' I realised that during my four weeks *curso intensivo* in Spain 20 years ago, I should have spent less time on *las fiestas y* San Miguel every night and more on studying vocabulary and the differing meanings of 'ticket' *en español*.

They figured out I was referring to 'entradas' and found the perfect interview partner for their report on thousands of ticketless supporters in town. 'Lo siento, pero hablo solo un poco español!' They just ignored the 'sorry, but … only a little … ' and focused solely on my confirmation ' … I speak … Spanish!' 'Perfecto, we do interview!' A waterfall in Spanish descended upon me that reminded me of Istanbul's taxi drivers. Could I get away with talking senselessly about any Spanish topic without addressing the issue of the question I didn't understand in the first place here again? I could refer to Rafa, the glory of Paris in 1981 or the 4-0 at Anfield. Sergio Ramos sprang to mind. What's 'Dirty fucking ****' in Spanish? They more or less prompted the answers, which I dutifully repeated in broken Spanish. A 'muchas gracias, señor!' saw me off without addressing my issue of a match ticket. Before I could ask for a spare journalist pass, they were gone.

Plaza Felipe II, otherwise known as Salvador Dalí Square, was already covered in red banners when I arrived at 10.30am. The sight of the mega stage was breathtaking. By 11am the entertainment programme had started and the square filled up quickly. 11am! This was almost ten hours before kick-off. The Spanish sun directly above a sea of Reds embedded in between the stage, an oversized Stonehenge memorial and block of flats on each side, heated up the square to over 30°C by midday and skins turned red. By the look of even more Reds around the square, it was easy to see that the number of supporters in town exceeded those who could have been in possession of a ticket. A couple of tens of thousands must have just turned up for the party. Videos of Shevchenko Park on social media the year before must have motivated supporters from all around the world to come to

Madrid to take part in the greatest party no other club in this universe could celebrate.

A week before, two London clubs had played out the UEFA Cup Final in Baku and couldn't even sell their allocations, a ticket distribution that Liverpool's Boys' Pen alone would have taken without asking their parents for permission to board the plane in the first place.

The entertainment programme included Timo Tierney, Kieron Molyneux, Chelcee Grimes, Colin Murray and John Power. John Barnes rapped The Sugar Hill Gang's 'Rapper's Delight' and the 'Anfield Rap' and told stories about sleeping rough in Liverpool's Concert Square on Saturday nights and other anecdotes.

The whole afternoon passed by in the best of positive moods. Tens of thousands of brothers and sisters, many of them ticketless, partied together in a typical Reds fashion. Respectful behaviour wasn't just demonstrated amongst one another, but to locals and the police. The *Anfield Wrap*'s Neil Atkinson, who wore a colourful long-sleeve jumper in the heat all day, gave various brilliant speeches and heated up the mood. He walked from one side to the other like a tiger in a cage just waiting to be let out. This underlying tension that built up from early morning to late afternoon came to a full explosion at the end of the final rendition of BOSS Night's 'Allez Allez Allez' when Jamie Webster screamed a raging red-faced battle cry 'UP … THE FUCKING REDS … FUCKING COME ON … GET TO THE FUCKING GROUND NOW … NUMBER FUCKING SIX!' punching his fists towards the cheering, ecstatic sea of Reds. His facial expression and gestures epitomised what every single Red felt inside.

The exhaustion could be seen on everyone's face. Thousands of Reds still had to find a space in a bar, just any bar! In between the party's ecstasy and panic in organising a place to watch the match, I missed out on meeting up with John, Brian and John, who had been lucky in the ballot and went to see the match. They avoided paying a fortune on expensive flights and accommodation around the Saturday by spending a whole week in Madrid in a rented camper van in someone's back garden.

The bar Frank & Furt at the corner right next to the stage served Reds with drinks all day. I kept asking whether they were staying open, but due to police orders they would have to close down. So they told me. I kept ordering my drinks with the same waitress and tried to flirt charmingly: 'C'mon, you stay open, don't you?' After a while she smiled and said, 'I have to speak to boss.' From then on, I focused on him, not in the same philandering way, but always courteously. After a while, he said 'I'll have to ask boss!' I thought he was boss? I was enlightened that he was only the shift manager, but it was the owner who made the decisions. When the owner arrived, wearing a Liverpool shirt, he gave me a hug and told me how much he loved Liverpool! He would have a word with the police, but we would be locked in and had to keep quiet until kick-off. There were about 20 Scousers, and me, left inside. Their husbands, sons, girlfriends and mates had gone to see the match. We must have had the most comfortable spot in Madrid that night with loads of space as well as easy access to and attention from the bar.

Our promised silence lasted up until the first minute when Mo scored from the penalty spot. After Divock scored the second and our trophy was safe in our hands, thousands poured back on to the streets to sing and party until all energy left me deep into the night. Some park bench would do just to sit for a while and recharge my batteries. When I woke up again, it was near check-in time. I got a taxi, drove to the airport and flew home.

Liverpool were champions, champions of Europe! In the league we had just finished the season with 97 points, the club's highest points total and the third-highest in the English top flight ever. 'Ever' as in since 1892, not since 1993. Liverpool had just finished the season as runners-up. The combination of words 'runners-up' and 'following season' sent shivers down my spine. Thoughts immediately crossed my mind of how we had fared each season after we had finished second the year before. Liverpool had come very close in 2002, 2009 and 2014 only to fall back every single time to finish the following season 5th, 7th and 6th. It wouldn't happen this time, would it? I convinced myself not to search for the nearest Betty Ford Clinic, but to believe.

I kicked off the new season with a trip to Geneva in the summer, where Liverpool played their last pre-season friendly against Olympique Lyonnais. In the stand around me I noticed many young couples in their early twenties with a Scouse accent. After a mass substitution after an hour, the guy behind me asked, 'Who's that young fella on the wing?' Before I could answer, the young girl next to me answered him: 'Harvey Elliott.' I was impressed to say the least. I would have thought she might know Mo, Virgil or Trent, but not a 16-year-old on his debut who we had signed for the U23s just three days before. I had a chat with them and realised that there were many young supporters from Liverpool who are real followers, but who are shut out from

279

matches as they have no access to tickets. Instead, they pick an attractive destination for a pre-season friendly, book an affordable EasyJet direct flight and make this their summer holiday's city break trip.

Four days later, my first visit to Wembley since mid-1980 was coming up. Brian could get hold of a ticket for me for the Charity Shield through a supporters' club. I was flying into London then back straight after the match. I was looking forward to walking up Wembley Way until I realised it was no more. Apartment blocks, shops and restaurants had taken over. You have to go with the times, I'm afraid but I was still buzzing to see the new Anfield South as I hadn't been there since its reconstruction.

As soon as I entered the arena, anticipation gave way to disillusionment. I noticed straight away that the toilet odour had disappeared, but at the same time the stadium had lost everything else, too. After about ten escalators, a sign told me I had arrived at the right floor. In the hallway, nothing would give you the impression you were inside a football stadium. On a positive note, the stadium management saw sense in picking the colour of the Reds for the seats. Sitting in that soulless plastic bowl, albeit admittedly with a very good view, I thanked the Almighty that we had never left Anfield, but had stuck to our home. The result didn't matter! There were bigger tasks awaiting us!

Losing our reliable goalie due to injury in the first half in the very first match of the league season wasn't the best of starts. I just knew something was going to happen that would cause us to lose points on the way. It would certainly be a different season to the one before and we couldn't achieve 97 points again, could we? After beating Norwich comfortably

4-1, wins against Southampton 2-1, Arsenal 3-1 and Burnley 3-0 gave us a perfect start.

We were on a winning streak, had just won our fourth match in a row, were topping the table with 12 points and bloodthirstily raring to go for the next match, which couldn't come soon enough. Studying the fixture list and the dates, I couldn't make any sense of the gap in between them and the following matchday. It suddenly dawned on me what stateless people like me had to be reminded of. It was the international break! Liverpool players have to mix with players from Mancland, London and other rural regions only to play matches against other cobbled together teams. The most senseless football matches would interrupt our march to number 19!

Shattered and gutted, I checked the later fixtures. I remembered that there would be another weekend in October when our run was to be unnecessarily halted again. The following break would be just before we played the Mancs away. My eyes wandered down the list to spot another gap, a third break, in November. I just sat there, lethargic, indifferent and watched the wall. I had read that symptoms of depression emerge gradually, they come and go, the disease flares and then has remissions, and you experience feelings of unhappiness, frustration, anger or just pure sadness. How was I going to cure myself? No matter how, I had better keep the contact details of that Betty Ford Clinic ready!

With the sun rising on my soul's horizon, a 3-1 win against Newcastle was followed by a 2-1 away win at Chelsea. A fighting spirit saw the Reds scrap to a 1-0 victory at Sheffield United before the Reds gained all three points in the 95th minute in a 2-1 win at home to Leicester. A 1-1 draw at Old

Trafford saw us lose our first points. Bloody international break! The refereeing performance in that match made me say things out loud in public that prompted bartender Mike to tell me for the first time ever: 'Carsten, we do have families and children in here this afternoon, you know!' In my defence, the Mancs should never have scored that goal as one of our players had been fouled in their half. We were simply robbed of our three points. I was sure, though, that the kids and their families were sympathetic.

A serious title fight was on and a serious fight for a long-anticipated away match ticket, too. If this was to be our season and it was to finally happen, I would have to be in the away end once, any away end! Soon I had to come to terms with the fact that I may be able to bunk into a European Cup Final, but every rural stadium in the country had a prohibition sign for me personally installed.

As Liverpool's away section had always been a closed shop, there was no alternative but to sneak into the home section somehow. I had studied stadia seating maps for 'neutral' sections next to the away end. I sent clubs emails with a subject header 'International guest request', narrating stories, such as my personal problem in regard to our '25th college anniversary get-together' in their town. I would be 'travelling from Germany on exactly the weekend that your club, which we have all followed since student days, coincidentally have a home fixture against Liverpool. My friends are Liverpool season ticket holders, who will all be sorted with tickets, but can't provide me with one. As I stay the weekend together with the Liverpool mates, I was wondering if it was possible for me to purchase one ticket in the section directly next to the away section.'

To underline my serious intention and proof of my enquiry, I included my German shipping address and credit card details straight away. What they all basically said in their replies was: 'We have to inform you with regret that unfortunately ... and at the same time we have to inform you that no away supporters are allowed in the home section ... thereby we suggest you refrain from ... as you'll be ejected from the stadium.' What they all basically meant in their replies was: 'Fuck off you ****! We know exactly what you Liverpool supporters are up to.' There was still the family section to look out for, but for an elderly bloke to insist on getting a single ticket to sit amongst youngsters might have rightly raised serious further queries on a rather different scale.

In the 2-1 win over Tottenham normal service was resumed. Liverpool had been rocking all season, sometimes grinding out results, but at Villa Park in the following match they would just never lose their spirit of belief. Four minutes from time we were still trailing. Four minutes into time added on the Reds turned the match around 2-1 and were back to winning ways yet again. When a week later we beat City 3-1, Liverpool were nine points ahead of them. We would be dropping points sooner or later, wouldn't we? No, we wouldn't! Next we beat Crystal Palace 2-1. In between beating Brighton 2-1 and Bournemouth 3-0, apropos of nothing, we squeezed in a 5-2 defeat of the Blueshite in midweek. Then another victory followed, 2-0 against Watford.

Having beaten Chelsea in the European Super Cup Final in August already, we also beat Flamengo 1-0 to lift the FIFA Club World Cup. It was nice to see us lift further trophies and

I was indeed happy, but my mind was already focused on the Boxing Day fixture away at Leicester. I wasn't nervous about the match, but aware that this would be the biggest challenge not to lose points. One of the busiest nights out in the UK is by far the quietest of all quiet evenings in Germany. As all pubs are closed, I had to watch the match at home. A 4-0 victory in the most superior way gave us a 14-point lead with a match in hand. I kept looking at the table for hours while listening to The La's, emptying the fridge and calculating what could still go wrong. The fact that we had won all but one of our matches, whereas City had already failed to win seven of theirs, made it clear that we were on the way to win the league, no matter what. Fulfilling our duty against Wolves 1-0, Sheffield United 2-0 and Spurs 1-0, it became crystal clear, even without mental support of Scouse music and cold booze, that we were going to win the league.

Not only did we accomplish what we couldn't for 30 long years, but we also won it in the most superior way! There wouldn't be a decisive moment in a tight title race when we would win number 19. There wouldn't be that one particular match or that one goal like Kenny's winner at Stamford Bridge in 1986. This team would tie in with the greatest-ever teams of 1979 and 1988. They knew at a certain early point they had won it and just had to walk over the line to be champions.

After such a long time, the celebration rightly endured over many enjoyable single moments that sent the Reds into frenzy. The ecstasy lasted from the first victory against Norwich, to Sadio's and Bobby's great strikes at Southampton, Joel's headed goal and Mo's solo run before scoring against Arsenal, Trent's intended cross that deflected and looped into the top corner at Burnley, as well as his free kick at Chelsea, Gini's shot from outside the penalty area that forced the ball through the Sheffield United's keeper's legs to secure victory, James's coolly converted 95th-minute penalty that secured three points against Leicester, Robbo's header and Sadio's winner at Aston Villa, Fabinho's strike against City, Virgil's two headed goals from Trent's free kick and corner against Brighton, the three brilliant assists for Ox, Naby lad and Mo at Bournemouth, Mo's unbelievable brace against Watford, to the Scouser in our team Trent's goal at Leicester on Boxing Day and many, many more!

I personally believe we all felt that one decisive moment when we clinched the title. For me it was Sunday, 19 January 2020. Alisson reacted quickly and passed the ball to Mo, who won a running battle to score for 2-0 in the last minute against the Mancs in front of the Kop. Alisson was the first to congratulate a half-naked Mohamed Salah before the whole of Anfield struck up the most emotional, convinced, unbearable 'we're gonna win the league!' That moment we won number 19!

I once asked John why the song 'A Liverbird Upon My Chest' hasn't really taken off on the Kop yet. The Scouser answered the learning wannabe Scouser: 'It's because of the refrain "that wins the championship in May". Once we win it again, you'll hear it!'

Liverpool are back where we belong! We're back on our perch and the whole world order has finally been restored.

* * *

I had fallen in love with Liverpool Football Club first, then the city and its people. I've developed a deeply rooted emotional bond, which has grown stronger and stronger over the decades. I don't have a specific reason or an explanation. I only know it's there. Is it the Liver bird on that red jersey? Is it the history, the heritage of our club? Is it the supporters' culture, the tradition, the Liverpool way? Is it what we do, but no one else does? Is it what we would never do, but everyone else does? Is it the unique, brilliant banners, the creative, inventive love songs? Is it Anfield's atmosphere, the European nights, the European Cup Final trips with or without tickets? Is it the Scouse spirit, the Scouse accent, the Scouse humour, the Scouse people? (Evertonians aside, of course. Still wondering what ship must have smuggled in those bitter genes!) Is it the unparalleled solidarity, the unbearability towards the bordering country called 'England'? Is it this never give up attitude, this never give in to the authorities mindset, this you better not mess with us approach? I guess it's not one single reason, but a combination of everything that makes what Liverpool is all about – a feeling, a mentality, a way of life!

The lyrics of that very first Bay City Rollers single from my mum sums it up somehow quite appropriately:

> I don't know what it is that makes me love you so.
> I only know I never want to let you go.
> 'Cause you started something, can't you see.
> Ever since we met you've had a hold on me.
> It happens to be true, I only want to be with you.

I'm writing these final words while listening to Jamie Webster's song 'This Place'. I'm repeatedly singing to myself: 'My city, my people, my heart. My city …' I've never lived in Liverpool and still to this day don't know how to properly say 'dey do dat dough, don't dey dough', but …

… the love you feel is not rooted in your origin, but in your identity.

I was born in a far foreign land, but the way my heart and soul perceive life, I'm told:

Not German, I am Scouse!

Also available at all good book stores

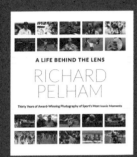

9781785315466

9781785313929

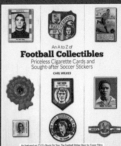

9781785315602

9781785313073

9781785310423

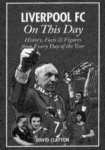

9781908051059

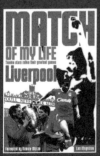

9781908051677

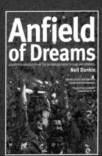

9781905449804

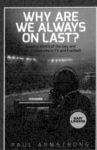

9781785314384